THE ARCHITECTURE OF
R.M. SCHINDLER

THE ARCHITECTURE OF
R.M.SCHINDLER

ORGANIZED BY ELIZABETH A.T. SMITH AND MICHAEL DARLING

The Museum of Contemporary Art, Los Angeles
in association with Harry N. Abrams, Inc., Publishers

ESSAYS BY
MICHAEL DARLING
KURT G. F. HELFRICH
ELIZABETH A. T. SMITH
ROBERT SWEENEY
RICHARD GUY WILSON

cover: HENRY BRAXTON AND VIOLA BROTHERS SHORE
RESIDENCE (project with AGIC), Venice, California, 1928

frontispiece: KINGS ROAD HOUSE, West Hollywood,
California, 1921–22. View towards Schindler's studio.
Photograph by Grant Mudford

this page: Schindler (front row, second from left),
aboard the Kaiserin Auguste Viktoria en route to the
United States, March 1914

back cover: Schindler, at an outing of the Palette and
Chisel Club, Chicago, 1915

TABLE OF CONTENTS

RESIDENCE : W. OLIVER · LOS ANGELES · CAL. : R.M. SCHINDLER. ARCHITECT

WILLIAM E. OLIVER RESIDENCE,
Los Angeles, California, 1933-34. Perspective elevation

DIRECTOR'S FOREWORD

What a wonderful phenomenon it is when an artist's reputation is pulled from the shadows and brought back into the light that it rightly deserves. Such is the case with R. M. Schindler, an architect of immense talent and sensitivity who nevertheless disappeared into brief obscurity after his death in 1953. Over the past few decades his reputation has gradually been restored, and in recent years an appreciation for his idiosyncratic brand of modern design has reached a level unattained during his lifetime. We are very proud to be able to contribute further to this critical reassessment by presenting the most comprehensive, retrospective exhibition of Schindler's work to date. "The Architecture of R. M. Schindler" is a long overdue examination of this seminal architect's oeuvre, and will doubtless convince wide audiences of the considerable merits of the work.

"The Architecture of R. M. Schindler" has been in development for many years under the careful nurturing of former MOCA Curator Elizabeth Smith, who is now the James W. Alsdorf Chief Curator at the Museum of Contemporary Art, Chicago. Elizabeth was ably assisted at MOCA by Michael Darling, assistant curator for this exhibition, and together they have crafted an intelligent and compelling portrait of this architectural pioneer. My predecessor Richard Koshalek was supportive of this project from its inception, and I am thrilled to have been able to shepherd it to completion. MOCA's Board of Trustees also has been instrumental in ensuring that important exhibitions continue to be at the heart of MOCA's programming, and Board Chair Audrey M. Irmas and Board President Gilbert B. Friesen in particular have been unwavering in their commitment.

No endeavor as ambitious as this would be possible without the financial support of generous corporations and individuals that have blessed MOCA's history from the beginning. "The Architecture of R. M. Schindler" has been supported by The Ron Burkle Endowment for Architecture and Design Programs; Gensler; Cynthia A. Miscikowski and Douglas Ring; Kelly Lynch and Mitch Glazer; and The Austrian Cultural Institute. In-kind support has been provided by Homasote Company. We also have been very lucky to have the assistance of an important group of lenders, foremost among them the University Art Museum at the University of California, Santa Barbara, from whose Architecture and Design Collection the bulk of this exhibition's materials was drawn. "The Architecture of R. M. Schindler" proves that cooperation and collaboration among committed individuals and institutions is not only possible, but that it has the potential to generate the sort of excitement that can galvanize entire communities to reflect on their cultural heritage and look ahead to their collective future.

JEREMY STRICK
Director
The Museum of Contemporary Art, Los Angeles

R. M. and Mark Schindler at Kings Road, summer 1923

ACKNOWLEDGMENTS

"The Architecture of R. M. Schindler" is an exhibition with an extremely long gestation period, requiring almost ten years from its original inception to its final realization. Over the course of this decade, many individuals have lent their support, encouragement, and expertise to the project. At MOCA, the exhibition was initially supported by former director Richard Koshalek, whose passion for progressive architecture resulted in a formidable legacy of architectural exhibitions and buildings during his tenure at MOCA. Enthusiasm for the project was sustained when Jeremy Strick assumed the directorship at the museum, making clear that "The Architecture of R. M. Schindler" will be the first of many exhibitions devoted to architecture and design under his leadership. Chief Curator Paul Schimmel has also been unflagging in his support of the project, recognizing Schindler's widespread influence over the creative community of Los Angeles.

Mounting an exhibition of this scope and depth would not have been possible were it not for the existence of the Schindler archives at the University Art Museum on the campus of the University of California, Santa Barbara—an archive astutely built by the late architectural historian, David Gebhard. Gebhard not only provided a home for these materials, allowing generations of scholars to delve deeply into the career of this pioneering architect, but brought to bear his own erudition and insight into Schindler's work. In the wake of Gebhard's death, Curator Kurt Helfrich has ably stepped in to maintain the integrity of the archive and indeed, improve upon its organizational structure, making it an even more valuable resource. Helfrich's professionalism, dedication, and attention to this project, coupled with his patient demeanor, have streamlined an extremely complex undertaking. The support of University Art Museum Director Marla Berns and former Chief Curator Elizabeth Brown for the loan of hundreds of valuable artifacts has been equally invaluable, and we are grateful for their generous spirit of collaboration. Additionally, the help of registrar Sandra Rushing and expertise of researcher Eric Lutz have made the University Art Museum an ideal institutional partner. Eric was primarily responsible for the valuable updating of the Schindler project list which appears at the back of this book.

Dramatically enhancing the quality of the exhibition, other generous individuals have loaned their own fragile Schindler artifacts. These lenders include Ann Caiger and Octavio Olvera of the Department of Special Collections at the University of California, Los Angeles, Library; Dion Neutra; Dr. Bobby Lovell; Robert Sweeney at the Friends of the Schindler House; Richard Guy Wilson; Judith Sheine; Dietmar Steiner and Monika Platzer of the Architektur Zentrum Vienna; Dr. Verena Karnapp of the Architektur Museum at the Technische Universität, Munich; Robert Nicolais; Gabrielle and Michael Boyd; Grant Mudford; Julius Shulman and Judy McKee; Marvin Rand; Frank and Jay Novak of Modernica; and Judith Throm at The Archives of American Art, Smithsonian Institution, Washington, D.C. New models of Schindler buildings were expertly constructed by students at California Polytechnic University, Pomona, and at Art Center College of Design under the guidance of Judith Sheine, Kris Miller-Fischer, John Chase, Chava Danielson, Rick Corsini, and Mark Dillon. Numerous drawings were conserved by Mark Watters and Bob Aitchison, and their contribution to the lasting legacy of Schindler's work is not to be underestimated.

The exhibition design has been handled with characteristic innovation and ingenuity by Annie Chu and Rick Gooding of Chu+Gooding Architects, supported by their creative team of Claudia Reisenberger, Sanjeev Patel, Michael Matteucci, Yu-Ping Chang, Kay Kollar, Michael Sy, Joseph Perazelli, Sky Kogachi, and Clay Holden. The clarity and material richness with which the drawings, photographs, models, and furniture are displayed in Chu+Gooding's design enhance the presentation of these materials and ensure their optimum eloquence for MOCA's diverse viewing public.

The exquisite catalogue which accompanies the exhibition owes its existence to the ever-sensitive design of Lorraine Wild and Amanda Washburn, and the complexities of catalogue production from start to finish have been handled with care and precision at MOCA by former Senior Editor Stephanie Emerson, Assistant Editor Jane Hyun, and Editorial Assistant Elizabeth Hamilton. Indispensable editorial feedback from Stephanie and Jane was complemented by a careful reading by Russell Ferguson, while the translation of letters by Thomas Stahl made a real contribution to the Schindler scholarship for those less than adept at German. The essays developed by Kurt Helfrich, Bob Sweeney, and Richard Guy Wilson, all of whom were also deeply involved in making this project a reality, bring new perspectives to bear on Schindler scholarship.

The content of the exhibition and catalogue has been built on the work of many dedicated scholars and architects who have turned their attention to Schindler's work over the years, and we have greatly benefited from their insights. Esther McCoy, David Gebhard, and Reyner Banham are among the great early champions of Schindler's architecture, ably followed by Judith Sheine, Lionel March, and Kathryn Smith. We are also grateful to Thomas S. Hines and Marco De Michelis for providing invaluable advice and assistance as to the content and direction of this exhibition and book. Further information, interpretation, and assistance have been offered by Mark Schindler, Dr. Mary Schindler, Stefanos Polyzoides, Peter Noever, Daniela Zyman, David Leclerc, Tim Samuelson, Randell Mackinson, Thomas A. Heinz, Bascha Batorska, Mark Robbins, Pavel Štecha, Ivan Wirth, Herbert Lachmayer, Brigitte Felderer, Mary Lee, Masachi Uchino, Bill Boehm, Manfred Kovatsch, Matthias Boeckl, August Sarnitz, Tom Buresh, Danelle Guthrie, Russ Leland, Adolph Tischler, Werner Brandstetter, Harald Gunther, Neil Denari, Joseph Giovannini, Erica Stoller at Esto Photographics, Graphische Sammlung Albertina, Frank

11   Escher at The John Lautner Foundation, Dennis Sharp, Hugh Oliver, Peter Loughrey, Mitch Glazer, and Kelly Lynch. The partnership of the National Building Museum in Washington, D.C., as a venue for the exhibition owes to the commitment of former Chief Curator Joseph Rosa, Executive Vice President G. Martin Moeller, Jr., and Director of Exhibitions Kathy Frankel. Likewise, the important presentation of the exhibition in Schindler's hometown of Vienna is the result of a longstanding interest in Schindler's work on the part of Director Peter Noever and Curator Daniela Zyman of the Austrian Museum of Applied Arts (MAK).

Others crucial to the realization of this multi-faceted project include Jane McNamara of the Los Angeles Conservancy who, with Daniel Lynch Milner, Amanda Seward, Jim and Erika Marrin, Cindy Olnick, Mary Barsony, Marlyn Musicant, and other volunteers, surveyed a range of Schindler-designed buildings and have organized a coherent and revealing tour for MOCA. The support of MOCA's Director of Education Kim Kanatani and Adult Programs Coordinator Caroline Blackburn in developing educational programming will doubtless make the intricacies of Schindler's achievement accessible to a wide audience. The complex logistics of organizing such an ambitious exhibition require the sort of staff that MOCA is privileged to count as members of its team, foremost among them Exhibitions Coordinator Stacia Payne, Chief Registrar Rob Hollister, Associate Registrar Rosanna Hemerick, Chief Exhibition Technician Jang Park, Exhibitions Production Coordinator Zazu Faure, Media Arts Technical Manager David Bradshaw, Secretary to the Exhibitions Coordinator Beth Rosenblum, and Exhibition Technicians Barry Grady, Jason Storrs, Joe Howard, Shinichi Kitahara, and Valerie West. Raising the financial support necessary for an endeavor such as this is also an integral part of the exhibition process, and the leadership provided by former Director of Delevopment Erica Clark, her enthusiastic successor Paul Johnson, and the talented team of Jillian Spaak, Ed Patuto, Jackie Kersh, and Michael Urban ensured a firm financial footing. Indeed, in the end it is the concerted effort of the entire MOCA staff that makes the museum's myriad programs possible, and we are ultimately indebted to every MOCA colleague for their industriousness and dedication.

The hard work of MOCA's development department was rewarded by major support received from The Ron Burkle Endowment for Architecture and Design Programs; Gensler; Cynthia A. Miscikowski and Douglas Ring; Kelly Lynch and Mitch Glazer; and The Austrian Cultural Institute, whose generous donations have made "The Architecture of R. M. Schindler" a reality. In-kind support has been provided by Homasote Company.

Finally, the ultimate thanks go to Rudolph Michael Schindler, whose consummately original and inventive work continues to inspire.

ELIZABETH A. T. SMITH
MICHAEL DARLING

1 PHILIP LOVELL BEACH HOUSE,
Newport Beach, California, 1922-26

ELIZABETH A. T. SMITH

R.M.SCHINDLER: AN ARCHITECTURE OF INVENTION AND INTUITION

Space architecture. To define it perhaps one would have to stand in the same relation to [Schindler's] methods of work as the witness stands to the height of a building in a perspective. To narrow and precise space you began with the contour map and building code; developed it through the character of the land and the way of life of the client. Space forms had their roots there, and were not arbitrary or extraneous to them.

—Esther McCoy, 1945

Active from the late 1910s to the early 1950s, R. M. Schindler occupies a place of profound significance as an innovator within the history of twentieth-century architecture. Although his work was primarily residential and the bulk of his practice limited to southern California, it has had a pronounced impact on the course of later Los Angeles architecture, one that has extended to architects abroad. Schindler's Philip Lovell Beach House (1922–26) *(fig. 1)* has long been considered a foremost example of early twentieth-century modernism due to its commonalities with the products of European contemporaries such as Le Corbusier and the architects of the Dutch De Stijl movement. During the years since his death in 1953, however, and especially since the 1970s, his entire corpus of work, in particular his Kings Road House of 1921–22, has been the subject of an increasing interest and attention on the part of historians and architects that has accelerated during the past decade.

Considered a figure of regional interest during much of his lifetime and for several decades beyond, Schindler can now be evaluated in terms of his contributions to and extensions of modernism away from an International Style orthodoxy and towards a sensibility of experimentalism and hybridization. This sensibility resonates within the work of many practitioners of a younger generation whose approach to the making of buildings demonstrates a kinship to that of Schindler. It is this spirit of quintessential experimentalism that motivated Schindler to disregard modernist conventions in favor of an approach to design and construction in which the intuitive and the pragmatic combine. The result was a body of work which can be understood as a series of inventive solutions that, far from being purely rational or prototypical, were generated as a set of unique responses to the needs of each client and site.

Following the pioneering studies of Esther McCoy, the consummate chronicler of California architecture who succeeded in establishing a basis from which to appreciate Schindler's work in the years preceding and just after his death, Schindler's career has been the subject of an ongoing reassessment during recent years. The subsequent scholarship and analyses of historians, critics, and architects—ranging from David Gebhard, Reyner Banham, and Barbara Giella, to August Sarnitz, Stefanos Polyzoides, Judith Sheine, and Margaret Crawford, among many others—have countered the dismissive assumptions of their 1930s and 1940s predecessors, namely Philip Johnson and Henry-Russell Hitchcock, surrounding the nature and direction of Schindler's work. Amidst the shifting terrain of revisionism and reinterpretation, these and other writers have put forth various opinions that his work anticipated postmodernism or the proto-expressionism of Frank O. Gehry and his followers, as well as a whole generation of younger architects in early and mid-points of their careers today.[2] What appears inarguable is that Schindler's restless experimentalism was the product of his inventive synthesis of numerous influences into the unique framework of an architectural language that was in many respects idiosyncratic and trailblazing. As Peter Blundell Jones wrote, "The more one scrutinizes the modern movement today, the more the exceptions seem to overwhelm the rules, the less valid seems the unified vision so unmistakable in books and magazines of the 1930s. Scratch the surface and the illusion of consistency disappears."[3] While it was not easily understood from a critical perspective during the first half of the century, the role of invention and intuition in Schindler's work can be more readily appreciated not only in terms of today's sensibility of pluralism in architecture, but also in light of developments in architectural history that have broadened the understanding of the parameters of modernism, particularly with regard to architecture in regional centers manifesting more expressionistic or hybridized characteristics.

Though the expressive and often idiosyncratic direction of Schindler's work set him apart from many of his contemporaries and led to his omission from such formative histories as The Museum of Modern Art's International Style exhibition in 1932 and the Los Angeles Case Study House program begun in 1945, he was not an isolated figure. Keenly aware of international architectural developments, Schindler articulated his own theories and responses extensively and thoughtfully. This exhibition and publication

examine the theoretical and pragmatic underpinnings of Schindler's practice and consider points of commonality and difference with such figures as Frank Lloyd Wright and Richard Neutra, both with whom Schindler had longstanding personal and professional associations, as well as with other architects of his own and of subsequent generations in Los Angeles. Building upon and extending the significant body of literature that now exists on Schindler, this book seeks to place him within a wider national and international context as well as to shed new light on the extraordinary social and cultural environment of the early twentieth-century Los Angeles in which he thrived.

Three broad phases can be identified in Schindler's work: his student years and early professional training in Vienna and, later, Chicago; his period in the office of Frank Lloyd Wright at Taliesin, near Chicago, and in Los Angeles; and his formative and mature years of independent practice after establishing his own office at the Kings Road House in Los Angeles. This latter phase of Schindler's work, spanning almost thirty-five years, can in turn be considered in three distinct periods, responding roughly to the decades of the twenties, thirties, and forties up to Schindler's death in 1953.

During the 1920s, a period which saw him establishing his own architectural identity and experimenting with construction materials and processes such as tilt-up concrete, Schindler produced some of his best-known works, including his own residence/studio and the Lovell Beach House. In this period he also developed a wide range of built and unbuilt projects spanning single- to multi-family residences, and undertook designs like the competition project for

2 JOHN J. BUCK RESIDENCE, Los Angeles, 1934.
Photograph by Julius Shulman

the League of Nations Building with fellow Austrian émigré Richard Neutra. In broad terms, the 1930s marked a move away from unorthodox construction techniques towards an increasing preoccupation with experimental approaches to space as a shaper of form, as well as an interest in the idea of the prototypical in buildings and furniture designs. Producing many significant homes during these years, ranging from the International Style-inflected John J. Buck Residence (1934) *(fig. 2)* to the expansive and formally complex Guy C. Wilson Residence (1935–38), Schindler also produced a number of commercial projects encompassing designs for shops and restaurants to motels and service stations. During the 1940s and early 1950s, an evolution toward increasingly expressive and idiosyncratic forms took place in Schindler's work, evinced by such designs as the Maurice Kallis Residence (1946–48) *(fig. 3)*, the Adolph Tischler Residence (1949–50), and the Bethlehem Baptist Church (1944–45). It was during these final years of Schindler's career, in which he forged a highly personal idiom, that his work seemed to diverge most sharply from that of his contemporaries and anticipate subsequent developments.

Born in Vienna in 1887, Schindler was trained in art and engineering at the Technische Hochschule and the Akademie der bildenden Künste. At the latter institution he studied under Otto Wagner from 1910 to 1913, with whom he developed a close relationship and whose impact on him was far-reaching. Wagner's advanced thinking about technology, form, and the importance of continuous experimentation as the basis for artistic solutions would underlie much of Schindler's subsequent approach to his own work.[4] The young Schindler was also considerably influenced by his contact with the architect Adolf Loos, whose theory of the *Raumplan*, in which space is articulated volumetrically depending on function, was to find correspondence in aspects of Schindler's later work. Perhaps even more important was the strong personal influence that Loos exerted; as Schindler's sister later commented, "Loos was his greatest idol, for whom he felt boundless admiration, and Loos had a very high opinion of Rudolf and foretold a great future for him; also it was reconfirmed in the last few days that mostly on Loos's advice he went to America."[5] Furthermore, like many young German-speaking architects of the day, he was impressed by the Wasmuth

3 MAURICE KALLIS RESIDENCE AND STUDIO, Studio City, California, 1946–48.
Photograph by Robert C. Cleveland

portfolios of Frank Lloyd Wright, published in 1910, which possibly furthered his desire to travel to the United States where he would later work for Wright himself.

Schindler's earliest projects—designs for a hunting lodge and a hotel (fig. 4), and a thesis project for a crematorium and chapel (fig. 5)—were academic and, for the most part, unremarkable in their symmetrical organization and geometric stylization. Their interest lies primarily in the fact that they reveal the attitudes of the Wagnerschule, an educational institution whose theories and practices were among the most progressive of its day. Already evident at this early stage of Schindler's career was his interest in architectural theory. In 1913 he authored a manifesto entitled "Modern Architecture: A Program," which spelled out a set of guiding principles about architecture that would in many respects provide an underpinning for the course of his later work. The most significant of these, and the one that most deeply reveals the impact of Loos's thinking, is Schindler's pronouncement that, "The architect has finally discovered the medium of his art: SPACE." Another prophetic articulation of principle is found in his statement that, "The modern dwelling will not freeze the contemporary whim of owner or designer into permanent tiresome features. It will be a quiet, flexible background for a harmonious life."[6]

While still a student Schindler joined the Viennese firm of Mayr and Mayer as a draftsman to gain practical experience. The most notable building he worked on, for which drawings in his own hand remain, was the reinforced, concrete structure of the Clubhouse for Actors, Vienna (1912) (fig. 6). Following the completion of his education and stimulated by Loos's advice, Schindler left Vienna in 1914 for America

to join the mid-sized, moderately progressive firm of Ottenheimer, Stern, and Reichert in Chicago. During his three years in their employ, Schindler worked on a variety of stylistically eclectic buildings, including the reinforced concrete Chicago Hebrew Institute (1914–15) and the Elks Club (1916–17), of which an interior watercolor exists that arguably manifests the presence of Schindler's hand in its design.[7] Other Chicago projects with which Schindler was involved include an unexecuted design for an eleven-story hotel with an unarticulated surface from which geometrically stylized windows protrude (fig. 7), the interior of a bar (fig. 8), and an unbuilt design for a Women's Club that betrays a Wrightian influence.

Schindler's most notable contribution to the architectural landscape of Chicago while in the firm's employ was the Buena Shore Club of 1916–18, located on the beachfront of Lake Michigan. The program for this private social club was a complex one, leading Schindler toward his first exploration of a synthesis of concerns that would later become central to his work—the relationship of the building to its site, the use of advanced structural materials and

4 HOTEL RONG (project),
Vienna, 1912.
Presentation drawing

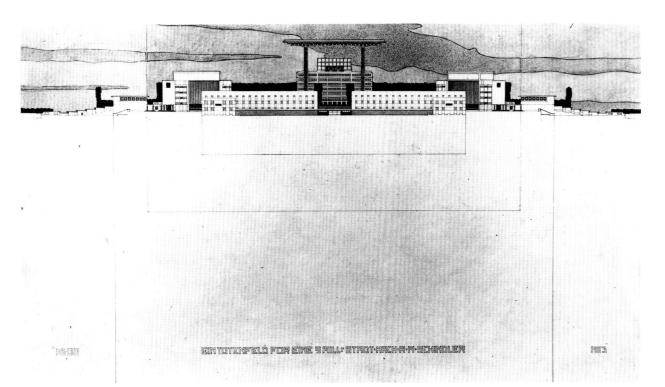

EIN TOTENFELD FÜR EINE 5 MILL · STADT · ARCH · R · M · SCHINDLER

5 CREMATORIUM AND CHAPEL FOR A CITY OF FIVE MILLION
(project), Vienna, 1912-13

6 CLUBHOUSE FOR ACTORS (for Mayr and Mayer),
Vienna, 1912

techniques, and an interest in complex interior spaces giving rise to a varied formal vocabulary. Indeed, Schindler considered the Buena Shore Club his first fully realized work. The L-shaped plan of the building *(fig. 9)* encompassed a series of interlocking spaces corresponding to their various functions and multiple changes in level based on the sloping beachfront site, yet its interior color scheme—gold, blue, and white—and its exterior façade manifested the persistent influence of Vienna.

Heralded in a Chicago newspaper upon its opening as "an architectural masterpiece ... [with] unique and artistic features which are not found in any other clubhouse in the country," the Buena Shore Club was also the subject of an essay by Schindler published in the same edition of the newspaper, in which he was given complete credit as designer of the building, apparently to the dismay of his employers at Ottenheimer, Stern, and Reichert. Due to the complexity of the scheme, however, construction of the building took more than one year, and Schindler left the employ of the firm to devote himself to completing construction on the clubhouse *(fig. 10)*.[8] In the

essay "The Buena Shore Club Described by its Designer," Schindler's words reveal overtones that manifest the increasing influence of Frank Lloyd Wright on his thinking:

On endless iron channels, the power emanated by the unexploited soil of all the North American prairies glides toward the western border of Lake Michigan, here to pile up in towering 20 stories–Chicago ... The beach and sea wall, the sunken garden with its banks and walks, the walls, the terraces and roofs–up to the street grade and still higher–up to four floors. All this one piling mass of concrete or of clay tile covered with gray plaster, except the long uncovered top line of red wall tile–calling way out into the lake; not with the broken red of the earth-born pressed brick nor with the lifeless pigment of the American builder's curse–the oil paint–but with the fresh transparent red of hard burnt clay ... go, see the house and enter it–breathe its air and touch its wallings and then read–read what life means to the architect– what the club means to its members and what the prairies could mean to humanity, if every artist tried to understand their teachings and their message.[9]

During his Chicago years Schindler continued an interest in fine art that he had earlier demonstrated in Vienna, engaging in drawing

7 HOTEL (project for Ottenheimer, Stern, and Reichert), Chicago, 1915. Presentation drawing

8 UNIDENTIFIED BAR (project), Chicago, c. 1915. Presentation drawing

CLUBHOUSE AT LAKE MICHIGAN

9 BUENA SHORE CLUB (for Ottenheimer,
Stern, and Reichert), Chicago, 1916–18.
Presentation drawing

10 BUENA SHORE CLUB (for Ottenheimer,
Stern, and Reichert), Chicago, 1916–18.
Photograph by R. M. Schindler

classes at the Palette and Chisel Club *(fig. 11)*. He participated fully in the progressive cultural life of Chicago, meeting his future wife, Pauline Gibling, at a musical performance there in 1919. To further his professional development, he gave a series of lectures at the School for Applied and Normal Art and at the Church School of Art on such topics as architecture and art, planning, the building and its location, the building and its time, form creation, and the building and its purpose, notes for which remain in the archives of his papers. Tellingly, he condemned Daniel Burnham's Plan of Chicago for attempting to reconfigure the appearance of the city as a traditional European one and for ignoring the implications of speed and the skyscraper. "Is this slick and common looking town Chicago? Why does it look so European? What makes the character of the American city?" were comments made during a lecture that revealed his perspective as a progressive European attempting to identify the characteristics of a truly American sensibility.[10]

Apart from his work with Ottenheimer, Stern, and Reichert in Chicago, Schindler developed a number of early independent designs. For a competition sponsored by the City Club of Chicago in 1914 he submitted a project for a neighborhood center of residences and roadways that, in its symmetrical organization, relates closely to his Viennese student work *(fig. 12)*. Increasingly, his work manifested the influence of Frank Lloyd Wright, whose buildings he visited and photographed throughout the environs of Chicago. Wright's theories and built works resonated for Schindler with ideas he had already absorbed in Vienna regarding the primacy of art in architecture, a commitment to geometric abstraction and stylization, and the desirability of the *Gesamtkunstwerk* as exemplified in Wright's Midway Gardens, which had opened in 1914 shortly after Schindler's

arrival in Chicago *(fig. 13)*. Schindler's increasing preoccupation with context—the role of the landscape and the site in determining the form and character of architecture—also can be understood as emanating from his contact with the work and ideas of Wright.

Of deep significance to furthering Schindler's feeling for the character of Americanness in architecture was a trip from Chicago to California via Denver; Salt Lake City; Taos, New Mexico; and the Grand Canyon in 1915. Upon his return to Chicago, he proposed to design for Dr. Thomas Paul Martin of Taos "a country house in adobe construction" that remains unexecuted. This design revealed the impact of pueblo architecture on Schindler, which impressed him as the only true indigenous architecture he had seen in the United States: "The only buildings [in America] which testify to the deep feeling for soil on which they stand."[11] His elevation drawings for this project pay homage to the pueblo style, while the plan's symmetrical organization recalls Schindler's academic training. The house, intended to be substantial in size, included three servants' bedrooms, servant dining quarters, a billiard room, and two guestrooms

11 Schindler, at an outing of the Palette and Chisel Club, Chicago, 1915

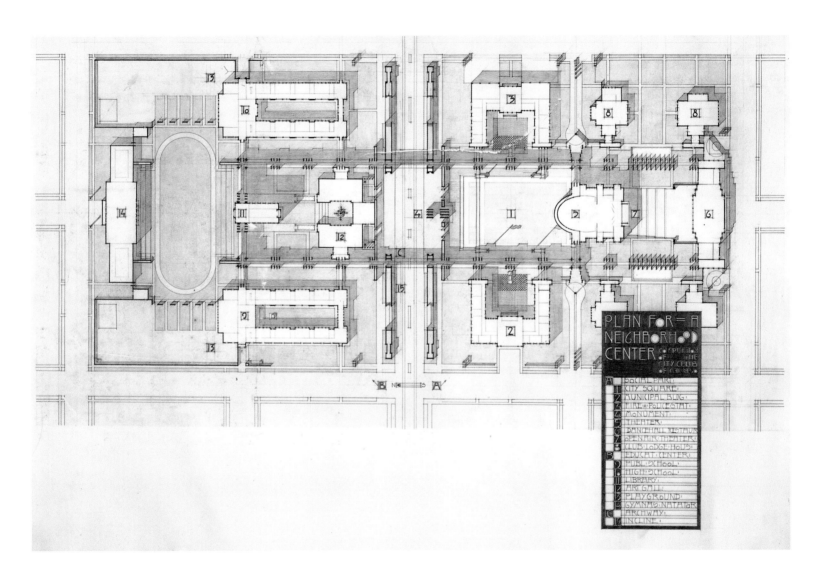

12 NEIGHBORHOOD CENTER (project),
Chicago, 1914

in addition to the kitchen, living, and dining rooms and master bed-room; it was also to encompass a small farm. The design synthesizes numerous influences stemming from Wagner, Loos, and Wright, with an enthusiasm for the adobe vernacular that Schindler felt to be an appropriate response to the demands of the site and its context.

Schindler's project for a Log House, begun in 1916, was the first in a series of vacation homes that Schindler would design over the years and represents his earliest experiment with the notion of modulari-ty *(fig. 14)*. The design manifests clearly Wrightian overtones, and in fact was finished at Taliesin in 1918 after Schindler had secured employment with Wright. Manifesting his growing dissatisfaction with work for Ottenheimer, Stern, and Reichert, Schindler had eagerly sought to join Wright's office. "If I had not found shelter with Wright not even the threat of hunger could keep me here any longer," he later wrote in a letter to Loos.[12] In February 1918 he went to Taliesin to work on the plans and construction documents of Wright's Imperial Hotel for Tokyo, returning later in the year to Chicago to work in Wright's office there and to live in the Oak Park

studio. There he worked on several projects for Wright, including the unbuilt J. P. Shampay Residence (1919) *(figs. 15, 16)*, the design of which has recently been attributed almost entirely to Schindler.[13] For Wright, he also devised a series of designs in 1919 for a development of "Monolith Homes"—low-cost, partially prefabricated homes for workers utilizing concrete construction. It was also through his association with Wright that Schindler met Louis Sullivan, for whom Wright himself had worked. Schindler actively assisted Sullivan in trying to find a European publisher for his book *Kindergarten Chats*; Schindler's writings reveal a respect and desire to provide assis-tance to this venerable figure, whose reputation was in decline at the time.[14]

Even while in Wright's employ Schindler continued to pursue inde-pendent designs such as a 1920 competition entry for the Bergen branch of the Free Public Library in Jersey City, New Jersey *(fig. 17)*. The square plan of the project *(fig. 18)* has been linked to that of Wright's Unity Temple (1905–08), yet it is spatially more complex while exhibiting a high degree of symmetry.[15] Schindler's own

13 Frank Lloyd Wright. Midway Gardens, Chicago, 1914

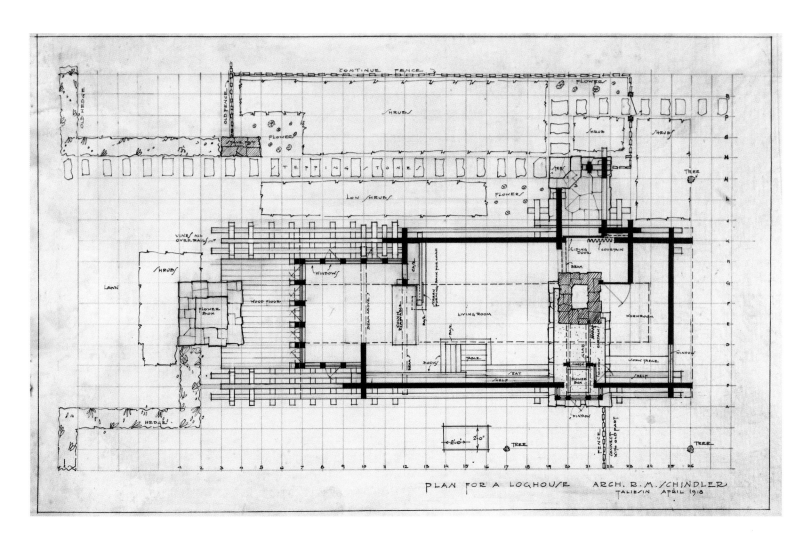

PLAN FOR A LOGHOUSE   ARCH. R. M. SCHINDLER
TALIESIN   APRIL 1918

14 LOG HOUSE (project), location unknown, 1916–18.
Floor plan

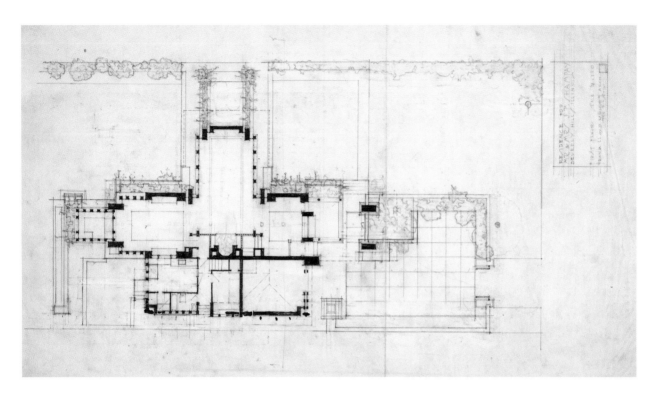

15, 16 J. P. SHAMPAY RESIDENCE (project for
Frank Lloyd Wright), Chicago, 1919

description of the project emphasized the importance of connecting it intimately with the garden, and doing away with any sense of monumentality generally associated with such a building type. "The library should become an organic part of the neighborhood, instead of standing apart, a strange-looking instrument of 'uplift' and a monument to the power of riches."[16]

In 1920, Schindler left the Midwest for Los Angeles to supervise the construction of Wright's Hollyhock House for Aline Barnsdall. He soon became heavily involved not only in the construction process but also in the design of several additional components of the overall complex envisioned by Barnsdall, including the Director's Residence *(fig. 19)*. Wright, preoccupied with the ongoing work for the Imperial Hotel, left Schindler almost fully in charge of this complicated project and client. While the relationship between Barnsdall and Wright became fraught with tension as the project progressed, Schindler remained on good terms with the mercurial Barnsdall, for whom he later designed an unbuilt home—the experimental Translucent House *(fig. 20)*—for a different site from 1927 to 1928.[17]

Initially, Schindler felt that his sojourn in Los Angeles would only be temporary. In mid-1921 his letters refer to a desire to return to Europe, because he couldn't imagine spending his entire life in Los Angeles, and to the possibility of going to Japan to assist Wright with the Imperial Hotel following completion of the Barnsdall complex. However, as 1921 wore on, Schindler became more firmly ensconced in California, taking a vacation in Yosemite, which he described as "one of the most marvelous places in America."[18] This formative experience was instrumental in seducing Schindler toward an appreciation of the landscape, climate, and way of life that seemed unique to California. Weighing the prospect of breaking with Wright to establish his own practice, and because commissions in Wright's office were dwindling, he began work on what was to become his most important early achievement—his own residence and studio on Kings Road in what is now West Hollywood, where he would remain for the rest of his life.

Los Angeles during the early 1920s was on the cusp of a population explosion fueled by the advent of newcomers drawn by the promise

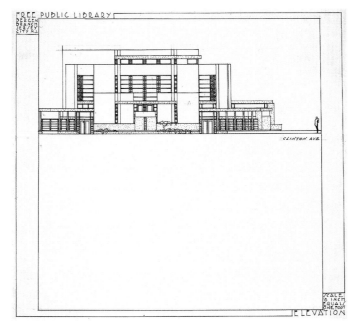

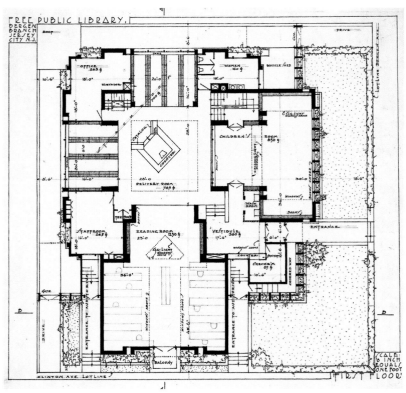

17, 18 FREE PUBLIC LIBRARY,
BERGEN BRANCH COMPETITION (project),
Jersey City, New Jersey, 1920

THE DIRECTOR'S HOUSE

FRANK LLOYD WRIGHT ARCHITECT

19 DIRECTOR'S RESIDENCE, OLIVE HILL, FOR ALINE BARNSDALL
(for Frank Lloyd Wright), Los Angeles, 1920

TRANSLUCENT · HOUSE
R·M·SCHINDLER · ARCH.
1927

20 ALINE BARNSDALL TRANSLUCENT HOUSE (project),
Palos Verdes, California, 1927–28

of the oil and film industries, and was still largely unformed from a physical standpoint—a dispersed horizontal spread that offered great possibility in terms of the need for new construction and housing. Eclecticism was abundant and Schindler's arrival coincided with the development of the popular Spanish Colonial Revival style. This period would see the arrival of many other German-speaking émigrés to Los Angeles, including artists, designers, architects, writers, and musicians, as well as the burgeoning of a bohemian culture in which Schindler and his wife Pauline became key participants.

In June 1922 Schindler wrote to his friend Richard Neutra, who was still residing in Europe, that his house was "finished—that is, I live in it and work on the interior. The money ran out before everything was finished and now I have to finish it myself."[19] Describing his "slab-tilt" construction technique of raising poured-in-place concrete walls by means of a tripod "with a block and tackle easily handled by two men" (fig. 21), Schindler pointed to his creation of a new feeling for the wall of a house: "The resulting wall has all the repose of the old type masonry wall, without its heavy, confining qualities."[20] As noted earlier, Schindler's previous experiments with low-cost houses and the idea to use concrete as a major structural material sprang from several sources. First, his European education and practical experience in Vienna and Chicago had provided him with extensive familiarity with the material and predisposed him towards structural experimentation. In addition, he had observed Irving Gill's work with tilt-up concrete (fig. 22) in San Diego during his earlier visit to California and later, in Gill's major building, the Dodge House (1914–16), located opposite the site of Schindler's own house on Kings Road.

Schindler described the house as "A Cooperative Dwelling for Two Young Couples." Interested in exploring alternative approaches to communal living as well as for reasons of economy, Schindler and his wife Pauline constructed their house/studio as a double residence to be shared with contractor Clyde Chace and his wife, Marian. The pinwheel-shaped plan for the house (fig. 23) utilized the entire 100-by-200-foot site and integrated areas for outdoor

21 KINGS ROAD HOUSE, West Hollywood, California, 1921-22.
View of construction, 1921

22 Irving Gill. La Jolla Woman's Club, La Jolla, California, 1912-14.
View of construction

living space, planting, and vegetation. This radical incorporation of the outdoors echoed the unconventionality of the plan itself—containing a communal kitchen to be shared by the two families, as well as private workspaces *(fig. 24)* for each of the four inhabitants and sleeping quarters that took the form of open-air porches rather than conventional bedrooms, which were added after the house had passed building inspection. Schindler commented, "Each room in the house represents a variation of one structural and architectural theme. This theme fulfills the basic requirements for a camper's shelter: a protected back, an open front, a fireplace and a roof ... The shape of the rooms, their relationship to the patios and the alternating roof lines, create an entirely new spatial interlocking between the interior and garden."[21] His use of a concrete floor and walls, while advanced technologically, derived from his idea of a cavelike enclosure that would also be part tent, hence the canvas walls and sliding panels to open the house to nature. The radicality of Schindler's vision to incorporate nature within the confines of a domestic setting has been unparalleled in subsequent residential architecture.

During the years 1922 and 1923, Schindler completed several significant early works both for single- and multi-family residences. Among these was the Charles P. Lowes Residence (1923) *(figs. 25, 26)* in Eagle Rock, situated on a steep hillside. While using conventional wood-frame construction with a stucco exterior, Schindler created a rhythmic vocabulary with the overlapping exposed joints of the wooden frame, which he exploited as a unifying feature alongside a play with textures—wood, plaster, glass, and velvet—and colors—sage green and burnt orange. The expressionistic details of the house and intense play with complex angles and volumes were developed further in the curious geometry of the 1924 John Cooper Packard Residence in South Pasadena *(fig. 27)*.

Furthering Schindler's exploration of ways to manifest a relationship between a house and its site, the triangular plan of the Packard Residence *(fig. 28)* was inspired by the shape of the lot itself. Its organization was derived, in part, from Schindler's approach to "dissolving the house into the outdoors" by closely relating the exterior walls with the garden. Schindler capitalized

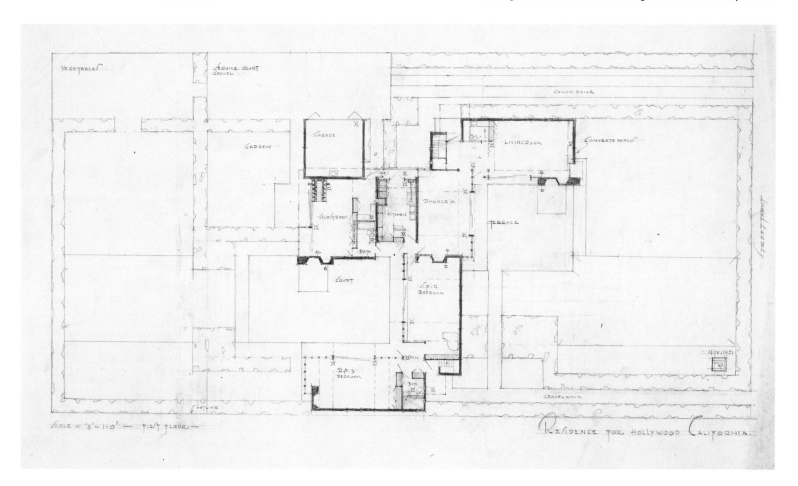

23 KINGS ROAD HOUSE, West Hollywood, California, 1921-22

24 KINGS ROAD HOUSE, West Hollywood, California, 1921-22.
View of Schindler's studio. Photograph by Grant Mudford

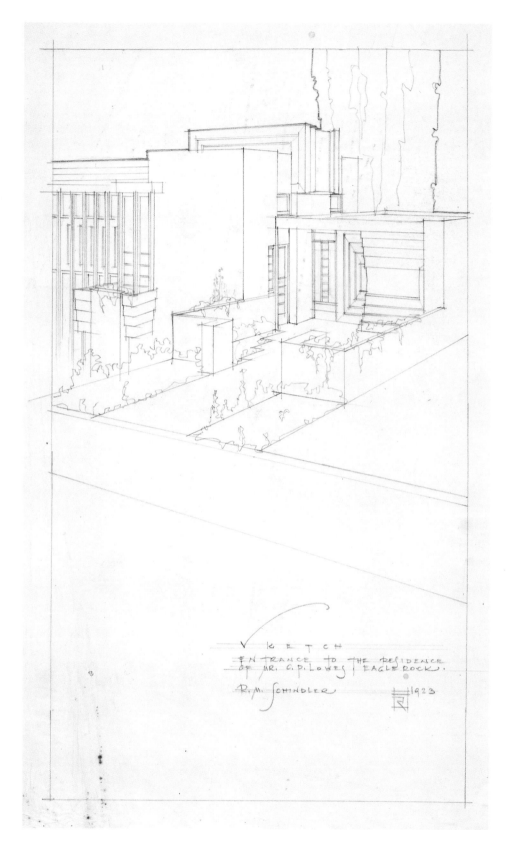

SKETCH
ENTRANCE TO THE RESIDENCE
OF MR. C. P. LOWES · EAGLE ROCK.

R. M. SCHINDLER   1923

25 CHARLES P. LOWES RESIDENCE, Los Angeles, 1923

on the clients' desire for a high-pitched roof by configuring it as an almost exaggerated slope, but flattening the top and mitering the sides to create "a new architectural form ... Although suggesting the high roof it has lost all of its utilitarian sheltering character *(fig. 29)*. Instead of protecting the house against threatening northern heavens it rather seems to open up towards a friendly southern sky."[22] Schindler used a modular proportioning system in the Packard Residence design to lend it visual cohesion and unity. For its construction, he utilized another experimental feature, his so-called "slab-gun" system consisting of the use of gunite, a high-grade cement mortar applied with an air gun, to eliminate the need for a wooden framework in concrete wall construction.[23]

The Packards—he an attorney and she trained as a Montessori teacher—were typical Schindler clients in their socially progressive attitudes; both had been founders of the American Civil Liberties Union in 1920. While certain of the house's unconventional structural features led to major and minor inconveniences documented in the early correspondence between Schindler and the clients, Rose Marie Packard later pointed to its adaptability and her satisfaction deriving from such elements as the closely related interior spaces and gardens as well as the unusual details.

As I think back over our lives in this house for nearly 29 years I believe these are the features that give it charm and satisfaction.

We have the maximum of privacy yet the entire house can be thrown open to large groups for entertaining—adaptability is the word that describes it.

Both daylight and moonlight pours into every room.

The solid slab floor all on one level has given the children much pleasure.

The closets with sliding doors forming partitions was unknown to most people at that time.

The rooms opening out into the garden making the two related is now generally accepted as "California Living."

A comment of a friend many years ago often comes to my mind—"This home has more interest and imagination than any I have ever known."[24]

The Pueblo Ribera Courts in La Jolla *(fig. 30)*, built between 1923 and 1925, are a compelling achievement in the application of

26 CHARLES P. LOWES RESIDENCE, Los Angeles, 1923

27 JOHN COOPER PACKARD RESIDENCE,
South Pasadena, California, 1924.
Photograph by Viroque Baker

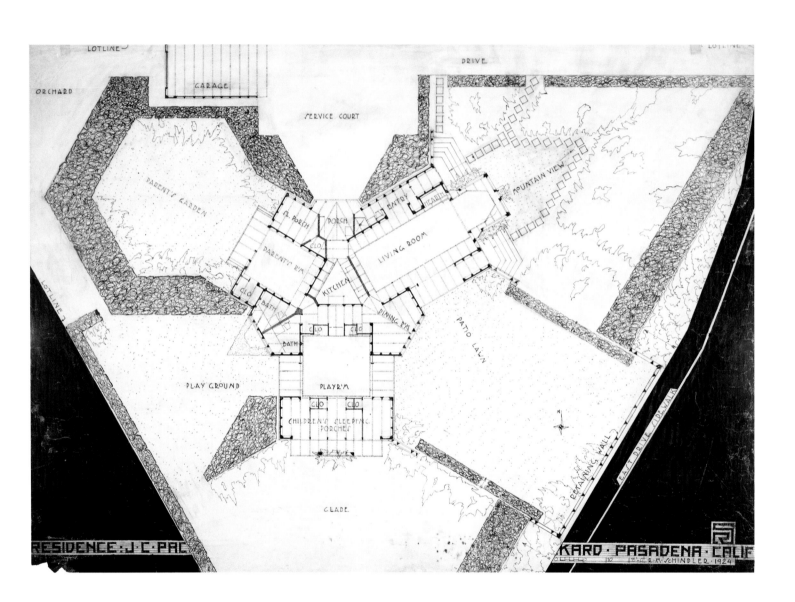

LOTLINE

ORCHARD

GARAGE

SERVICE COURT

DRIVE

ORCHARD

LOTLINE

PARENT'S GARDEN

LOTLINE

MOUNTAIN VIEW

ENTRY

HEARTH

Pt. PORCH

PORCH

CLO

LIVING ROOM

PARENT'S R'M

KITCHEN

CLO

BATH

DINING R'M

PATIO LAWN

CLO

CLO

BATH

PLAY GROUND

PLAYR'M

CHILDREN'S SLEEPING PORCHES

CLO

CLO

N

RETAINING WALL

EAST DRIVE SIDEWALK

GLADE

RESIDENCE · J.C. PAC

KARD · PASADENA · CALIF

10   1"=10'   R.M. SCHINDLER · 1924

28 JOHN COOPER PACKARD RESIDENCE,
South Pasadena, California, 1924. Plan and site plan

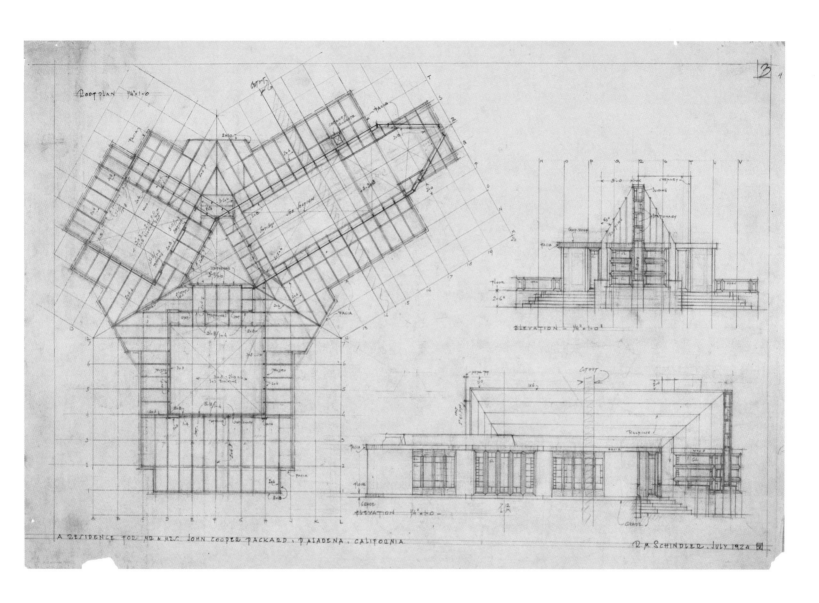

29 JOHN COOPER PACKARD RESIDENCE,
South Pasadena, California, 1924. Roof plan and elevations

Schindler's ideas about experimental, low-cost housing. The project integrated a group of twelve essentially identical units into a harmonious relationship with one another and with the site on a bluff overlooking the ocean, organized to expand and enhance the private outdoor space afforded to each unit. Here Schindler continued to utilize his experimental "slab-cast" system of concrete walls to create simple, easily replicable components that could be manipulated in terms of their siting and positioning.[25] Letters between Schindler and the client, W. Llewellyn Lloyd, reveal numerous difficulties encountered in securing financing for the project as well as the desired degree of finish and waterproofing in the concrete.[26]

Two projects for cost-efficient workers' housing designed in 1924—the Gould & Bandini Workmen's Colony and Harriman's Colony projects, both for the Los Angeles area—depended strongly on the ideas applied and realized at Pueblo Ribera, but envisioned on a larger scale. Harriman's Colony was conceived as a town containing a college with surrounding parks and public spaces—an almost utopian conception on the part of the client, Job Harriman, articulated in correspondence with Schindler in 1924. Both of these large-scale designs, however, remain unbuilt.

The James Eads How Residence of 1925–26 (fig. 31), built for the progressive clients Dr. James Eads How and his wife, Ingebord, is one of Schindler's most intriguing and coherent early achievements. It succeeds in embodying his ideas about "Space Architecture" with its sequencing and interrelationship of dynamic spaces and forms and its complex geometries and sections, and has been described by its current owner and resident, the architect Lionel March, as "a masterful demonstration of *raumplan*, the spatial idea that Schindler's mentor, Adolf Loos, had formulated but had not by 1925 executed with such audacity."[27] Conceived to adapt to its steeply sloping hillside site and to take advantage of dramatic views, the four-story house was built with an understructure of concrete according to Schindler's "slab-cast" system (fig. 32). The house's uppermost level, made of redwood, rests above the concrete understory; the whole is unified by concrete fireplaces and chimneys extending up through the entire house and serving to "interlock" the

COURT
UNIT
LA JOLLA
STRAND
PLANNED BY
R. M. SCHINDLER
JULY 1923 CAL.

30 PUEBLO RIBERA COURTS FOR W. LLEWELLYN LLOYD, La Jolla, California, 1923–25. Perspective elevation

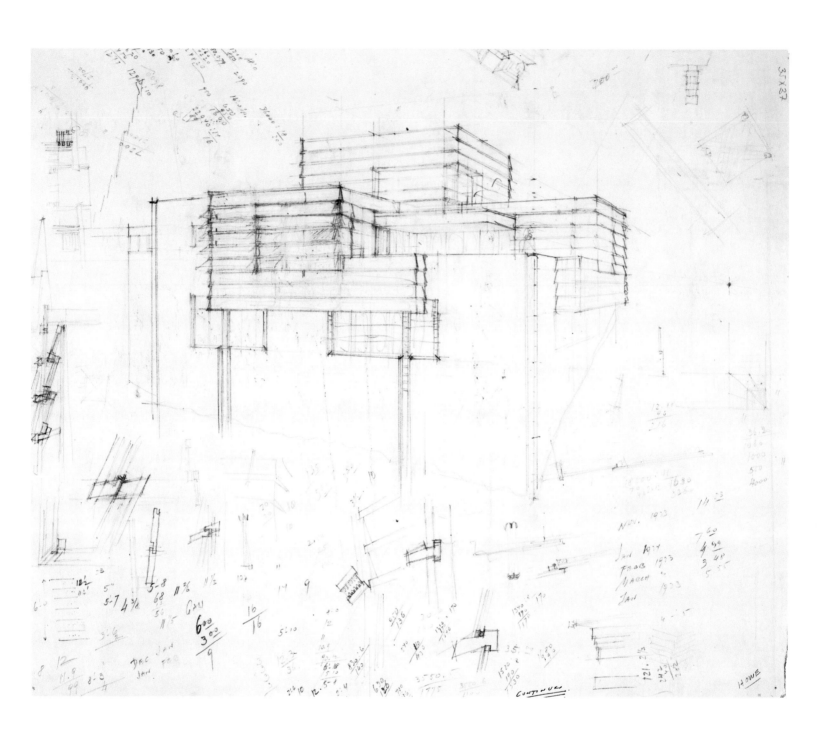

31 JAMES EADS HOW RESIDENCE, Los Angeles, 1925–26.
Perspective elevation

39 materials of the structure.[28] Schindler achieved additional design unity through horizontal stratification on the exterior and interior and by means of a natural color palette—tan, yellow, gray, and gray-green—derived from the foliage and bark of eucalyptus trees which dotted the site *(fig. 33)*.

Meanwhile, Schindler had begun work in 1922 on a beach house for Philip and Leah Lovell in Newport Beach *(fig. 34)*. Dr. Lovell, a naturopath, was a well-known figure in Los Angeles due to his column in the *Los Angeles Times*, "Care of the Body." Sharing the Lovells' commitment to the pursuit of healthful, outdoor-oriented living, Schindler himself contributed several writings to this column during his period of work on the beach house.[29]

Completed in 1926, the Lovell Beach House was a highly complex design for a structure supported by and inserted within five reinforced concrete frames. Raised up to overlook its beachfront set-

ting, the design provided both views and privacy. The house's double-height interior spaces offered a variety of interior configurations, enclosures, and window shapes, with extensive built-in components and modular proportions *(fig. 35)*. Aspects of the house demonstrate an affinity to other pivotal modernist residential works executed around the same time period, including Le Corbusier's Villa Savoye and the houses of the Weissenhofsiedlung in Germany; as such it took its place in the annals of modern architectural history relatively early after its construction. Yet it is characterized by a rusticity and complexity of space and detail that is unique to Schindler and a departure from the purity and rationality of International Style modernism. In fact, Schindler's point of departure for the concrete supporting structure originated from the functional pile structures commonly found in beachfront locations. This was, however, to be Schindler's final building in which reinforced concrete was extensively employed.

Schindler extended the rustic complexity of the Lovell Beach House in the design of another vacation home begun the following year—the multi-story Charles H. Wolfe Residence (1928–31) on Catalina Island—which adapts itself to a steeply sloping hillside overlooking the ocean *(fig. 36)*. He had met the clients, Charles and Ethel Wolfe, the proprietors of the Wolfe School of Costume Design, through the Lovells. Here, for reasons of cost, Schindler employed a wood-frame structure over floors and terraces of concrete, and used sheets of corrugated iron, painted golden bronze, for the ceiling material. He described the home as follows:

The character of the house as a play house is emphasized by its form. It appears light and airy and all vertical supporting members are architecturally suppressed. No excavating was done to speak of; instead of digging into the hill the house stands on tiptoe above it. The design consciously abandons the

32 JAMES EADS HOW RESIDENCE, Los Angeles, 1925–26.
Photograph by Viroque Baker

33 JAMES EADS HOW RESIDENCE, Los Angeles, 1925–26.
View of living room. Photograph by Grant Mudford

34 PHILIP LOVELL BEACH HOUSE, Newport Beach,
California, 1922-26. View of construction.
Photograph by R. M. Schindler

35 PHILIP LOVELL BEACH HOUSE, Newport Beach,
California, 1922-26. View of living room

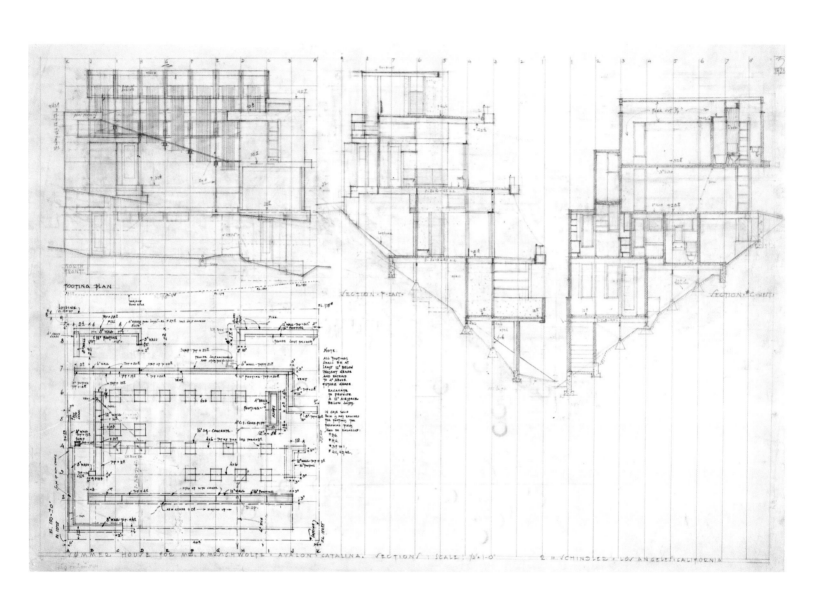

36 CHARLES H. WOLFE RESIDENCE,
Avalon, Catalina Island, California, 1928-31.
Plan, elevations, and sections

43 *conventional conception of the house as being a carved mass of honeycombed material protruding from the mountain, for the sake of creating a composition of space units in and of the atmosphere above the hill. Only the foliage from an abundance of flowerboxes all over the building laces it back into the ground.*[30]

Consisting of three levels—the top floor for the owners, the second floor for guests, and the lower floor for servants' quarters—it provided wide balconies at each level and also utilized the roof as a garden space incorporating a sheltered fireplace *(fig. 37)*.[31] Stemming from Schindler's evolving ideas about asymmetry in composition as well as his growing dependance on practical considerations—adapting to views, site conditions, and client preferences—the elevations of this house differed substantially from one another. In this respect the Wolfe Residence foreshadows later works by Schindler in which extremes of asymmetry and contextualism are manifested in radically divergent elevations within the same building.

By the end of the 1920s, after executing several significant and groundbreaking residences, Schindler had succeeded in solidifying

his reputation in Los Angeles as a foremost practitioner of modern architecture. During the second half of the decade he had also become involved in the design of additional multi-family as well as institutional and commercial projects. These ranged from the Manola (Manolita) Court Apartments in Silver Lake for Herman Sachs (first phase, 1926–28) and his joint entry with Richard Neutra in the competition for the League of Nations Building in Geneva (1926), to the execution of small storefront buildings such as the Leah-Ruth Garment Shop (1926) in Long Beach *(fig. 38)* and the Henry Braxton Gallery (1928–29) in Hollywood *(fig. 39)*. The latter, an interior remodel in a Mediterranean-style building, accomplished a visual extension of the small space by means of screens placed at angles to correct awkward proportions and similarly angled display shelves for sculpture and other small artworks. In addition, Schindler designed furniture for the gallery and employed other devices and materials such as black oilcloth as coverings for walls and ceiling to lend an artistic character to the space. Schindler's relationship to modern art circles led to his involvement with Braxton, for whom he also designed an unrealized house *(fig. 40)*, a connection made through the German art collector and enthusiast Galka Scheyer, who also resided at the Kings Road House for a brief period during the 1920s.[32]

Schindler and Richard Neutra had maintained extensive correspondence during the years before Neutra's arrival in the United States. Neutra and his wife, Dione, took up residence with the Schindlers at the Kings Road House from 1925 to 1930 *(fig. 41)*. Neutra and Schindler even initiated a joint practice with city planner Carol Aronovici in 1928, calling themselves the Architectural Group for Industry and Commerce (AGIC), with the intention of attracting large commissions. The AGIC pursued several designs for buildings and

37 CHARLES H. WOLFE RESIDENCE,
Avalon, Catalina Island, California, 1928-31

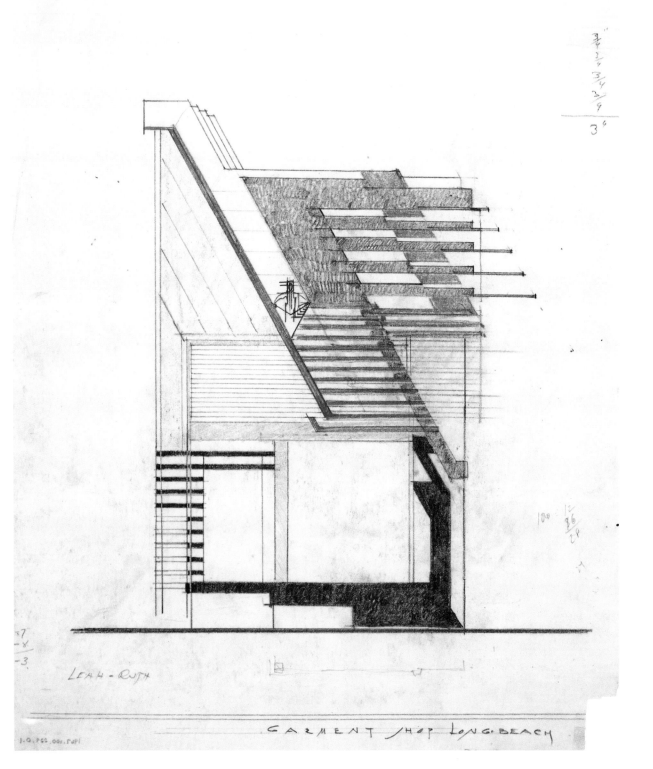

GARMENT SHOP LONG-BEACH

38 LEAH-RUTH GARMENT SHOP (with AGIC), Long Beach, California, 1926

39 HENRY BRAXTON GALLERY, Los Angeles, 1928–29

RESIDENCE: V.B. SHORE R.M. SCHINDLER ARCHITECT

40 HENRY BRAXTON AND VIOLA BROTHERS SHORE RESIDENCE
(project with AGIC), Venice, California, 1928

47 complexes ranging from a civic center to apartments. Schindler and Neutra's competition entry for the League of Nations Building was one of three projects selected from the competition's international submissions to be included in a touring exhibition in Europe *(figs. 42–46)*. This project's drawings reveal the contributions of both architects in developing its design, a notable feature of which was the placement of an auditorium space dramatically projecting out over Lake Geneva. Circumstances surrounding this unexecuted project, however, contributed to the beginnings of a rift between Schindler and Neutra, when documents of the design attributed only to Neutra toured in the European exhibition.[33]

Besides Neutra, Schindler's Los Angeles contemporaries included Lloyd Wright, Julius Ralph Davidson, and Jock Detloff Peters; all pursued various strains of and approaches to modernism. Yet the distinctiveness of Schindler's work was already beginning to contrast with that of his fellow modernists. Writing in the magazine *Creative Art* in 1932, Pauline Gibling [Schindler] described Schindler's work as "lyric" and "organic" in contrast to the "arch-functionalist" Neutra:

The work of Schindler results from a life picture which is revolutionary, and which differs strongly from the current mechanistic view of life which the new functionalism, perhaps abjectly, serves.... Schindler conceives of the architectural form as the space enclosed, rather than the flat surfaces of wall which encase it. The feeling of forms so conceived is radically different from the inverse, and adds a dimension to space-experience.

The residences of Schindler are intimately related to the earth. Meant for a life which flows naturally from the house out of doors, but which at the same time maintains an intense privacy, they are woven into their gardens, and the gardens themselves become rooms.[34]

By the beginning of the 1930s, Schindler's works of the previous decade had been published in several books on modern architecture by authors including the Germans Bruno Taut and Ludwig Hilberseimer and the American Sheldon Cheney, as well as in books and articles by Neutra.[35] In 1932, however, Schindler experienced deep professional disappointment at his exclusion from MOMA's International Style exhibition. More than once he wrote to the exhibition's curators, Henry-Russell Hitchcock and Philip Johnson,

41 Richard Neutra, Schindler, Dione Neutra, and Dion Neutra (clockwise from top left) at Kings Road House, c. 1928

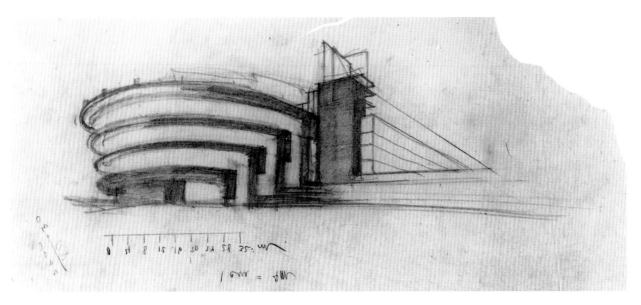

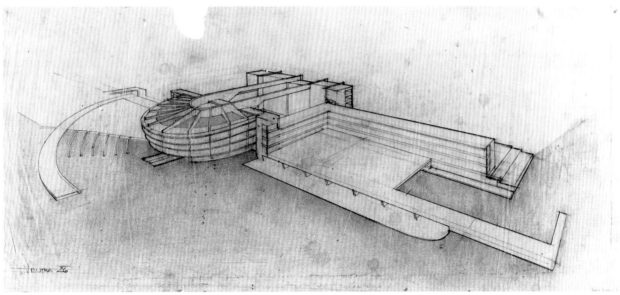

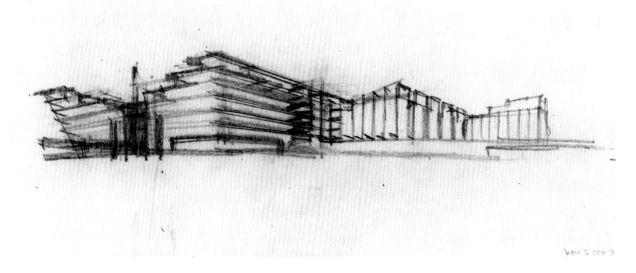

42–46 LEAGUE OF NATIONS BUILDING (project with Richard Neutra),
Geneva, Switzerland, 1926

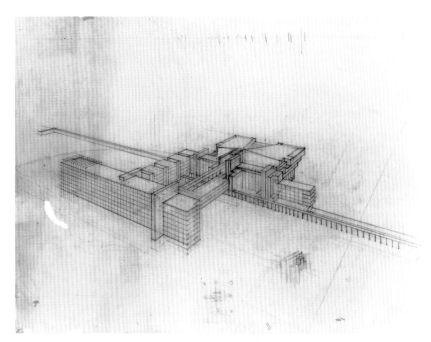

RESIDENCE·W.OLIVER·LOS ANGELES·CAL.:R.M.SCHINDLER.ARCHITECT

47 WILLIAM E. OLIVER RESIDENCE, Los Angeles, 1933-34.
Perspective elevation

48 WILLIAM E. OLIVER RESIDENCE, Los Angeles, 1933-34.
View of living room

inquiring about the inclusion of his work but was ultimately unable to convince them of its suitability to their thesis. Johnson later commented that, at the time, he had only visited one work by Schindler, the Kings Road house and studio, and had not been impressed with it. Furthermore, in his view it did not adhere to the tenets of the International Style articulated as a coherent movement with certain clear stylistic features. Both Hitchcock and Johnson compared Schindler's work unfavorably with the aesthetic principles of his European counterparts—Hitchcock having commented in 1929 that "he has paralleled with mediocre success the more extreme aesthetic researches of Le Corbusier and the men of *de Stijl*" and, in the catalogue essay for the International Style exhibition, designated him as a follower of Wright.[36] Although later included in the MOMA exhibition entitled "Modern Architecture in California," which toured throughout the country for several years, Schindler revealed in his writings an increasing awareness of being overlooked and misunderstood by the East Coast architectural establishment.

Perhaps in response to this shift of emphasis which had bred critical success for many of his contemporaries, especially Neutra, certain Schindler houses of the 1930s manifest elements of, or affinities to, International Style modernism which had not appeared earlier in his work. Historian Barbara Giella has characterized the majority of his output of this decade as an aberration in which he unsuccessfully sought to overlay formulaic International Style elements onto his own far more intuitive and inventive architectural vocabulary, resulting in what she has termed a distinctive "Thirties Style."[37] For example, distinctions between such works as the William E. Oliver Residence (1933–34) *(fig. 47)* and the John J. Buck Residence (1934) are revealing in this regard. Positioned at an angle on a sloping site to eliminate the need for excavation, the earlier Oliver Residence was made of wood-frame construction covered with tan and yellow stucco. A simple design encompassing Schindler's most extensive built-in components to date and a gently pitched roof to increase the ceiling height within the main part of the house *(fig. 48)*, the Oliver Residence also incorporated the unusual feature of a sinuous curving exterior handrail manifesting overtones

49 WILLIAM E. OLIVER RESIDENCE, Los Angeles, 1933–34.
Photograph by Axel F. Fog

50 JOHN J. BUCK RESIDENCE, Los Angeles, 1934.
View from rear garden. Photograph by Grant Mudford

53 of Streamline Moderne *(fig. 49)*. Schindler's Buck Residence represents a much more pronounced application of an increasingly International Style bias in his work. Presenting a simple façade to the street of planar walls and ribbon or clerestory windows, the rear of the house opened to a garden by means of sliding walls of glass—a device used infrequently by Schindler elsewhere in his work *(fig. 50)*. The design was further distinguished by Schindler's incorporation of a second-story apartment with its own separate entrance alongside the main house. A 1930s publication described Schindler's aim in the design as eliminating partitions to give a continuous form to all the rooms, and that his use of flat roofs suggested rainsheds instead of simply being just a solid flat slab.[38]

In 1929, Schindler had begun work on a model home for a tract development near Los Angeles called Park Moderne for William Lingenbrink *(fig. 51)* (also referred to as Camp Moderne by Schindler), for which all the prototype homes were designed in a modern idiom by local architects. This design anticipated his Schindler Shelters, a series of low-cost prototypes, on which he

worked from 1933 to 1939. Like many architects of his generation in the 1930s, Schindler was fascinated with the problem of prefabricated housing. Schindler copyrighted his design for the "Schindler Shelter," which provided for a factory-made unit consisting of a kitchen, bathroom, and laundry facilities, around which a simple shell enclosure of thin slabs of concrete would be constructed. All internal divisions within this house could be accomplished by standardized partitions, allowing for maximum flexibility. Schindler designed special windows with sheet-metal sashes and conceived of many other space- and labor-saving features that anticipated those of the standard, postwar modern home. He described his vision for the Schindler Shelters as follows:

The Schindler-Shelter proposes a solution for the housing problem which is ready for use here and now and need not wait for mass production. It is a solution which not only meets the challenge of our time for low cost but answers it with a thoroughbred product fulfilling the demands of advanced architectural thought: space design, flexibility, individualization, and practicability.[39]

51 PARK MODERNE MODEL CABINS FOR WILLIAM LINGENBRINK,
Calabasas, California, 1929-38. Perspective elevation

52 HANS N. VON KOERBER RESIDENCE,
Torrance, California, 1931-32

55 Besides Schindler's seeming reliance on International Style devices during the 1930s, certain works of this decade also manifest the continuous experimentalism that marked his entire career. One of the most extreme was the Hans N. Von Koerber Residence of 1931-32 (*fig. 52*). Mandated by restrictions of the Torrance, California, tract on which it was constructed, Schindler utilized tile, the material of the popular Spanish Colonial Revival style, to clad the roof, even extending this material to portions of the exterior walls. The Elizabeth Van Patten Residence (1934–36) was designed to provide a private bedroom and studio for each of the three ladies who would utilize a common living room and kitchen. Schindler used the requirement for a sloping tile roof due to building restrictions on the site as the basis of a series of dynamic converging rooflines. This energetic treatment served to mark three separate garage spaces facing the street and to mask additional variations in pitch that occurred over the main portion of the house (*fig. 53*). Seen from the rear, the divisions of this house are strongly articulated as the volume appears to splay out from a closed form to an open one (*figs. 54, 55*). In the Van Patten house, Schindler first used his designs for

"Schindler Units"—semi-standardized elements of furniture conceived as being adaptable to any space and condition of individual preference (*fig. 56*).

Schindler built a double residence for music historian John DeKeyser in Hollywood in 1935 (*figs. 57, 58*). Sited on a steep hillside lot, the house consists of a main residence in a single story with a one-bedroom apartment below. Here Schindler's use of unusual cladding materials encompasses strips of green composition roofing over portions of the house, combined with areas of light-colored stucco and contrasted with dark-red painted trim to produce a vibrant compositional effect. The interior, characteristically, manifests complex spatial volumes, structural exhibitionism, and extensive built-in furnishings.

Expressive characteristics were often found in Schindler's treatment of roof structures, as in his designs for the Warshaw (*fig. 59*) and William Jacobs residences of 1936. In the Warshaw scheme in particular, Schindler employed a curving roof plane that extends

53 ELIZABETH VAN PATTEN RESIDENCE, Los Angeles, 1934–36.
Photograph by Julius Shulman

54 ELIZABETH VAN PATTEN RESIDENCE, Los Angeles, 1934-36.
Photograph by Julius Shulman

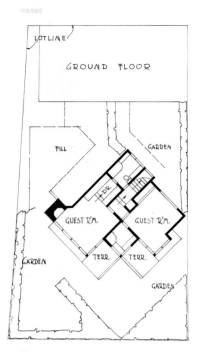

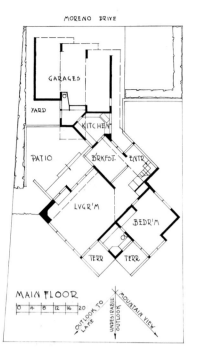

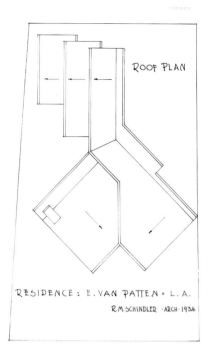

55 ELIZABETH VAN PATTEN RESIDENCE,
Los Angeles, 1934-36. Plans

56 ELIZABETH VAN PATTEN RESIDENCE,
Los Angeles, 1934-36. View of living room.
Photograph by W. P. Woodcock

57 JOHN DEKEYSER DOUBLE RESIDENCE, Los Angeles, 1935.
Photograph by Grant Mudford

59 emphatically downward to form the rear wall of the house, but also wrapped it around to define and enclose space on the street façade. Schindler once commented to Esther McCoy, who had remarked on the integral nature of his roofs to his buildings, "You don't set a roof on a house. A house is its roof. Just as a house is its foundation."[40]

In 1935 Schindler began work on a three-story residence and furniture designs for Ralph G. and Ola Walker in Silver Lake (figs. 60, 61). Compositionally, the Walker house exemplifies much of Schindler's approach to design during this period in that it is formally complex and without apparent unity from one elevation to the next. Indeed, the design seems additive and almost arbitrary. Its orientation, placement of windows, pacing of levels, and various other features depend on a variety of environmental conditions concerning the site and views. With wood-framing and stucco as the predominant building materials, Schindler utilized sloping ceilings in the interior to cover the roof beams and to mitigate a boxy character. He also used illusionistic devices such as silver paint to suggest that metal rather than wood had been used for framing. The incorporation of specially designed and built-in furnishings was also deeply important to the design as a whole (fig. 62).[41]

A residence and remodel for the Guy C. Wilson family, begun in 1935 and completed in 1938, was also sited in the Silver Lake area of Los Angeles. While slightly less complex than the Walker design, it contains a number of similar features—including a modest entry from the street side masking the character of a multi-level design articulated on the rear side oriented to the views beyond. In the disposition of their rear elevations, the Walker and Wilson houses are among the most restrained of Schindler's 1930s houses, departing from such designs as the Victoria McAlmon Residence (1935–36) or others in which the various elevations spring emphatically from the articulation of space within. A broad roof overhang shelters the compact living room, situated on the uppermost story in a complex spatial interrelationship with the kitchen and dining room. Interior circulation to the levels below, via an asymmetrically positioned interior staircase, results in a dynamic and rich spatial experience.

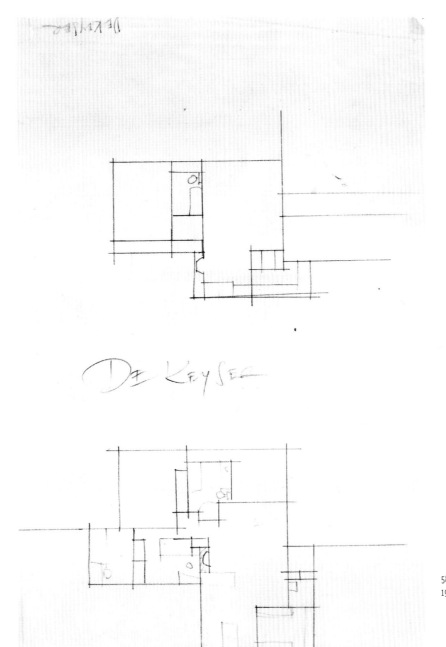

58 JOHN DEKEYSER DOUBLE RESIDENCE, Los Angeles, 1935. Floor plans

R. M. SCHINDLER , ARCHITECT   LOS ANGELES CAL

WARSHAW
RESIDENCE   ARCHITECT 37

59 WARSHAW RESIDENCE (project), Los Angeles, 1936–37

60 RALPH G. WALKER RESIDENCE, Los Angeles, 1935–41

61 RALPH G. WALKER RESIDENCE, Los Angeles, 1935-41.
Photograph by Grant Mudford

62 RALPH G. WALKER RESIDENCE, Los Angeles, 1935–41.
View of dining room. Photograph by Julius Shulman

Schindler began work on a residence and furniture designs for Mildred Southall, a musician-teacher, and her family in 1938 (fig. 63). Responding to the need for a combined residence and workshop for teaching music, he organized the house around a flexible main living space, a multi-purpose room designed to be used as a classroom, as well as to meet the family's own needs, keeping bedrooms and kitchen to minimum dimensions (fig. 64). To further maximize the desired spatial efficiency, much of the furniture was built-in; other pieces such as a folding plywood stool were collapsible and designed to be easily stored. McCoy has described the Southall House as one of the first all-plywood houses (fig. 65). In addition, Gebhard has pointed out how the use of wood became increasingly apparent in Schindler's work during the later 1930s and how he, like others of his generation including J. R. Davidson, William Wurster, Harwell Harris, and even Richard Neutra, were drawn to the quasi-industrial qualities of plywood.[42] Schindler used this material extensively in the built-in cabinets and furniture for the Southall House.

During the first half of the 1930s Schindler pursued several commercial projects. These included a design for the Lavana Studio Building in Beverly Hills (1929-30) (fig. 66), the Highway Bungalow Hotels of 1931, and two unbuilt projects for service stations for Standard Oil Company (1932) (fig. 67) and Union Oil Company (1932-34). He shared an enthusiasm for buildings oriented to the needs and nature of the emerging highway culture with Neutra and Lloyd Wright, who also designed service station projects and motels during a time when the pervasiveness of the automobile was beginning to transform the American landscape, especially in Los Angeles.

Schindler's foremost commercial building of the 1930s was his remodeling of Sardi's Restaurant (1932–34) in Hollywood (fig. 68), a building that evinced a Streamline Moderne architectural styling in keeping with the predominant tenor of the period. Sardi's was distinguished by its glass and metal façade which incorporated a stylized marquee and a dramatically suspended canopy over its front entrance. The interior of the main dining room, conveying an overall

RESIDENCE:SOUTHALL
R.M.SCHINDLER·ARCHITECT

63 MILDRED SOUTHALL RESIDENCE AND STUDIO, Los Angeles, 1938-39.
Exterior elevation

64 MILDRED SOUTHALL RESIDENCE AND STUDIO, Los Angeles, 1938-39.
Main-level floor plan

65 MILDRED SOUTHALL RESIDENCE AND STUDIO, Los Angeles, 1938-39.
Photograph by Maynard Parker

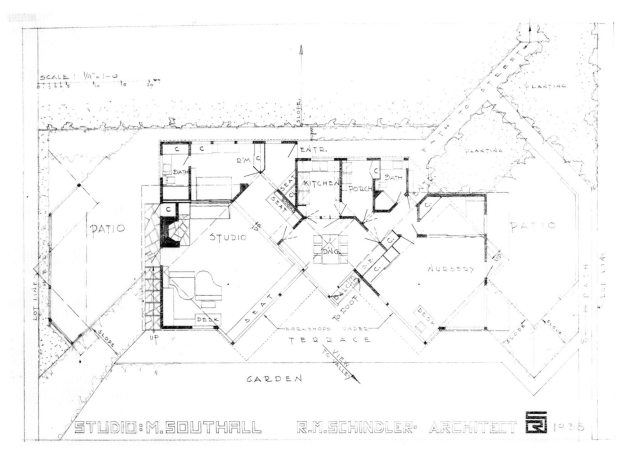

STUDIO: M. SOUTHALL   R.M.SCHINDLER· ARCHITECT   1938

66 LAVANA STUDIO BUILDING (project with AGIC),
Beverly Hills, California, 1929-30. Perspective elevation

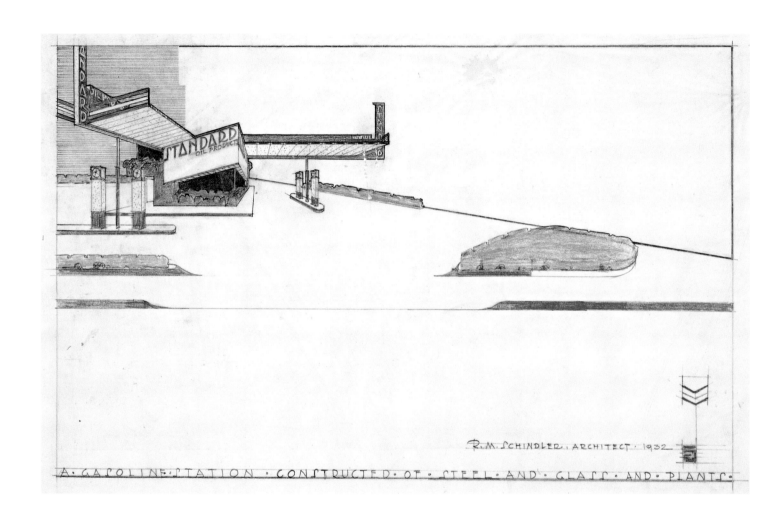

A·GASOLINE·STATION·CONSTRUCTED·OF·STEEL·AND·GLASS·AND·PLANTS·

R. M. SCHINDLER, ARCHITECT · 1932

67 STANDARD OIL COMPANY SERVICE STATION (project),
location unknown, 1932. Perspective elevation

68 SARDI'S RESTAURANT REMODELING FOR A. EDDIE BRANDSTATTER,
Los Angeles, 1932–34. Perspective elevation

69 effect of spaciousness and luminosity, contained circular dining alcoves and furniture designed by Schindler *(fig. 69)*. Sardi's was a commission of great importance for Schindler due to its central location in Hollywood, where prominent members of the film community frequented it. However, beyond a handful of other small commercial restaurant projects, including Schindler's design of another for the same client, Lindy's Restaurant Number I of 1932–34, it did not lead to any significant expansion of Schindler's commercial practice.

Schindler's multiple-housing efforts of the 1930s were limited, yet several stand out as noteworthy continuations of his experimental approach. In 1937 he designed a project for a beach colony for client A. E. Rose *(fig. 70)*. Arranged in two semi-circular configurations, a number of small wood-framed, stucco, and canvas beach cottages fronted onto the sand, offering privacy within their confines but at the same time easy access to communal space. While a portable mockup was made of one of the cottage designs *(fig. 71)*, the project was never realized due to the high cost of beachfront property.[43] If built, it would have represented a unique synthesis of Schindler's casual approach to materials and construction in tandem with a highly organized and structured plan for the entire complex.

Among Schindler's best-known multi-family designs is that of the A. and Luby Bubeshko Apartments *(fig. 72)*. Begun in 1938 and finished in 1941, it contains visual similarities to Schindler's private houses of the 1930s, but foreshadows the siting and orientation of later designs such as the unbuilt T. Falk Apartments (1943) *(fig. 73)* and the Laurelwood Apartments (1945-49) *(fig. 74)*. In the Bubeshko design, Schindler was able to accomplish his goal of providing out door open spaces for each unit by utilizing roof terraces and extending his approach to interlocking space with somewhat more regularity, whereas elements of the Falk Apartments become more angled and expressive both on the interior and exterior. His Laurelwood Apartments were also sited in an irregular manner to correspond to the site's topography and to provide a diversity of internal floor plans and outdoor spaces.

69 SARDI'S RESTAURANT REMODELING FOR A. EDDIE BRANDSTATTER,
Los Angeles, 1932-34. Photograph by Mott Studios

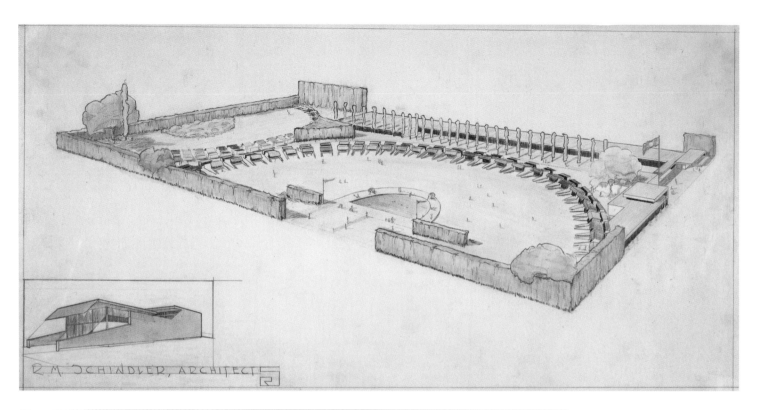

70 A. E. ROSE BEACH COLONY (project), Santa Monica, California, 1937

71 A. E. ROSE BEACH COLONY PROTOTYPICAL UNIT, built in West Hollywood, California, 1937.
Photograph by Julius Shulman

The forties was a decade of consummate experimentalism for Schindler, in which he cast off the need to develop extensive working drawings, instead preferring to concentrate on the details of construction directly in the field.[44] Increasingly, his buildings took on unusual and sometimes even exaggerated forms and properties that departed from conventional approaches and from the acceptable preoccupations of other modernists. Schindler's residence for José Rodriguez in Glendale, California (1940–42), was one such design. With a generously scaled L-shaped plan, its combination of wood and stone and its expressively angled wood members endow this house with a sense of dynamic articulation. Extensive use of plywood on the interior for built-ins and paneling contrasts with the use of stone, slate, and copper for a richly textured effect that appears almost additive.

A building for a Baptist congregation in south Los Angeles, the Bethlehem Baptist Church was completed in 1945 *(fig. 75)*. This low-budget commission was organized in a simple yet effective manner to make the most of a small rectangular lot. Placing the church at the corner of the lot rather than in the center and marking its presence by means of an abstracted cruciform tower, Schindler organized his design to enable flexible use of both indoor and outdoor spaces. Lacking a conventionally monumental front door, the modest exterior, which provides visual privacy from the busy street it fronts, is faced with wide, horizontal bands of stucco into which planters and other openings for natural illumination are inset *(fig. 76)*. Earlier, Schindler had created a version of a church design with similar features for another congregation in Hollywood; however, the design remains unbuilt.

In 1946, following the lifting of postwar building restrictions, Schindler began work on several houses. These included a residence and furniture for Richard Lechner in Studio City (1946–48) *(fig. 77)*; a desert house for Maryon E. Toole in Palm Springs (1946–48); and a house for Maurice Kallis, also in Studio City, completed in 1948. The Kallis Residence (1946–48) *(fig. 79)* is one of Schindler's most forcefully expressive in its combinatorial approach to the use of angled walls as well as rusticated

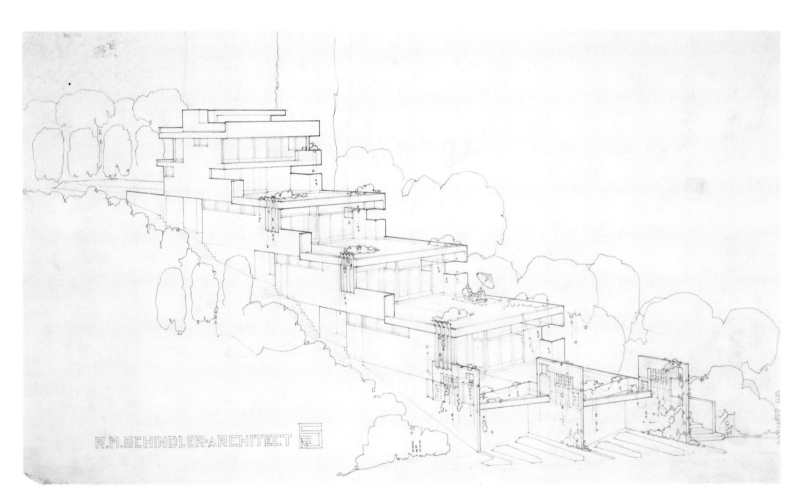

72 A. AND LUBY BUBESHKO APARTMENTS, Los Angeles, 1938–41

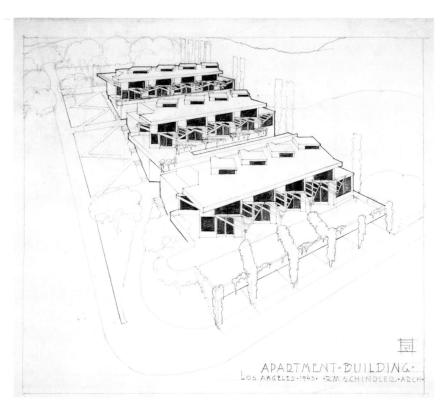

APARTMENT·BUILDING·
LOS ANGELES·1943· ·R.M.SCHINDLER·ARCH·

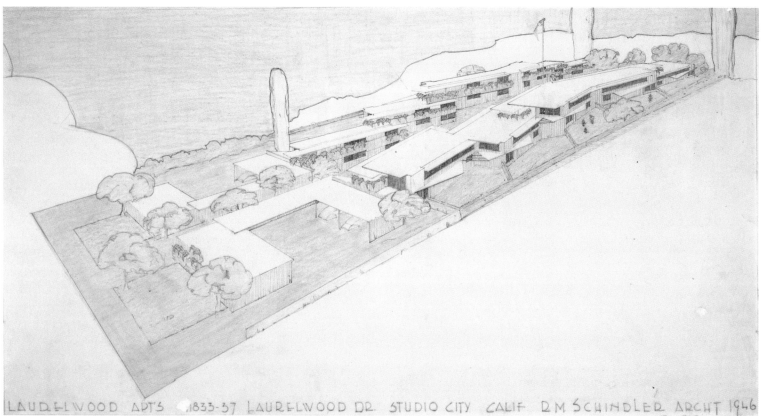

LAURELWOOD APTS 1833-37 LAURELWOOD DR. STUDIO CITY CALIF R.M SCHINDLER ARCHT 1946

73 T. FALK APARTMENTS (project), Los Angeles, 1943

74 LAURELWOOD APARTMENTS FOR HENRY G. SCHICK
AND MAXIM H. BRADEN, Studio City, California, 1945-49.
Aerial perspective

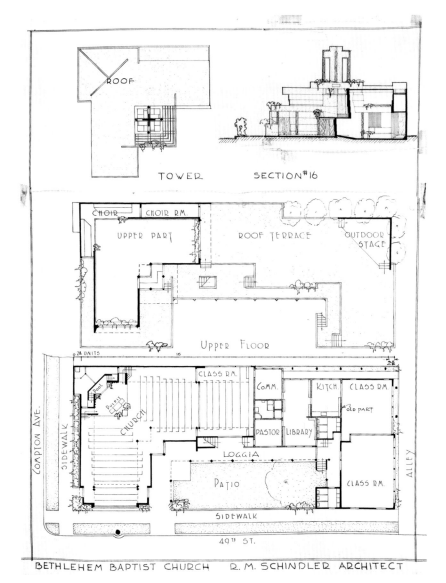

TOWER   SECTION #16

BETHLEHEM BAPTIST CHURCH   R. M. SCHINDLER ARCHITECT

75 BETHLEHEM BAPTIST CHURCH, Los Angeles, 1944-45.
Floor plans and sections

76 BETHLEHEM BAPTIST CHURCH, Los Angeles, 1944-45.
Photograph by Julius Shulman

strips of split-stake fencing to create exterior screening and wall surfaces. These elements endow the house with a sense of dynamism, yet as a whole it remains a remarkably cohesive statement. Describing his own intentions for the house, Schindler commented that he had attempted to create "spatially satisfying rooms by using in-and-out sloping ceilings in a balanced way," and he also referred to the genesis of the design as site-specific, "deriving from the oak trees and the hills."[45] Its open V-shaped plan *(fig. 78)* corresponds to the contours of the sloping site, and its connection to the landscape is underscored by the predominant blue-green tonalities of its color palette. Originally designed as two small, detached structures—a studio space and the main residence—connected by an outdoor terrace, the connection has since been enclosed.

Schindler's designs for his final houses were among his most intuitive and unconventional. These include the Ellen Janson Residence in the Hollywood Hills (1948–49), the Adolph Tischler Residence in Westwood (1949–50), the Maurice Ries Residence in Los Angeles (1950–52), and the design of a house and furniture for Samuel Skolnik (1950–52). The tenuous appearance of the dramatically sited Janson house *(fig. 80, 81)*, seemingly hovering over its plunging downslope site, depends on the presence of a lattice-like series of supports that appear superficial rather than structural. This feature and the extreme casualness of its composition and materials—its appearance of incompleteness, fragility, and even roughness— departs radically from work by other modern architects in Los Angeles of the time. Likewise, the Tischler house *(fig. 82, 83)* was marked not only by a highly original form in plan and organization, but by an extreme experimentalism with low-cost materials—in this case blue corrugated fiberglass used extensively as roofing material *(fig. 84)*. Schindler's material experiments in this house seem to echo that of his earlier design of a Translucent House for Aline Barnsdall (1927–28).

In 1940, the problematic character of interpreting Schindler's work had once again become the subject of critical commentary by Henry-Russell Hitchcock:

77 RICHARD LECHNER RESIDENCE, Studio City, California, 1946-48.
Perspective elevation

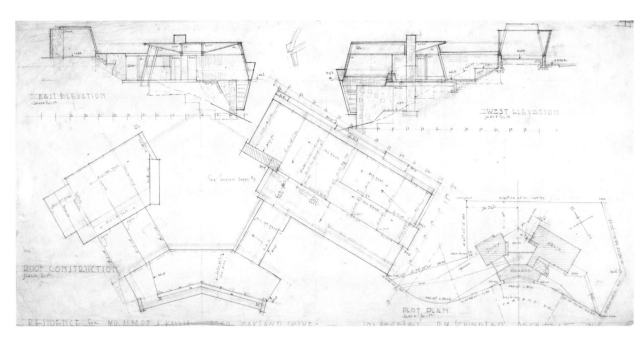

78 MAURICE KALLIS RESIDENCE AND STUDIO, Studio City, California, 1946-48.
Floor plans and sections

79 MAURICE KALLIS RESIDENCE AND STUDIO, Studio City, California, 1946-48.
View of façade from terrace. Photograph by Robert C. Cleveland

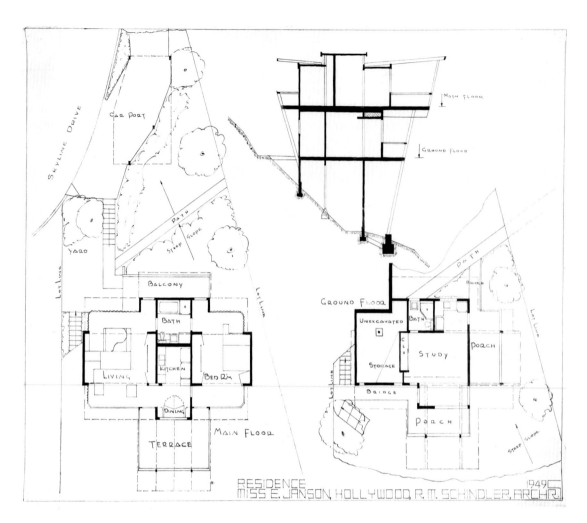

80 ELLEN JANSON RESIDENCE, Los Angeles, 1948-49.
Floor plans and sections

81 ELLEN JANSON RESIDENCE, Los Angeles, 1948-49.
Side view. Photograph by Lotte Nossaman

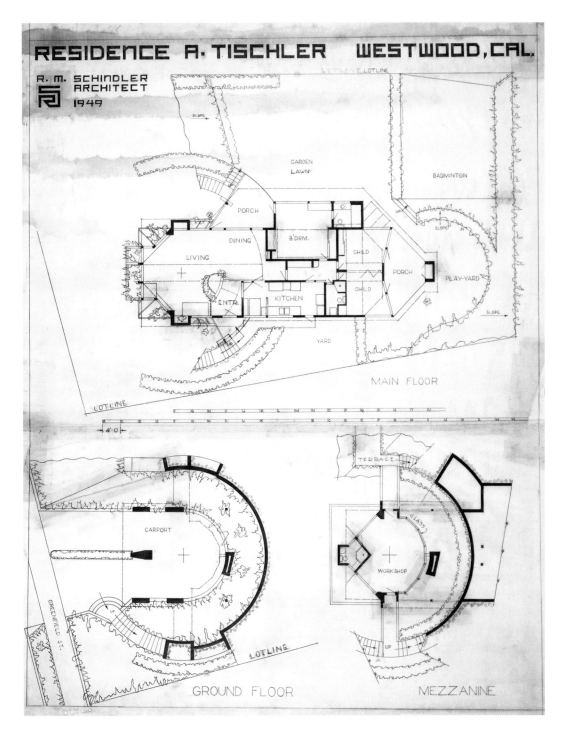

RESIDENCE A·TISCHLER   WESTWOOD, CAL.

R. M. SCHINDLER
ARCHITECT
1949

E. LOTLINE

SLOPE

GARDEN
LAWN

BADMINTON

PORCH

UP

SLOPE

DINING

B'DRM.

CHILD

LIVING

CHILD

PORCH

PLAY-YARD

ENTR.

KITCHEN

CHILD

SLOPE

UP

YARD

LOTLINE

MAIN FLOOR

4'-0"

TERRACE

CARPORT

GLASS

WORKSHOP

GREENFIELD ST.

UP

LOTLINE

UP

GROUND FLOOR

MEZZANINE

82 ADOLPH TISCHLER RESIDENCE, Los Angeles, 1949-50.
Floor plans and site plan

83 ADOLPH TISCHLER RESIDENCE, Los Angeles, 1949-50.
Photograph by Grant Mudford

84 ADOLPH TISCHLER RESIDENCE, Los Angeles, 1949-50.
Photograph by Grant Mudford

The case of Schindler I do not profess to understand. There is certainly immense vitality perhaps somewhat lacking among many of the best modern architects of the Pacific Coast. But this vitality seems in general to lead to arbitrary and brutal effects ... Schindler's manner does not seem to mature. His continued reflection of the somewhat hectic psychological air of the region, from which all the others have attempted to protect themselves, still produces something of the look of sets for a Wellsian "film of the future."[46]

A similar skepticism about the merits of Schindler's work may have led to his exclusion from one of the foremost vehicles for dissemination of information about experimental postwar modern architecture in California—the Case Study House program. Despite the interest in prototypical solutions to housing that he had demonstrated earlier in his career, indeed one that continued to preoccupy him at various stages throughout, Schindler was never asked to contribute a design to this program for *Arts & Architecture* magazine. Conceived by editor John Entenza in 1945, the Case Study House program continued into the mid-1960s with a series of designs by mostly Los Angeles architects for low-cost, modern houses that could serve as prototypes for mass production. Whether Schindler's exclusion from the program was due to antipathy on Entenza's part toward the anti-rational character of his work, or to Entenza's closer connection to Neutra, who contributed several designs to the program, is unclear. Both explanations may be plausible, however, since participation in the program resulted from personal invitations by Entenza. Schindler's absence from the program further removed his work from the international recognition and critical esteem accorded to other participating architects in the program through the vehicle of its widespread publication and promotion in local, national, and international journals and later, books and exhibitions.[47]

Exclusion from the Case Study House program during the late phase of Schindler's career resulted in the further solidification of his reputation as an architect outside of the mainstream—one preoccupied with seemingly arbitrary effects in wood and stucco while others pursued the use of steel and techniques of prefabrication. It was a shortsighted view that overlooked Schindler's radical experiments with concrete, as well as the more conventional materials of wood and stucco, and with extremes of indoor/outdoor living that would indeed become a standard feature of the "postwar California home." Most significantly, such assessments overlooked Schindler's fundamentally social goals in rethinking how architecture could foster not only physical but also psychological health, as well as a spirit of egalitarianism and flexibility that he considered hallmarks of life in the twentieth century. He had written in 1926, "The house will have to cease to squeeze us through narrow door jambs, to keep us dodging among pieces of furniture, and perch us on top of scaffolds. It must permit us to indulge in the free harmonious motions of a walking and resting animal, which we are."[48]

Late in his career, Schindler became preoccupied with articulating his ideas and clarifying how his work and approach differed from that of other architects. Writing in 1949, Schindler pointed to what he felt were his pioneering innovations. Among these were a variety of structural systems that he had developed from an empirical standpoint to facilitate the efficient construction of his designs. For instance, he designated his use of wood framing, covered with plaster in many of his 1930s houses, as a system of "Plaster Skin Design," conveying the rational basis with which he pursued the experimental use of even this commonplace material.[49] In 1941 he had described his own work as "the only distinctly Californian development in modern work. Different from the European importations of the 'Internationalists' like Neutra, etc., and from the derivations of the 'midwestern Prairie' style of Frank Lloyd Wright produced by Harris, etc."[50] He wrote in 1943:

My early realisation that a house is not an international but a local product meant for local use, lead [sic] towards the exploration of the character of California. Therefore I abandoned the "modern" as imported from Europe (Lescase [sic], Neutra A.S.F.) and tried to develop a contemporary expression of California ... I believe that outside of Frank Lloyd Wright I am the only architect in U.S. who has attained a distinct local and personal form language ... You will find its traces even in the work of my friends and coworkers as: Gregory Ain, E. [Ed] Lind, H. [Harwell] Harrison [sic].[51]

And toward the end of his life, Schindler wrote, "I came to live and work in California. I camped under the open sky, in the redwoods, on the beach, the foothills and the desert. I tested its adobe, its granite, and its sky. And out of a carefully built up conception of how the human being could grow roots in this soil—unique and delightful—I built my house. And unless I failed it should be as Californian as the Parthenon is Greek and the Forum Roman."[52]

Schindler's historiography has most recently been the subject of insightful study by Margaret Crawford[53] and is also evaluated by Richard Guy Wilson elsewhere in this book. Reassessment of his career was set in motion by writer and former Schindler draftsman Esther McCoy, who published a group of tributes to Schindler the year after his death that revealed the nature of his impact on younger architects such as Gregory Ain, and the extent of how his work was appreciated by architects and critics at home and abroad.[54] McCoy's extensive writings on Schindler, beginning in 1953, were followed by a 1967 exhibition of his work organized by the historian David Gebhard, who became the foremost Schindler scholar after McCoy and before Judith Sheine. Additionally, British historian Reyner Banham, whose sympathetic studies of Los Angeles architecture first evaluated the revolutionary character of much of the work produced there from the unique revisionist standpoint of respect for idiosyncrasy and the role of climate and popular culture, asserted Schindler's pioneering role in the development of modern architecture. Banham also authored the first unequivocally admiring analysis of the Kings Road House:

Schindler's architecture has been an unsettling revelation, undermining ... their long-held preconceptions about the nature and history of the Modern Movement ... Persistently ignored by the standard literature it remains one of the most original, and ingenious domestic designs of the present century—and one of the most gratifyingly habitable.[55]

In 1969, when Schindler's work was the subject of an exhibition that traveled to the Royal Institute of British Architects in London, a writer expressed the opinion that Schindler's contribution lay in his early and unhesitating application of the ideas he had absorbed from Loos, producing designs that were uncompromisingly modern from the start. When the same exhibition was seen in The Netherlands, architect Herman Hertzberger wrote of Schindler:

There is no doubt that he in [sic] one of the earliest of the true constructivists, since everything he touches he makes in such a way that it explains clearly how it works, and why. He makes only what has to be there, in answer to every individual demand; the whole structure becomes the complexity of all demands together.[56]

A distinct yet related assessment of the importance of construction to Schindler, and his role in this tradition within the architectural trajectory of his Los Angeles context, is found in a 1986 text by Kurt Forster, who commented: "the qualities of the best California architecture are more than skin-deep. From Gill to Mack, from Schindler to Gehry, they spring from an effort to give the practical side of architecture its due without falling short on the side of architecture as architecture."[57] The issue of Schindler's place within the history of California architecture and within a continuum of expressive experimentalism is an intriguing one. Although he himself pointed to only a few architects with whom he felt some sense of commonality (such as Gregory Ain and Ed Lind, who had worked for him as draftsmen), aspects of Schindler's work can be related to that of his contemporaries and members of a slightly younger generation such as Lloyd Wright, Harwell Hamilton Harris, and the young John Lautner, all of whom were also pursuing personal variants of modernism that depended on expressive, dynamic treatments of form and space *(fig. 85)*.

One of the most insightful analyses of Schindler's aesthetic, directly countering Hitchcock's dismissive assessment in 1940 of Schindler's "brutal and arbitrary effects," is one offered by Barbara Giella in 1985:

Schindler's artistic ambitions impelled him to manipulate an uncommonly large number of variables and, at times, rendered it difficult to integrate space and form ... although he clearly desired unity, he did not demand absolute consistency. He was tolerant of any problems created by the gap between his goals and the available means to achieve them, between whatever ideal notions he may have had and the practical realities he had to accept. Schindler tolerated inconsistency and awkwardness because, above all, he was interested in space and in space-molding form rather than in materials, workmanship, detailing or structure per se. Inconsistency, conflict, ambiguity and contradiction, when they occurred, were the by-product either of practical necessity or of a value system which did not hold consistency as an absolute.[58]

It is clear that from today's standpoint, the variety and expressive character of Schindler's work which confounded partisans of a rigorous rationality in modern architecture has found an audience that is sympathetic to and even inspired by this architect's relaxed yet restless experimentalism *(figs. 86, 87)*. Schindler's avoidance of formulaic solutions, and his emphasis instead on a pragmatic

85 John Lautner. Carling House, Los Angeles, 1949

83 intuitiveness, can be appreciated as a virtue in today's architectural culture. Even the qualities of roughness in detailing and hybridity in juxtaposing materials conveys an immensely satisfying sense of vitality and invention that seems extraordinarily well-suited to the architectural culture of Southern California. Architect Philip Johnson, author of the 1932 International Style exhibition within which Schindler's work had not been deemed suitable for inclusion, has recently expressed a shift in his thinking about the merits of this singular architect based on the evolutions in his own work as well as in architectural culture in general. Now comparing Schindler and Neutra to their Dutch contemporaries Gerrit Rietveld and J. J. P. Oud, Johnson has commented that he finds a similar relationship in the work of these two pairs of architects—Oud and Neutra representing the rational, rigorous, and machined, and Rietveld and Schindler the expressive and individualistic—and that historical revisionism fed by shifts in the culture at large demonstrates that both approaches are equally valid ones and that the latter, from today's standpoint, might even be the more valuable and interesting one.[59]

86 Frank O. Gehry. Gehry House, Santa Monica,
California, 1978. Photograph by Tim Street-Porter

87 Chu + Gooding Architects with Michael Matteucci.
Gabbert House, Santa Monica, California, 2000.
Photograph by Benny Chan

Notes

1 Esther McCoy, "Schindler, Space Architect," *Direction* 8, no. 1 (Fall 1945): 15.

2 While several noted architects in Europe such as Hans Hollein, Herman Hertzberger, and Enric Miralles have documented their interest in Schindler's work, it is in Los Angeles, where Schindler's influence has been strongest, that architects of the post-Frank Gehry generation (ranging from Michael Rotondi, Frank Israel, and Stefanos Polyzoides) to a younger, less-established spectrum of architects now in their thirties and forties (including Judith Sheine, Guthrie + Buresh, Chu + Gooding, Barbara Bestor, Escher GuneWardena Architects, Anthony Unruh, and Paul Randall Jacobson, among many others), have manifested an active interest in and responsiveness to the nature of Schindler's work.

3 Peter Blundell Jones, "From the Neoclassical Axis to Aperspective Space," *Architectural Review* 183 (March 1988): 18.

4 August Sarnitz, in his *R. M. Schindler, Architect: 1887–1953* (New York: Rizzoli, 1988) and "The Wagnerschule and Adolf Loos," in Lionel March and Judith Sheine, eds., *R. M. Schindler: Composition and Construction* (London: Academy Editions, 1993), 21–37, provides extensive analyses of the climate in which Schindler was educated in Vienna. Barbara Giella, "R. M. Schindler's Thirties Style: Its Character (1931–37) and International Sources (1906–37)" (Ph.D. diss., New York University, 1985), devotes considerable emphasis to the importance of Schindler's education at the Wagnerschule.

5 Franziska Bojczuk to Esther McCoy, 2 September 1958, Box 15/Schindler/Notes and Research Material/Vienna to Los Angeles, Esther McCoy Papers, Archives of American Art, Smithsonian Institution, Washington, D.C.

6 This manifesto is published in its entirety in several sources, including in Sarnitz, *R. M. Schindler, Architect*, 42; and March and Sheine, eds., *R. M. Schindler: Composition and Construction*, 10–12.

7 I am grateful to Tim Samuelson, Curator of Architecture at the Chicago Historical Society, for providing concrete evidence that the Elks Club interior seems to demonstrate the hand of Schindler, thus reinforcing Esther McCoy's suggestion that Schindler had played a strong role in its design. I also thank him for his helpful assistance with original documents relating to the Buena Shore Club.

8 "To Open New Buena Shore Club Tomorrow," *The Chicago Israelite*, 22 December 1917. Barbara Giella, "Buena Shore Club," in March and Sheine, eds., *R. M. Schindler: Composition and Construction*, 39–47, gives a detailed analysis of this design.

9 "The Buena Shore Club Described by its Designer," *The Chicago Israelite*, 22 December 1917. David Gebhard, in *Schindler* (1971, reprint San Francisco: William Stout Publishers, 1997), 21, describes this project as paralleling avant-garde Dutch work of the late 1910s/early 1920s, but Barbara Giella, in "Buena Shore Club," 47, stresses that it predates these and states emphatically that the Club should be recognized as one of the more advanced buildings in Europe and America of its day.

10 Handwritten notes in the Rudolph M. Schindler Collection, Architecture and Design Collection, University Art Museum, University of California, Santa Barbara (hereafter "RMS at ADC/UCSB").

11 Text by Schindler of 1920 or 1921, reprinted in Esther McCoy, *Vienna to Los Angeles: Two Journeys* (Santa Monica, Calif.: Arts + Architecture Press, 1979), 129.

12 Schindler to Loos, reprinted in McCoy, *Vienna to Los Angeles*, 143.

13 Judith Sheine, "R. M. Schindler 1887–1953," *2G,* no. 7 (1998): 9.

14 This correspondence is detailed in McCoy, *Vienna to Los Angeles*, 143–49.

15 Jin-Ho Park, in his "Schindler, Symmetry and the Free Public Library, 1920," *Arq* 2 (Winter 1996): 72–83, analyzes this project extensively.

16 Text by Schindler in RMS at ADC/UCSB.

17 Letters from Aline Barnsdall dating from 1925, and the records of a lifetime subscription to *New Masses* that she had given him as a gift in 1926, document the ongoing friendly nature of their relations and her desire to seek his advice and involvement with matters related to remodeling and upkeep of the Olive Hill property. RMS at ADC/UCSB.

18 RMS to Richard Neutra, October 1921, reprinted in McCoy, *Vienna to Los Angeles*, 137.

19 RMS to Neutra, 16 June 1922, reprinted in McCoy, *Vienna to Los Angeles*, 139.

20 Text by Schindler in RMS at ADC/UCSB.

21 *Ibid*.

22 *Ibid*.

23 The system is described in detail in a text by Schindler in RMS at ADC/UCSB.

24 Rose Marie Packard, in a 1953 statement, RMS at ADC/UCSB.

25 The system is described in detail in *Architectural Record* (July 1930): 17–18, in an article on Pueblo Ribera and in a 1949 statement by Schindler on this project developed for the School of Architecture at the University of Southern California.

26 A group of letters spanning May 1923 to August 1926 detail the complexities and frustrations of realizing the project from the client's point of view, particularly with regard to securing financing and establishing a solution for the deficiencies in waterproofing the concrete. RMS at ADC/UCSB.

27 Lionel March, "R. M. Schindler: The Residence of Dr. and Mrs. James Eads How, Silver Lake, Los Angeles, California, 1925," *G. A. Houses* 56 (1998): 35.

28 *See ibid.*, in which March provides a penetrating analysis of this building's complex structure.

29 These included "Ventilation," *Los Angeles Times*, 14 March 1926; "Plumbing and Health," *Los Angeles Times*, 21 March 1926; "About Heating," *Los Angeles Times*, 4 April 1926; "About Lighting," *Los Angeles Times*, 11 April 1926; "About Furniture," *Los Angeles Times*, 18 April 1926; and "Shelter or Playground," *Los Angeles Times*, 2 May 1926. These texts were reprinted in *Oppositions* (Fall 1979): 74–85.

30 Text by Schindler in RMS at ADC/UCSB, and reprinted in part in Esther McCoy, "Schindler Houses of the 1920s," *Arts and Architecture* (September 1953): 31.

31 P. Morton Shand, "A Cantilevered Summer-House," *The Architectural Review* (March 1933): 117.

32 This relationship is discussed by Naomi Sawelson-Gorse, "Braxton Gallery, 1928–29, Hollywood," in Marla C. Berns, ed., *The Furniture of R. M. Schindler* (Santa Barbara, Calif.: University Art Museum, 1997), 85–89.

33 The relationship between Schindler and Neutra is detailed in Thomas S. Hines, *Richard Neutra and the Search for Modern Architecture* (New York and Oxford: Oxford University Press, 1982). In addition, the Lovells' choice of Neutra as the architect for their house in Los Angeles, a commission that Schindler had hoped to receive after having designed and built their beach house, may have contributed further to a cooling of relations between these formerly close friends.

34 Pauline Gibling, "Modern California Architects," *Creative Art* 10, no. 2 (February 1932): 113.

35 The specific contents of books and articles by Taut, Hilberseimer, Cheney, Neutra, and others who published designs by Schindler early in his career are detailed in Giella, "R. M. Schindler's Thirties Style," 26–27.

36 Henry-Russell Hitchcock, *Modern Architecture: Romanticism and Reintegration* (New York: Payson & Clarke, 1929), 204–05; and Hitchcock and Philip Johnson, *Modern Architecture: International Exhibition* (New York: The Museum of Modern Art, 1932). Johnson's tart replies to Schindler's queries about the MOMA exhibition can be found in RMS at ADC/UCSB.

37 Giella, "R. M. Schindler's Thirties Style."

38 Patrick Abercrombie, ed., *The Book of the Modern House: A Panoramic Survey of Contemporary Domestic Design* (London: Hodder & Stoughton, 1939).

39 Text by Schindler dated 1933 in RMS at ADC/UCSB. His Panel-Post Method project related to this desire to develop standardized methods of construction to ensure efficiency in the time and cost of residential construction. Schindler further articulated his ideas about a scientific and cost-effective approach to construction in his writings about "The Schindler Frame," published in *Architectural Record* in May 1947. Most recently, his methodology with regard to construction is analyzed by Judith Sheine in "R. M. Schindler 1887–1953," *2G*, no. 7 (1998): 10–13.

40 McCoy, "Schindler, Space Architect," 14.

41 The Walker House is the subject of a detailed analysis by Barbara Giella in "R. M. Schindler's Thirties Style."

42 Esther McCoy, *Five California Architects* (New York: Praeger Publishers, 1975), 178; and David Gebhard, *Schindler*, 129–32.

43 Gebhard, *Schindler*, 122.

44 Esther McCoy has written most extensively about Schindler's working methods as she had the opportunity to observe these first-hand while a draftsman in his office in 1944.

45 Text by Schindler in RMS at ADC/UCSB.

46 [Henry-]Russell Hitchcock, "An Eastern Critic Looks at Western Architecture," *California Arts & Architecture* (December 1940): 41.

47 For the most extensive discussions of the Case Study House program, *see* Esther McCoy, *Case Study Houses, 1945 – 1962* (Los Angeles: Hennessey & Ingalls, Inc., 1977), and Elizabeth A. T. Smith, ed., *Blueprints for Modern Living: History and Legacy of the Case Study Houses* (Cambridge, Mass.: The MIT Press, 1989).

48 R. M. Schindler, "About Furniture."

49 Schindler to the School of Architecture, University of Southern California, 10 October 1949, in RMS at ADC/UCSB.

50 Schindler to E. [Elizabeth] Mock [The Museum of Modern Art, New York], 20 May 1941, in RMS at ADC/UCSB.

51 Schindler to Mock, 10 August 1945, in RMS at ADC/UCSB.

52 Schindler to McCoy in RMS at ADC/UCSB.

53 Margaret Crawford, "Forgetting and Remembering Schindler: The Social History of an Architectural Reputation," *2G*, no. 7 (1998): 130–43.

54 "R. M. Schindler," *Arts & Architecture* (May 1954): 12–15. The Schindler Collection at ADC/UCSB also contains the original statements by architects and historians including Ain, Neutra, Harwell Harris, William Wurster, Whitney Smith, Juan O'Gorman, Talbot Hamlin, and Philip Johnson.

55 Reyner Banham, "Pioneering without Tears," *Architectural Design* 37 (December 1967): 578, 579; reprinted in his *Los Angeles: The Architecture of Four Ecologies* (New York: Harper and Row, 1971), 182.

56 Herman Hertzberger, *Bouwkundig Weekblad* 87, no. 8 (April 1969): 187.

57 Kurt Forster, "California Architecture: Now You See It, Now You Don't," *UCLA Architecture Journal* (1986): 6. In this essay Forster pointed to Schindler as a foremost predecessor of the early work of Frank O. Gehry.

58 Giella, "R. M. Schindler's Thirties Style," 82, 85.

59 Philip Johnson, in Peter Noever, ed., *MAK Center for Art and Architecture: R. M. Schindler* (Munich and New York: Prestel, 1995), 26, and in conversation with the author, Fall 1999.

1 KINGS ROAD HOUSE, West Hollywood,
California, 1921–22. Presentation drawing

ROBERT SWEENEY

LIFE AT KINGS ROAD: AS IT WAS 1920–1940

[I am] grateful to you, r.m.s.... for ... this house, which has been so dear to me that in a way it has determined life.

—Pauline Gibling Schindler to R. M. Schindler, 9 July 1953[1]

Eighty years hence, R. M. Schindler's Kings Road House (1921–22) radiates brilliance, provocation, and resolution: it has the inevitability of a masterpiece *(fig. 1)*. It is an informed distillation of many sources and influences—architectural, structural, and philosophical—that resulted from the union of two free spirits: a gifted modern architect and his socially conscious wife. If ever a building determined life, this is it. Comfort is intellectual, beauty subjective. No other house so thoroughly challenging ingrained behavior patterns and expectations comes to mind. Yet the forces that coalesced to realize the vision all too soon destroyed it. It is a story with moments of exhilaration tempered by periods of agony—and it all seems very contemporary today.

Esther McCoy offered the initial critical assessment of Kings Road in 1960; most that followed accepted her judgment. Now, with the new availability of an extensive collection of correspondence preserved by Pauline Gibling Schindler, we can move beyond McCoy's pioneering work and tell a substantially more revealing and satisfying story. From a revisionist perspective, most intriguing is the realization that the house is the embodiment of an ideal lifestyle Pauline conceived as a young woman. The seeds of Kings Road can be found in a letter she wrote to her mother from Hull-House in 1916:
One of my dreams, Mother, is to have, some day, a little joy of a bungalow, on the edge of woods and mountains and near a crowded city, which shall be open just as some people's hearts are open, to friends of all classes and types. I should like it to be as democratic a meeting-place as Hull-House, where millionaires and laborers, professors and illiterates, the splendid and the ignoble, meet constantly together.[2]
R. M. Schindler's achievement was to express this ideal in brilliant architectural form. In a sense the building was Pauline's; though physically often away, in spirit she never left.

Pauline was a lively correspondent. We now have accounts of the Schindlers' initial explorations and impressions just after their arrival in southern California in December 1920. After the house, at 835 North Kings Road, was completed, she wrote exuberantly of the frequent social gatherings there and of the beauty of the building. From this early period we also have the recorded impressions of Pauline's parents and sister, Dorothy. Though far from adventurous in their taste, they spoke with amusing approbation of the building's merits and the Schindlers' rigorous aesthetic standards; Dorothy observed in early 1923 that "835 has *many* notions as to just how everything must be done."[3]

The correspondence also frankly reveals a dark side of the personal chemistry at Kings Road. Pauline left in 1927 and, for the next decade, she led a gypsylike existence before returning more or less permanently in the late 1930s. During this period numerous individuals occupied the house as tenants; the most notable include John Cage, Galka Scheyer, and several Hollywood personalities. All left a record for posterity.

Through it all, R. M. Schindler has remained an elusive personality. He was at once in the forefront of progressive architectural and social thought while curiously remaining an outsider. He was taciturn in demeanor, rarely seeking conflict but quietly challenging the establishment. Dione Neutra remembered him as "a very difficult character, very noncommunicative, hiding his true feelings behind a smiling face." Conversely, he had "a very winning personality ... such an infectious laugh." Pauline observed "the wonderful quiet that R.M.S. has when he is at work."[4]

Pauline was a genteel rebel, another study in contradiction, though easier to assess. Clues to her personality emerged early on: when she was seven her father, Edmund Gibling, observed that she "seems likely to gradually outgrow her nervous & excitable disposition and may develop into a loveable girl. She is certainly bright." Her years at Smith College gave her an air of privileged authority of which she never lost sight, yet some of her most vivid early recollections were of work in the slums of Boston and at Jane Addams's Hull-House in Chicago. She was high-minded and ambitious and at the same time self-defeating in her activities. In 1915 her father summarized behavior patterns that continued throughout her life:

It is unfortunate that you should have repeated at Hull House the mistake you made at Smith of attempting too many things, as a result of which you seem to be continually rushing from one thing to another and apparently have little time for reflection ... you jump into active work ... concerning which you cannot possibly be really well posted ... you seem anxious to delve into the darkest and unclear things of social life ... you identify yourself in an official way with a collection of "Hoboes", on the impulse of the moment.

In the end, her son Mark remembered her as a woman who "knew she was right."[5]

Pauline and a Smith College friend, Marian Da Camara, extended their relationship beyond graduation with shared experiences at Hull-House and teaching assignments at Ravinia in North Shore Chicago. Important coalitions were formed during this period. In

December 1917, Marian married Clyde Chace, and Pauline and Schindler were married in August 1919.[6] Schindler was then working in Frank Lloyd Wright's office and, after their marriage, he and Pauline lived alternately in Wright's former home in Oak Park, Illinois, and at Taliesin near Spring Green, Wisconsin. The Schindlers moved to Los Angeles in late 1920; the Chaces followed in July 1921 (figs. 2, 3).

LOS ANGELES

The Schindlers arrived in Los Angeles on 3 December. They spent the first few days at the Hotel Woodward, which still stands today on Eighth Street. They subsequently moved to suburban Highland Park then, in March 1921, to an apartment in Los Angeles overlooking Echo Park. Pauline explained to her parents that they were "taking this studio in town, because ... we want a preliminary period in which to entertain the few interesting people we are meeting ... and to establish definitely a little of our own atmosphere, tangibly."[7]

With her innate sense of urgency, Pauline began at once "prowling about the city every day, meeting people and trying to get in touch with things." She announced straightaway that she was "hunting up Upton Sinclair," the socialist author, but that "he has to be written to,—hides from the telephone book, even!" Sinclair responded, inviting Pauline and Schindler to lunch; Pauline commented afterward that he "was AWFULLY good to us,—and is going to introduce me to all sorts of interesting people and groups ... began at once, in fact."[8]

Shortly thereafter Gaylord Wilshire invited the Schindlers and several others to tea. Wilshire was a prominent land developer in Southern California (Wilshire Boulevard was named for him). But that was not of the Schindlers' interest. More compellingly, he was also a prominent socialist. Between 1900 and 1915 he published *Wilshire's Magazine*, which had the largest circulation of any socialist journal at the time. Even though the gathering included several individuals "who admit themselves to be the world's most distinguished," the Schindlers "confessed [them]selves not superlatively impressed...."[9]

Within the next few months, the Schindlers formed various associations and became affiliated with a number of organizations that gave structure to their early years in Los Angeles. Pauline summarized in June 1921:

2 KINGS ROAD HOUSE, West Hollywood, California, 1921–22. Marian Chace's studio. Photograph by Grant Mudford

3 KINGS ROAD HOUSE, West Hollywood, California, 1921–22.
Marian Chace's studio. Photograph by Grant Mudford

We are so far and so deeply "in" the radical movement these days that we never have an evening at home any more ... Committee meetings for the Worker's Defence [sic] League, for the Walt Whitman School,—conferences large and small,—supping in odd places with folk who tell us news impossible to get except "from hand to mouth",—lectures; meetings at which we stop only long enough to make an announcement before going on to the next; visits to the printer to read proofs for the school; trips with the car for a committee of a doctor, a lawyer, and and [sic] alienist, to the hospital to visit an I.W.W. who has been a month in jail waiting for trial, and so violently and brutally treated by the authorities that in addition to serious bodily injuries he seems to suffer mentally, and is in the observation ward of the psychopathic, suspected of insanity....

Then on top of it all today ... we speed out to Pasadena...to a meeting at the private residence of a wealthy radical ... to hear Max Eastman ... Everybody was there,—and we had awfully good talk afterwards ... Upton Sinclair introduced me to his wife ... Eastman was delightful ... And a good time was had by all ... Really a much better time than I have found possible in Chicago, in general....[10]

The Workers' Defense League was "concerned with cases prosecuted under the vicious criminal syndicalism law,—a law planned to destroy the labor unions eventually." Although Pauline mentioned that both she and Schindler were active, it is easier to imagine her zeal more than his. She had become passionately involved in a 1915 garment workers' strike in Chicago, joining in a picket line and ultimately being arrested—for her an exhilarating experience. Discussing the Workers' Defense League six years later, she explained that "this movement completely consumes my energies ... my mind is ... too much concerned with the absurd details of mass-meetings, and the raising of funds to defend workingmen prosecuted for working class activities."[11]

The Walt Whitman School was an impoverished "working men's children's school" in Boyle Heights, then Los Angeles' Jewish ghetto; according to Pauline, the students were mainly Russian Jews. She described it as the "one very real thing which I have found here ... a very crude undertaking,—but done in so fine a spirit that I have promised to give a part of my energies to the creating of a satisfactory physical environment there...." Later, she elaborated:
I have found our aristocracy ... among the proletariat ... My comrade and I have recently plunged into their activities,—for instance a school originated by libertarians who rejected the idiotic slavery of the public school system.... The Walt Whitman School ... gives each child such complete freedom, that

one walks about the buildings and gardens wondering where the school is,—for there are no formal classes! No assigned lessons, no rewards, no punishments, no authority, and no discipline!

The parents, of course, are redicals [sic] ... and are giving the children at home something of the feeling tht [sic] is needed for the revolution.
For a while there was hope of selling the old school property on Boyle Avenue and rebuilding elsewhere. Schindler prepared plans for a new structure, but lack of funds precluded any real progress.[12]

If the involvement with the Workers' Defense League and the Walt Whitman School—with their focus on seamy social ills—seems attributable to Pauline, an alliance with the Hollywood Art Association was perhaps more in line with Schindler's sympathies. In October 1922, Pauline mentioned that Schindler was "very active on half a dozen committees," and continued: "Except that they are rather fun, they would be a waste of time if they did not also mean interesting contacts...."[13]

Formed in 1920 with the primary goal of establishing an art museum in Hollywood, the association also sponsored an ongoing program of exhibitions and lectures. Schindler spoke on several occasions. Perhaps his most tangible contribution was a polemic entitled "Who Will Save Hollywood?," published under the group's auspices in *Holly Leaves*, a weekly newspaper. Subtitled "A Plea for the proper respect for and treatment of our wonderful endowment of nature," Schindler argued against the mutilation of the landscape by developers, significantly anticipating Frank Lloyd Wright's similar condemnation in his autobiography a decade later.[14]

Schindler also provided architectural services. Each summer between 1922 and 1924, the organization sponsored fundraising fiestas at the Hollywood Bowl. Schindler worked on the first two, notably designing an "old Spanish Village" for the 1923 event. Proceeds from the fiestas were destined to establish a community art gallery at the Hollywood Public Library. Schindler completed drawings for a "skylight screen" for the gallery, which was described as "the largest, most important and most costly single item for the room." Whether the work was completed remains unclear.[15]

Although there was ongoing talk of a trip to Japan with Wright, the Schindlers clearly intended to settle in Los Angeles; they began looking for a building site almost immediately. In October 1921, a frustrated Schindler commented that further work with Wright was uncertain. He concluded that the time had come to establish himself in Los Angeles, and the "period of study and work for others shall have to end."[16] By then the Chaces were also in Los Angeles; the couples jointly acquired a lot on Kings Road in Hollywood and embarked on their cooperative venture.

A LITTLE OF OUR OWN ATMOSPHERE, TANGIBLY ...

The house was constructed between February and June of 1922. Work was far enough along on 12 May for the Chaces to move into the guest-studio. Creature comforts were few, but still there was undeniable romance, as Pauline recorded:

we all spent most of our time here,—Clyde and R.M.S. working till midnights....
Both in huge overalls,—their hair grey with concrete dust or sawdust ...
All very very strenuous. Clyde and Kimmie [Marian] were almost comfortably
arranged in the guest-studio,—and all of us supping about its open fireplace.
No electric power in of course—and no gas,—but weather and sun and salads
kept us all going hard and merrily.[17]

Ten days later, the Schindlers were occupying their apartment at Kings Road. Again from Pauline:

we're really camping,—and you'd never see how folk could live at all in such
a—rough and incomplete household, it's quite wondrous ... tho we've been too
busy even to note the dramatic moment moving into our own ought to be.

Indeed, although the house was unfinished and there was almost no furniture, Pauline commented that, "People are constantly turning up.... At all hours they fall upon us ... and sometimes, when R.M.S. happens not to be at home, I am hard put to it to guess whether or not they are guests he has invited to dinner...."[18]

Edward Weston, one of the earliest visitors, became a lifelong friend; the Schindlers are mentioned frequently in his daybooks. They had heard him lecture and seen his work and found him "exceedingly interesting." They called on him in July 1922; later, "when the evening was ripe," the group moved over to Kings Road. Weston "[was] of course very much excited about the house, and wanting to see it by daylight."[19]

The births of Ann Harriet Chace on 17 May and Mark Schindler on 20 July of 1922 increased the head count at Kings Road, but the social pace seems hardly to have been affected (*figs. 4, 5*). As Pauline admitted, life at Kings Road was strenuous. A "Bohemian dress-up party" in November was followed by a week of activity. "One night a committee meeting to plan the rescuscitation [*sic*] of the Modern School ... Next night some rather 'arty' people.... And last night Lloyd Wright brought over his cello,—and played with me till another midnight.... We had really lovely music together."[20]

The earliest first-hand accounts of life at Kings Road, other than those provided by the Schindlers themselves, come from Dorothy Gibling, Pauline's sister. Dorothy was in Los Angeles for three years, between late July 1922 and summer 1925, teaching women's physical education at the University of California, Southern Branch (precursor to UCLA). She lived briefly in the Kings Road guest-studio in 1922 before moving closer to the campus on Vermont Avenue, although she returned often to help with household chores and to care for Mark and, soon enough, Pauline.

Initially, Dorothy was enthusiastic about the Kings Road experiment, writing: "The studio is really very lovely inside—but so different from

4 R. M. and Pauline Gibling Schindler,
Sophie and Edmund Gibling, Dorothy Gibling,
and Mark Schindler at Kings Road, summer 1923

5 Pauline and Mark Schindler at Kings Road, summer 1923

anything I've ever seen that it's hard to describe without pictures." She added that her room "is the most complete of the lot—even to bookshelves—matting-& many pillows—also lamp shade. But they haven't an ice box yet between them!" A day later, her excitement had tempered a bit: "I s'pose it's R.M.S.'s queer ideas that have gone to make my room so lovely—& so entirely in keeping—but to me they're most tremendously un understandable when they interfere with comfort & peace of mind." She added that she was sitting by "stretchy sliding doors—all slid open & looking out to a bank of scattered lights about a mile away across fields" *(fig. 6).*[21]

Dorothy's early letters confirm Pauline's descriptions of an agreeably unorthodox lifestyle. It was "an artistic household, unhampered by regular hours." Even though "It takes a reorganization of your whole living scheme," Dorothy concluded that the Schindlers "live a very delightful life." She mentioned "sitting & sleeping almost next to the floor—fishing crickets out of the tub before washing—being hostess to friendly cats & *toads* who travel across my doorsill at all hours of the night." She followed up with photographs of the guest-studio, the earliest interior shots available *(figs. 7, 8).*[22]

Dorothy also provided intriguing detail into how the house was actu- **94** ally used. In early August she accounted for nine people living at Kings Road, including Marian Chace's mother, Mrs. [Kathryn] Da Camara, and a nurse for Ann Harriet; the house was "a little nation all its own." Meals were served from the kitchen on trays; Marian always cooked the evening meal. Dorothy observed that even though "It still continues about a hundred and sixty five during the day ... with six inch cement walls, the *inside* of this house stays reasonably cool." Finally, she demolished a myth about the infamous rooftop "sleeping baskets." At least in the beginning, the Schindlers slept downstairs, in Pauline's studio.[23]

By all accounts, Pauline was a superb hostess. After attending a recital at Kings Road in April 1923, Dorothy Gibling recorded her mock astonishment:

It's really too bad you couldn't have been here on Friday evening—for the recital—I never dreamed 835 could look so truly lovely and impressive. As folks rambled through the various rooms—& across the courts with their open fires—I'm sure quite several of them were highly impressed. At any rate, I was. There seemed to be hundreds of people—but probably not more than fifty or

6 KINGS ROAD HOUSE, West Hollywood, California, 1921–22.
Photograph by Werner Moser, 1924

7, 8 KINGS ROAD HOUSE, West Hollywood, California, 1921–22. Photographs by Dorothy S. Gibling

sixty—and such a mixture—from the most formal to the long haired variety, though Helen Barr & I were both rather disappointed to find how comparatively few really funny types there were! We knew no one so had planned to just watch the "passing show"—but were surprised rather by the high toned air of it all than the Bohemianism we had gleefully expected. [24]

Indeed, the number of now prominent personalities passing through Kings Road House is extraordinary. The Swiss architect Werner Moser and his wife Sylva were early guests *(figs. 9, 10)*. Pauline commented that they were "two very rare and delightful people, who have stimulated in our house much discussion on questions of art and architecture."[25] Moser, yet another European modernist architect to pay homage to Frank Lloyd Wright, was en route to Taliesin.

Maurice Browne, a founder of the Chicago Little Theatre, recalled perspicaciously in his autobiography that Pauline, "brilliant, warmhearted, bitter-tongued ... was trying to create a *salon* amid Hollywood's cultural slagheap." Browne lived briefly in Hollywood in 1925; in October, he lectured on Keyserling at Kings Road. Pauline was effusive in anticipation: "[the party] ... is going to be huge. We have never had more than a hundred guests before ... But this will be overflowing." Later she recalled "all the fires burning brightly ... and the evening warm enough for the house to be wide open. Many exceedingly interesting people were among the guests,—and the evening had great charm."[26]

There is a dichotomy—impossible to ignore—between the Schindlers' decidedly radical house and progressive attitudes and associations, and their demonstrations of old-fashioned traditionalism. The European avant-garde architect and his firebrand wife didn't eschew traditional Thanksgiving and Christmas celebrations; they embraced them *(figs. 11, 12)*. The first Thanksgiving at Kings Road was celebrated in 1922. Dinner was served on the west patio on a table constructed "of two horses with boards between—& the chairs perhaps similar to the telephone stool which is a grocery box." The following year was more elaborate:

Edith [Howenstein] did all the ordering and cooking, including a monster turkey; [E.] Clare [Schooler] being potato masher and chief kettle washer—Brandy [Brandner] making a special kind of eggnog; ... an outdoor table was constructed by Karl [Howenstein] for the occasion with ditto benches, and immense poinsettias & fruit decorations at either end ... ; place cards made of bamboo; Mr. [Max] Pons turned up in the midst of dinner and of course stayed—and just as the 4 o'clock chill started in we were "through enough" to move in around the fire to stay till time to go home.

Schindler was typically laconic:

With a wonderfully set table in the court and 12 people incl. Mr. Pons Thanksgiving proceded [sic] in order. [27]

The Christmas-carol evenings Pauline organized for three years, between 1922 and 1924, seem, even more than the Thanksgiving celebrations, to be a collision between sentimentality and the New World aspirations of Kings Road House. She described the first:

9 Schindler and Werner Moser at the Kings Road House, April 1924

10 Sylva Moser in the guest-studio of the Kings Road House, April 1924

97 *The house was really quite lovely in the evening,—despite lack of the usual comforts of chairs and things ... with masses of branches in the strategic spots, and bowls of great red roses ... and the fireplaces inviting. We sang the old old English carols, and the German ones ... and after the rest were gone, Lloyd Wright brought forth his 'cello, and we sang again, he giving us the melody in rich tone ... while Edith, and Kimmie, and I sang ... (Dorothy had of course characterisitcally [sic] gone to bed!)*[28]

Throughout the twenties there are reports of high spirits and hard times at Kings Road. Seemingly indefatigable in the beginning, Dorothy soon reached her threshold:

They make me quite cross sometimes—for the minute everything is going smoothly, they start in having much company & staying up till all hours.... their attitude is more as though days were a succession of holidays, where things just fall from Heaven & the other fellow does the work.... they're in the clouds most of the time—& then suddenly come to earth.

It had fallen to Dorothy and Edith Howenstein—then living with her husband Karl in the guest-studio—to organize Thanksgiving dinner in 1922 and again in 1923. Both years, Pauline succumbed to a ner-vous instability that would plague her throughout her life; Dorothy commented in 1922 that "she got to a regular queen bee state...."[29]

Pauline suffered from what her mother described as "white heats of intensity that send you to hospitals and sanatariums [sic]." Her hair-trigger emotions led to at least one suicide attempt, on 21 June 1924; though the specific provocation is unknown, there were preliminary signs of trouble. Schindler was away in Connecticut, working with Helena Rubenstein on a proposed remodeling of her house in Greenwich. On 3 June, he wrote that "it was not fair—being jammed into an entirely strang [sic] and unsympathetic surrounding—trying to do 3 months work in one—work which can never become a satis-faction—and on top receive missils [sic] of despair—!"[30]

CHANGE

Clyde and Marian Chace's role in the early social life of Kings Road is unclear; their participation is seldom mentioned in the correspon-dence. They were away for periods of time in 1922 and 1923 while

11, 12 Thanksgiving at Kings Road, 1924

13 KINGS ROAD HOUSE, West Hollywood, California, 1921–22. Clyde Chace's studio.
Photograph by Grant Mudford

Clyde was building Schindler's Popenoe Cabin (1922) in Coachella and Pueblo Ribera Courts (1923–25) in La Jolla. After only two years, they left Kings Road for good in the summer of 1924, terminating their contract with the Schindlers on 26 July. The Chaces then moved to Florida—Marian's home—where Clyde and his father-in-law formed the Da Camara-Chace Construction Company in West Palm Beach.

Ostensibly without fanfare, the circumstances of the Chaces' departure are debatable. There may have been economic motivation; Schindler commented in April 1924 that Clyde's "family increase [the birth of his son Thomas on 5 April] has wrecked his finances." Late in life, Clyde contended that the move was for business reasons, and that there had been no rupture in the relationship with the Schindlers.[31] Indeed, returning to California in the thirties, he served as building contractor for several of Schindler's houses. Still, it is easy to speculate that other issues were at play. The Chaces left almost immediately after Pauline's attempted suicide, suggesting that her emotional volatility may have become intolerable. This the-

sis is supported by the virtual cessation of communication between Marian and Pauline, two soul mates who had shared so much: Smith College; Hull-House; Ravinia; and finally, Kings Road.

Upon the Chaces' departure, their apartment at Kings Road became a rental unit *(fig. 13)*. The first of many tenants were Arthur and Ruth Rankin. Arthur Rankin was a silent-screen actor of modest accomplishment *(fig. 14)*. He is remembered in *Who's Who in Hollywood, 1900-1976*, as a "Good-looking secondary leading man." By today's standards, the motion-picture industry of the teens and twenties moved with alacrity: films were produced quickly; actors' contracts typically were of few weeks' duration. In the approximate two years Arthur Rankin lived at Kings Road, nine films with his credits were released.

There was another aspect of the Rankins' tenancy: they responded well to Schindler's work and for a while there was discussion of their purchasing the E. J. Gibling Residence (1925-28) in Westwood that Schindler had designed for Pauline's parents. Although anxious to sell, Edmund Gibling observed that Rankin's "occupation renders him an uncertain quantity financially." Talk of selling to the Rankins continued for nearly two years. Meanwhile, their impecuniousness aside, Schindler designed another house for them in 1925, although nothing of this project is known.[32]

The Rankins established an "industry presence" (in today's parlance) at Kings Road that has gone unnoted and yet is unsurprising, given the concentration of motion-picture studios nearby. On 9 January 1925, while they were living in the Chace apartment, Pauline wrote that "Mr. George O'Hara, another moving picture actor,—one with an enormous car, and a two-year acting contract" had moved into the guest-studio. She continued that he "is supposed to be bookish and musical" and that "Our little car besides his in the garage (it must be a Rolls-Royce 'or something') feels very much overshadowed and humbled."[33]

In 1922, *Variety* observed that O'Hara "stands out as a distinct find. He is a combination of the Charles Ray-Richard Barthelmess type and troups [*sic*] and photographs like the mint" *(fig. 15)*. At the time he lived at Kings Road, he was best known as the featured player in Film Booking Office's two-reeler series *Fighting Blood*; he was "cast as an ex-champion of the prize ring."[34] His personal traits—"bookish and musical"—were entirely out of character with his screen persona.

14 Arthur Rankin (seated) in *Broken Laws*
(Film Booking Office, 1924)

15 George O'Hara, in *Film Year Book 1926*

On 2 February 1925, Dorothy Gibling wrote to her parents that the Schindlers were having "'some noble but poor' architect (*and wife and 1½ yr old son*) come live with them." She was referring to Richard, Dione, and Frank Neutra *(figs. 16, 17).* The initial plan was to let them use the upstairs sleeping basket *(fig. 18).*[35] By the time they reached Kings Road, however, George O'Hara had left the guest-studio and the Neutras took that space instead.

The Neutras arrived in Los Angeles on 7 March 1925. Schindler met them at the train station and drove them to Kings Road. Initially, Mrs. Neutra reported that "Mrs. Schindler is extraordinarily helpful and both of them show great friendship and help us a lot." She confirmed reports of the Schindlers' frequent social gatherings and, in September, commented that "We are slowly drawn into the whirl of social activities, although we are only starting to make acquaintances." Soon, however, they were in stride:
Yesterday I had my second "party" with forty invited guests. Can you picture your Dionchen as a successful hostess? If I had not met Pauline, this would have been unthinkable. I imitated her and Richard says I even surpassed her.

Come to think of it, I really can be proud that all went so smoothly and with no help whatsoever, especially considering the fact that Doris [Dione's sister] and I were the entertainers.[36]

The Neutras remained in the guest-studio through 1925, then moved into the larger Chace apartment *(fig. 19).* The progressive dancer John Bovingdon and his companion, Jeanya Marling, replaced them, remaining for approximately one year. Bovingdon performed in the Kings Road garden on several occasions; Mrs. Neutra described one event in October 1926:
they would dance together. And they would dance practically in the nude, which was, of course, at that time for Hollywood quite an event. But it was very beautiful. At night they would illuminate the garden and for music they had gongs, which were hung on ropes, and they would hit the gongs. And I remember one dance where he danced The Ascent of Man; *first, man was crawling on all fours and then slowly, slowly he became erect and then walked on his legs, and this he danced. So that was quite thrilling.*[37]

16 Frank, Dione, and Richard Neutra
at Kings Road, 1925

17 Dione and Richard Neutra at Kings Road, 1926

18 KINGS ROAD HOUSE, West Hollywood, California,
1921–22. View of the Schindlers' sleeping basket.
Photograph by Grant Mudford

Like Pauline Schindler, Dione Neutra had a strong sense of personal history and saved her correspondence. The letters reveal an optimism tempered by the difficulty of becoming established professionally, and a concomitant lack of money. Neutra and Schindler did not at once establish a formal partnership; Neutra instead took a series of jobs with other architects. Only in 1926 did he and Schindler form the collaborative Architectural Group for Industry and Commerce. Schindler explained that they wanted "to undertake larger industrial buildings."[38]

If the large commissions were not forthcoming, the chemistry of the Schindler/Neutra association nonetheless resulted in a period of unsurpassed architectural vitality at Kings Road; the seedbed of California modernism is here. Independently and collaboratively, Schindler and Neutra produced the seminal Lovell houses (1922-26 and 1929, respectively); the Jardinette Apartments (1927); the Translucent House for Aline Barnsdall project (1927-28); and the Charles H. Wolfe Residence (1928-31). Collectively these rank among their finest works. It is unthinkable that either was working in creative isolation: the bohemian and the technocrat coalesced in the rarest of synergistic partnerships. Could the dynamism of the Lovell "Health" House have been conceived without the pure sculpture of the Lovell "Beach" House? Would the formally retardi-taire but structurally provocative Translucent House have been imaginable without the influence of one who overburdened his first book with the mechanics of building the Palmer House in Chicago?[39]

Still, each man retained his identity. Schindler was inventive but built crudely; Neutra was formulaic but technically proficient. Dione Neutra commented half a century later:

[Schindler] *was such an individualist ... Mr. Neutra always believed that prefabrication would eventually have to be the road for the architects ... But Schindler was very much interested in space exploration, so all his houses were—Each house was again completely different, and designed for a particular space.*[40]

And there were competitive instincts. When things came to a head in 1927, Galka Scheyer was mediator. Scheyer immigrated to America in 1924 as a representative of the Blue Four—the painters

19 KINGS ROAD HOUSE, West Hollywood,
California, 1921–22. View of Marian Chace's studio.
Photograph by Ernest M. Pratt and Viroque Baker, c. 1926

Lyonel Feininger, Alexej von Jawlensky, Wassily Kandinsky, and Paul Klee—and in October 1926 organized the first Los Angeles exhibition of their work at the Los Angeles Museum in Exposition Park. She stayed briefly in the Kings Road guest-studio during the summer of 1927. The circumstances of her acquaintance with the Schindlers, the Neutras, and Kings Road are unknown but, if Dione Neutra's contemporary account is accepted, Scheyer's presence changed the course of modern architecture.

Schindler had designed three vacation houses for Philip and Leah Lovell and was anticipating receiving the commission for a large residence in Los Angeles. Whatever the complexities of the relationship between Schindler and Lovell—there are various accounts—the commission for the Los Angeles house went to Neutra. Reportedly, Neutra was initially hesitant to accept the project, but Scheyer interceded. Dione Neutra described the course of events:
Then Mrs. Scheyer appeared on the scene, saying that Richard's consideration was ridiculous. She worked on Schindler, on Lovell, on Richard, and finally, the preliminaries were started.[41]

Much speculation surrounds the Neutras' departure from Kings Road in 1930. Dione Neutra, reminiscing in 1978, cast aside venomous conjecture about a rift between Schindler and Neutra. "It was never acrimonious. It was just a slow, slow abating of working together. We were vacating the apartment. I don't remember anything—that we left in anger or anything like that." On a personal level, Mrs. Neutra was generously overlooking difficulties that surfaced early in their occupancy at Kings Road. In 1926, she commented on "how intertwined our lives are." She had "found a very different set of values" which led to "an uncomfortable situation,"

although she was able to report: "Conditions are improving."[42] Still, a casual familiarity with the polemics suggests that a break was inevitable: history shows that, ideologically, the differences between Schindler and Neutra far outweighed the similarities.

Neutra was moving ahead in a way that Schindler never did. Pauline commented in 1932 that "neutra has become *the* prominent figure in town among modern architects ... while r.m.s. remains the mysterious and romantic 'michael'." Schindler followed up in 1935:
It is not jealousy towards Neutra but opposition to what he stands for—I would not object to your going to the end of the world for Frank Lloyd Wright—or Mies van der Rohe—But Neutra's steril [sic] go-getter-type, whose main force is a shrewd understanding of the publicity-market—is poison to any real art development. It is not a question of whether his things are little better or worse—He is essentially a racketeer & you can not be naïve about this....[43]

SOPHIE GIBLING, PAULINE'S MOTHER, was another regular correspondent from Kings Road during the twenties. She made at least five trips to California between 1923 and 1928, customarily remaining for several months. Her letters to her husband in Chicago are at once appreciative and contemptuous: not unlike Dorothy, she was charmed by the artistic lifestyle at Kings Road and put off by aspects of the Schindlers' personal conduct.

Mrs. Gibling was quick to recognize the magic of the night at Kings Road. She described a dinner in September 1926:
[It was] *somewhat of a party, the Neutras and John [Bovingdon] being present, the dinner served around the open fire in patio, and in almost total darkness. They had carried out the big sofa and it was all very effective and*

temperamental.... John was beautifully clad in fine white silk, long, wide plus four trousers and an RMSque shirt waist to match. We discussed among other things an approaching possibility of John's doing something in the movie line. R.M. suggested taking as his basic theme "Breath" showing it in all its relations to life and the universe, joy, love, fear, etc. I said begin with the Breath of God breathing on chaos.[44]

After another party in December for Leo Katz, a Viennese painter whose work was on display at the Los Angeles Museum, Mrs. Gibling commented that "when company drops in [Pauline] is a most fascinating hostess. Sunday evening it struck me again how much atmosphere, uniqueness and charm there is about her parties, and what interesting people she collects." She reiterated after a Christmas party three days later: "[the evening] was quite a success.... The place looks its most artistic when dressed for entertaining, in the half light there is a glamour about it."[45]

At the same time, Mrs. Gibling was witnessing the ongoing personal imbalances at Kings Road. She at once commented that, "It all seems so easy and effortless and life to be flowing so smoothly [*sic*] at 835," but continued, "Alas that there must be that seamy side...." While the Schindlers outwardly had carved a niche for themselves in radical Los Angeles society, the undercurrents of discord between them ultimately destroyed their lifestyle. Schindler commented in 1925 that Pauline's "moods change as lightning." Later, after Sophie Gibling observed a period of "peace and quiet," Schindler retorted, "Oh no ... not peace and quiet, it has simply been a little less violent."[46] Correspondence retained by the Schindler family reveals the extremity of emotion between Schindler and Pauline though, after repeated blowups, states of equilibrium seem to have returned.

The break came in the summer of 1927. In July, Dorothy Gibling commented on unspecified "disturbing news from Los Angeles." Then, in August, Pauline left Kings Road. Dione Neutra was witness: *These last weeks were too exciting. Pauline has left. She packed her belongings and I did not even see her go. Everything had to be done in secrecy to avoid a confrontation between the couple.*[47]

Pauline went first to Halcyon, a utopian community south of San Luis Obispo. Founded in 1903 by a small group of Theosophists from Syracuse, it was established as a healing center, on a site cho-

sen for its cosmic intersection of natural lines of force. A temple, dedicated in 1923 and still in use today, was built at the center of town "on lines of mathematical and geometrical symbolism." Four years later a social hall, Hiawatha Lodge, was completed.[48]

Halcyon was a place of retreat to which Pauline returned often. Possibly she learned about it from Maurice Browne and Ellen Janson, who spent much of 1924 there. It appealed to Pauline less for its religious teachings than as:

a strange odd little settlement with an astounding quality ... if you were impervious to the thing called "spirit" which so palpably, almost visible, governs here, you would say that the houses were drab little shacks. And yet again and again ... down to Halcyon ... will flee from the civilization of cities, people of cultivated minds and tastes,—for a day or a week in Halcyon.

There are theosophists here, and a temple,—but it is not that which causes it all. It is a quality as universal as light. Can it be a climatic thing,—the radiation at Halcyon of forces from the earth which produce a human type of unusual harmoniousness and serenity,—as the climate of Carmel by contrast produces in its inhabitants over-stimulation and cerebral scintillation?[49]

Although Pauline was offered the use of Ellen Janson's house for the winter, she left Halcyon on 19 October, moving north to Carmel where she would remain for two years. Carmel-by-the-Sea on the Monterey Peninsula was blessed with extraordinary physical beauty. Its quaintness and small size belied its sophistication. Home to a group of artists and poets, the city also hosted ongoing concerts and plays by visiting performers at the Theatre of the Golden Bough and the Carmel Playhouse. Pauline described it as "a democratic and non-commercial community.... People are poor and it doesn't matter; rich, and they are forgiven."[50]

By mid-December, Pauline had rapidly entered "into the center of Carmel life." She spent her time there writing and editing. Soon after her arrival, she began contributing an unsigned column, "The Black Sheep," to the *Carmel Pine Cone*, a local paper. Described as a "new critical department which does not promise to behave itself too well," it nonetheless would be "young, fearless, honest, and vital." The column appeared eleven times between November 1927 and March 1928; although it addressed various local issues and events, the primary focus was music. At about the same time, Pauline was also appointed drama critic from Carmel for the *Christian Science Monitor*.[51]

Most importantly, Pauline formed an association early on with *The Carmelite*, a newly established progressive weekly. Two regular columns, "Stage and Screen" and "With the Women," and numerous other miscellaneous articles appeared under her byline in early 1928. Soon enough, she became editorial assistant and, by mid-April, was anticipating becoming managing editor. On inception, *The Carmelite* was presented as "a periodical which will without fear or favor give voice and light on both sides of a mooted question affecting the artistic or practical in village life." In fact, it was a politically charged vehicle generated to counter the deeply entrenched *Carmel Pine Cone*: editorial fisticuffs began before the first issue of *The Carmelite* appeared. On 3 February, the *Carmel Pine Cone* questioned the true ownership and motivations of the upstart. *The Carmelite* retorted with references to "journalistic mud ... cowardly innuendo and implication...."[52]

The Carmelite survived sixteen weeks under its original ownership. The "Swan Song of 'S. A. R.'" [Stephen A. Reynolds, the editor] in the 30 May issue announced "the last number," while contending that "the *Carmelite* ... has not failed ... has fought a good fight ... and now retires honorably from the journalistic field unless other capable hands care to take on the burden." Indeed, other hands were in the wings: a postscript to Reynolds's statement revealed that "arrangements have been made whereby the *Carmelite* will pass into the possession of a group of local people."[53]

The "group" was Pauline Schindler and her fluid editorial board. An unsigned editorial in the 6 June issue partially explained the transition: *With this number, the* Carmelite *enters a new adventure. It comes today under the editorship of a new group. But why should any new group undertake such a task, and what is their purpose?*

They undertake it first as an adventure; second, in order to open new channels through which life may flow; and third, in active disbelief of the view commonly held that a news periodical must assume a higher intelligence on the part of any community.[54]

Under Pauline's guidance, *The Carmelite* became "a liberal-radical weekly, in whose pages the visiting or resident intelligentsia, from Lincoln Steffens to Robinson Jeffers, all had a word." Predictably, Pauline used *The Carmelite* to express her own views and interests, both artistic and political; she told her father that she wrote about half the paper, though many of the pieces were unsigned.[55] Music was a major focus, and she regularly reviewed concerts by progressive composers who passed through Carmel, most notably Henry Cowell. She also covered activity at the Theatre of the Golden Bough and the Carmel Playhouse assiduously *(fig. 20)*. Jane Addams's visit to Carmel in 1928 was front-page news. Photographs by Edward Weston and poems by Robinson Jeffers and Ellen Janson Browne appeared alongside editorials about prison conditions, another of Pauline's special concerns. Many of the issues included woodcut illustrations by Virginia Tooker, an early guest at Kings Road.

If *The Carmelite* was vanity press, it also was distinctly high-toned, functioning as "a channel of liberal opinion through which the minds and energies of the new age may find expression." Doing so, it provided a forum for editorial discourse. The validity of modern art was defended; a library tax was contested; growth and traffic issues in Carmel were challenged; the "ecstasy of bees" was debated.[56]

Though it had triumphs editorially, like many small publications *The Carmelite* was sadly underfinanced and burdened with contentious personal relationships. In January 1929, the muckraking author Lincoln Steffens, one of the contributing editors, tried to wrest control of the paper from Pauline and turn it over to his wife, Ella Winter, using an unpaid printer's bill as leverage. Pauline published Steffens's view of the incident in *The Carmelite*:
There are rumors in circulation of a conspiracy ... to oust me and my gang from the Carmelite*. We are leaving of our own free, mechanistic will. You have always been glad to have us do all the work we would, as long as what we did was up to the high-flying standard you kept mentioning.*

The alternative report that we were trying to take the paper away from you or rather that we were trying to take you away from the paper is as true as history. It is not exact. It is hardly correct to call it a conspiracy since I was all

20 John Bovingdon, reviewed in *The Carmelite*, 4 July 1928

JOHN BOVINGDON
OFFERS FOUR FRIDAY EVENING
PROGRAMS OF RESEARCHES INTO
THE NEW DANCE BEING
EXPERIMENTS TOWARD A LIFE
DANCE ROOTED IN HYGIENE . .

HYGIENIC ROOTS OF A FUNCTIONAL DANCE . JUNE 6
REVOLTS OF A ROBOT-AND HIS DISCOVERIES . JUNE 13
DANCE PAGEANT OF THE CRAFTS . . . . . . JUNE 20
EPISODES IN THE RE-CREATION OF MOODS . JUNE 27

AT THE PATIO THEATER
835 KINGS ROAD, TEN
BLOCKS WEST OF FAIR-
FAX BETWEEN MELROSE
AND SANTA MONICA
BOULEVARD . . . . . .
8:30 PROMPT AND AT
THE DOOR A DOLLAR

. . . THESE PROGRAMS MARK THE RETURN OF JOHN
BOVINGDON AND HIS WIFE JEANYA MARLING FROM A
YEAR'S EUROPEAN TOUR DEVOTED TO STUDY, PRESEN-
TATIONS AND TEACHING . . . AND THE OPENING OF
THEIR DANCE STUDIO-LABORATORY AT THE ADDRESS
ABOVE GIVEN

21 Sadakichi Hartmann reading Edgar Allen Poe
at Kings Road, 8 January 1928. Drawing by Boris Deutsch

22 Announcement for Sadakichi Hartmann talk
on modern art, 22 February 1930

23 Announcement, John Bovingdon and The New Dance,
June 1930

24 Galka Scheyer at Kings Road, early 1930s

alone in the plot—I and you.... I soon saw that an editor and owner who went off singing carols and sitting at the feet of dancers that danced the philosophy of life ... who rebuilt advertisements into architectural syntheses without the knowledge and the correct addresses of the advertisers and wrote music in bed when the city council waited to be written—I lifted up my highbrows and thought that such an editor would be happier and more useful to the paper if she had time to dance and sing and compose music and music criticism unhindered by and unhindering the mere business of journalism.... I did trust you to go right on forgetting to meet the printer's bills until he would press you to deliver the Carmelite *to some one else....*[57]

Steffens made two valid points. He paid Pauline a backhanded compliment in acknowledging her very real skills as a graphic designer, a talent she would further pursue. At the same time, he correctly observed that she was not a business person. Pauline acknowledged the criticism, writing to her father on 4 December 1928, that she had "heard a lot of slams recently about my business capapacities [*sic*]. There seems to be plenty of agreement that there are certain departments of life in which I am simply no good!"[58] Still, with a combination of community support and assistance from her father, Pauline weathered the crisis temporarily.

Pauline remained at *The Carmelite* for several more months, maintaining its undeniably high standards and handsome appearance. She lost control of the paper in 1929; a decisive meeting was held in *The Carmelite* office in the Seven Arts Building on 16 September. Pauline called the meeting, expecting financial support. Instead, the group challenged her ownership:
Cooly, almost coldly then, the deal was put through. New papers were drawn, strictly legal; a pen was placed in the shaking hand of Mrs. Pauline Schindler; "Sign on the dotted line," came the command. And Mrs. Schindler signed.

Pauline left Carmel a short time later, explaining to her father that it was "time for the next step." Sophie Gibling followed up, reflecting on the "strong political influence, afraid of her fearless spirit ... which arrayed against her.... She never fully realized its force...."[59]

MEANWHILE, IN PAULINE'S ABSENCE, life at Kings Road retained its rhythm, at least for a few years. Sadakichi Hartmann, a self-described "mad, bad, sad and slightly red poet," was there often during the late twenties. He lived a penurious existence, regularly asked Schindler for a dollar or two, and was described by Edward Weston in 1928 as "a sad old ruin ... [who was] paying for a dissipated, malicious life." Still he obviously amused Schindler, who allowed him to use the house for "readings" to which the public was invited. At "A Poe Evening" in January 1928, Hartmann announced that he would read "A Tell-Tale Heart" and other short stories, "provided he does not change his mind." The announcement continued that "Mr. Hartmann will endeavor to look like Edgar Allen Poe" *(fig. 21)*. On another evening the topic was modern art; the public was advised: "This will be the most amusing Art Talk of the season; miss it if you can" *(fig. 22)*.[60]

In early 1930, John Bovingdon returned to Kings Road to live in the Chace apartment, recently vacated by the Neutras. In June, as he had in the twenties, Bovingdon danced in the garden on four sequential Friday nights *(fig. 23)*. Later that year, Galka Scheyer *(fig. 24)* contacted Schindler, explaining that she was about to return to Los Angeles from Bali and that she needed a big room with light and wall space in which to live. She had purchased "a marvelous collection of Bali things—mostly paintings," which she wanted to display. Scheyer moved into the apartment in March 1931, unhappily sharing the space with Bovingdon for a short time. She explained a short time later to Lyonel Feininger that she intended "to pick up some of my relationships with some movie people in Hollywood, for which reason I rented a lovely little modern house built by the architect Schindler and where my pictures show to great advantage."[61]

Dudley Nichols *(fig. 25)*, a motion-picture scriptwriter, and his wife, Esta, took over the Chace apartment after Scheyer's departure in October 1932. His first film, *Men without Women*, directed by John Ford, appeared in 1930. Success was immediate: between 1930 and his move to Kings Road, thirteen films with Nichols's credits were released. In the nine months or so he was in residence, four additional features appeared.

25 Dudley Nichols, in *The 1932 Film Daily Year Book of Motion Pictures*

While the Nichols occupied the Chace apartment, Mary MacLaren, yet another Hollywood personality, was living in the guest-studio. While Nichols's star was ascendant, MacLaren's was in decline. She had been a teenage star, playing the lead in her first film, *Shoes*, in 1916. Although MacLaren had extensive screen credits, her overnight success was short-lived, her ability increasingly questioned. By 1922, she had lost her footing:

It is only a couple of years ago that this girl looked like the biggest bet that the screen had had in some time, but evidently association and an aptitude of assimilating mannerism through it seemingly has stopped her from going forward as she should have.[62]

Two years later, MacLaren married and moved to India, where she lived for several years. She returned to Los Angeles and the screen in the early 1930s and worked through the forties, although she was reduced to playing minor supporting roles *(fig. 26)*. But even those roles were unpredictable. She wrote to Pauline: "not that I have been working every day by any means, but the days I am not working I am compelled to stay at home in the hopes of getting a call to work."[63] She left Kings Road after a fire in October 1935.

The Nichols vacated the Chace apartment in May 1933. Pauline then took the space for three months. Eric Locke, another industry insider, and two of his friends followed her in turn. Locke worked behind the camera, first in wardrobe on a Metro-Goldwyn-Mayer (MGM) film, *The Student Prince in Old Heidelberg*, released in 1927. In 1933, he was credited as assistant director for a Paramount production, *Midnight Club*, and then in 1934 as business manager for another MGM movie, *The Merry Widow*. Locke remained at Kings Road a scant three months. On 15 December, he wrote to Pauline that "In looking over the damage done by the recent rain to the house and to my own personal belongings, I made up my mind today that I will terminate my occupancy of your house on Dec. 31."[64]

Although disgruntled with conditions at Kings Road, Locke entertained a dialogue with Schindler about building a new house on Griffith Park Boulevard. Schindler prepared two schemes, both dated November 1933. The more developed of the two is a composition of emphatic vertical and horizontal planes separated by large glazed voids. One feature, the rounded intersections of the geometry, breaks sharply from the tenets of the International Style.[65]

John Cage and his friend, Don Sample, took over the Chace apartment on Locke's departure. They were there on the fringe;

to paraphrase Thomas S. Hines, "Cage was not yet Cage." The actual duration of Cage's occupancy of Kings Road contradicts his memory: in 1992 he recalled staying "for probably a little less than a year." In reality, he and Sample were there for nine days, between Locke's departure on 31 December 1933 and 9 January 1934. Cage returned to Kings Road in April 1935 to host a concert of classical shakuhachi music by a visiting Japanese musician. Cage reported to Pauline that "Schindler was marvelous ... And Kings Rd [*sic*] was utterly magnificent. I'm afraid that it quite 'ran away with the evening.' The entire effect was one of horizontality and a sort of organic calm which was not exciting but rather full and complete."[66]

Betty Kopelanoff in turn displaced John Cage at Kings Road. She had long been a member of the Schindlers' inner circle, but her position in history was better secured by her participation in Edward Weston's attic series; "Betty in Her Attic" (c. 1921) was widely exhibited. In an undated letter, Weston stated his intention to make more prints of the attic series and quipped that they "may make us both famous—or rather—more famous!"[67]

Betty had contacted Pauline in early January 1934, looking for a place to live. Pauline responded "Move right in tell Michael boys temporarily there must immediately depart." Soon enough, the apartment at Kings Road became "too much of a good thing." Betty importuned Pauline "you know how cold and dreary the other room can be in the rain ... to say nothing of the fact that it was raining there as well as in other parts of the house."[68] She left after two months.

THE POSTHUMOUS LUMINOSITY of various occupants and events at Kings Road overshadows a sad reality: virtually from the onset, the house was in a state of decline. The Schindlers' personal affairs were unsettled, money was a constant problem, and the house was not maintained. Sophie Gibling was captious about the condition of the property in 1926, commenting that "the place is just going to rack and ruin." Pauline followed up in 1931 mentioning Schindler's "atrocious administration" in her absence. Later, she concluded: "r.m.s. has simply no talent for cherishing a property once it is built. only for designing and executing them. they are different functions."[69]

While Schindler remained at Kings Road, Pauline led a nomadic existence. After leaving Carmel in 1929, she drifted for a decade between

26 Mary MacLaren (right) in *Escapade*
(Metro-Goldwyn-Mayer, 1935)

Halcyon and neighboring Oceano; Ojai, where Mark was in school; Santa Fe; the San Francisco Bay Area; and Los Angeles. In Los Angeles, Pauline's habit was to obtain living space away from Kings Road, although she did stay there temporarily on several occasions. She explained to her father in October 1931 that she wanted to live at Kings Road, not to necessarily stay there, but to be able to return. Several months later, she expressed that she did not "set aside the sense of the kings road house as our home. that is where mark and i will return, where we will make our own atmosphere.... i do not like los angeles, but mark and i do love the house ..."[70]

Pauline typically used either the Chace apartment or the guest-studio during her intermittent visits though, on at least one occasion, she stayed with Schindler in his apartment. She took advantage of the opportunity to rekindle a lifestyle previously abandoned, entertaining as she and Schindler had during the twenties. In June 1933, she mentioned that:

last night there was one of the old kings road parties here in my apartment. dr. alexander kaun ... who recently returned from a sabbatical year in Europe ... spent three weeks with kerensky in paris, talked long with trozky [sic] in turkey ... spoke to an informally gathered small group and there was an evening of discussion.

On another occasion she described:

[A] *tea to be given here next week at the house, by the women's committee of the league against war and fascism. on saturday evening we are to have here also a discussion of the situation in spain.... this is the third large party to be held here this summer. the house is perfect for such discussion, there is a very interesting group which gathers, and in these times it is good to have such a center available. i shall regret giving it up to tenants,—have greatly enjoyed it these months.*[71]

Mark attended the Ojai Valley School between October 1932 and June 1935; Pauline was there with him intermittently, living in a series of rented cottages. From this base, she traveled to Santa Barbara and, more regularly, to Halcyon and the neighboring Dunes at Oceano. Described by Pauline as "a strange and separate region ... with a hidden life little known," the Dunes had long been a destination for drifters seeking refuge from urbanity—"a community of solitaries."[72] A constantly reconfigured, windswept oasis overlooking the Pacific Ocean, it offered both solitude and freedom from all but the most rudimentary man-made intrusions.

Life in the Dunes became somewhat more structured in September 1931 when the grandson and namesake of President Chester A. Arthur began work on a utopian community. "Gavin" Arthur retained powerful political connections in Washington while drawing around himself at "Moy Mell", as the place was called, a ragtag group of artists, poets, intellectuals, and dropouts who lived in an odd assortment of shacks and gathered in the evenings by an open fire for conversation *(fig. 27)*.[73]

Pauline Schindler's first recorded visit to Moy Mell was in September 1933. She had been invited along with Ellen Janson to become associate editor of *Dune Forum*, Gavin Arthur's new publishing venture. Ostensibly based on the fireside conversations, it was to be "a westcoast [sic] magazine of culture and controversy ... [that] would publish both the conservative and the radical points of view." The editors' contributions aside, the most significant article to appear was Schindler's "Space Architecture," published in February 1934; it guided his work for the remainder of his career. In it, Schindler distinguished between spaces that resulted as a by-product of sculptural exploration and structural necessity, and those of true spatial creation, "the real medium of architecture."[74]

During the thirties there was a gradual evolution from Socialism to Communism in Pauline's political ideology, possibly coinciding with American recognition of the Soviet Union in 1933. In December she recommended a subscription to the *Daily Worker*, "a communist newspaper," to her mother. Two years later she was writing for the *Western Worker*, "the Western Organ of the Communist Party USA."[75]

One of the more bizarre—yet personally rewarding—manifestations of this philosophical shift was a brief sojourn in July 1935 at Commonwealth College in Mena, Arkansas. Commonwealth is

remembered today as "a subversive organization" that operated for seventeen years—between 1923 and 1940—a period of expansive farm and labor organization. Commonwealth's mission was "to recruit and train leaders for unconventional roles in a new and radically different society—one in which the workers would have power and would need responsible leadership." The methods used, including "Repeated forays by Commonwealth faculty and students into the Eastern Arkansas plantation country, into the coal mine fields and into other regions, always with intent to incite disorders of one kind or another," led the Arkansas House of Representatives to investigate "alleged 'Communism' at Commonwealth."[76]

Pauline arrived shortly after the investigation was concluded, "Voted Down by Large Majority When Protested by Entire Nation." Initially she was asked to teach English, but the assignment subsequently was expanded to include "labor journalism." Pauline was ready:
i have long had an idea that the revolutionary periodicals i occasionally see would do much better if they told their story more quietly. the facts are enough. they need no comment and no exclamation point. no adjectives and no ranting. i hope they will let me teach the course this way.[77]

The experience at Commonwealth meant much to Pauline "in development of a certain sort."
certainly here ... one has the impression that the revolution is being prepared for scientifically and practically. and that it is inevitable. most of the students this summer are young communist college graduates, some of whom have been active in radical activities in their colleges and are seriously preparing for revolutionary leadership. there is a high degree of idealism among them. in the afternoon you will find a dozen of us ... either discussing some marxian point concerned with dialectical materialism, or perhaps reading the communist manifesto. many come from working class environments (they can bear the living standards here better than some of the rest of us, whom they think bourgeois).
She concluded:
that i am NOT a communist in their sense. this to my surprise.... many men ... fail to realize the extremity of suffering which the capitalist system brings to millions and millions of human beings.... it is a cruel system which must be superseded [sic]. now we must come to an economic system based upon production for use and not for profit....

communists believe that the possessing classes will not give up the system without a struggle. they therefore believe that th [sic] class war is inevitable.... if it really is true that capitalism will not surrender without a struggle, then I shall fight on the side of the workers.[78]

Commonwealth proved to be as physically debilitating as it was personally rewarding. The "humid and totally motionless heat" and absence of acceptable food soon took their toll. Pauline and Mark remained in Arkansas less than a month. Driving back to California they stopped in Shawnee, Colorado, for a reunion with Marian Chace. Marian was by then running Po-ah-Tun, a center for the Harmonious Development of Mankind, "with daily classes and a wise man etc." Pauline was decidedly unimpressed: "i'm not interested in the wisdom, the wiseman [*sic*], or the classes."[79]

Much can be made of Pauline's wandering during the thirties. Her high-minded idealism collided with pragmatic reality: the need to be at the forefront of progressive thought seldom reconciled with a corollary need to achieve emotional and financial independence. Still, if there were too many false starts, there remains a record of accomplishment. Pauline aggressively submitted articles to magazines and newspapers on subjects ranging from the weighty to the whimsical; many were published. Architecture was a favorite topic, although it seems fair to observe that it was the "idea" of architecture rather than an intuitive understanding that drove her.

Pauline consistently praised Schindler's work both privately and publicly, and was arguably his most significant pamphleteer. She announced a special issue of *The Carmelite*, though ultimately unrealized, devoted to modern architecture that undoubtedly would have showcased Schindler prominently. Well into the thirties she used her associations with *California Arts and Architecture*, *Architect and Engineer*, and other venues to feature his work, though at one point Carol Aronovici chided her for failing to clarify Schindler's significance. As late as 1936, she considered "him the most brilliant of all the modern creators in architecture known to me; am going to write an article on schindler alone; and am discussing with him again the possibility of a book now on his work. he is at last ready for this; was not before. but is now wildly busy."[80]

Pauline's personal comments on Schindler more closely reflected the trajectory of their relationship—she could be both charitable and damning. Shortly after leaving Kings Road in 1927, she spoke of "recovering from the shock and pain of the summer." By the early thirties she was able to express "enormous respect for the genius and personality of r.m.s.,—and as long as we keep things totally impersonal i shall be glad to work with him." Two months later she stated that Schindler "is a very strange man,—a great artist, but with

113 the divergence from norms which accompanies genius." Soon enough, Pauline's venom resurfaced: on one occasion, Schindler was "an incredible liar ... no scruples whatever." Two weeks later, he was "outrageously unthinking and inconsiderate of people ... a man of great talent, glowing charm, totally irresponsible,—and who lies as easily as he tells the truth."[81]

Reflecting on his daughter's marriage in October 1928, Edmund Gibling looked in vain for the "hope or desire on either side for complete reconciliation." He concluded that it was "better that they should never again live together;" that they "have caused one another unforgivable suffering." The Schindlers were not immediately so decisive. Significantly, they both maintained a tenacious grip on Kings Road; it was both a rallying point and source of contention. In 1931 Pauline proposed that Schindler transfer title of the house to her. Schindler, seemingly acquiescent, responded that he was "trying to arrange for another place for myself ... might take ... a few months. In meantime I will stay at Kings Road."[82]

In November 1934, after seven years' estrangement, Pauline admitted to her mother that the marriage had ended. The protracted legal dissolution, however, began only in August 1938; divorce was granted in February 1940.[83] Schindler and Pauline wound up sharing Kings Road *(fig. 28)*, each displaying proprietary instincts. Even as adversaries they continued to work on the building, separately and together. Numerous unfortunate changes were made. Her seeming insensitivity was mitigated by Schindler's willingness to compromise the original concept.

Schindler and Pauline were strangely together to the end. She composed an exceptionally fine tribute two months before his death in 1953: *I am ... grateful to you, r.m.s.... for what you have given to architecture all these years, while forbidding myself personal feeling, i have been free nevertheless to respond fully to your work, to feel and know its richness and perhaps even sometimes its meaning.*

Gregory Ain speaks sometimes of the house at Kings Road as though it were a sort of miracle,—bringing to architecture the same miraculous freshness of creation which the Sacre du Printemps does to music. As I have seen your work over the many years it seemed to me that your central preoccupation was the evocation of that which had never before been imagined. A sort of uncoiling of dimensions in space. I recognize the elements of greatness in this life; and now ... am at last ready to acknowledge it to you freely.[84]

Late in life, Pauline gained increasing recognition as "Mrs. Schindler," wife of the architect, a role she played handsomely. It was no accident that she finished her years in so unworkable a house, no accident that she left such an extraordinary collection of letters.

28 Pauline Schindler at Kings Road House, November 1941

Notes

Unless noted, all correspondence cited is in the Pauline Schindler Collection, currently on deposit by the Schindler family in the Architecture and Design Collection, University Art Museum, University of California, Santa Barbara [hereafter "ADC/UCSB"]. R. M. Schindler is identified as RMS; Sophie Pauline Gibling Schindler as SPG; Sophie S. Gibling as SSG; Edmund J. Gibling as EJG; and Dorothy S. Gibling as DSG.

1 SPG to RMS, 9 July 1953.

2 SPG to SSG, n.d. [9 May 1916]. I thank Maureen Mary for bringing this letter to my attention.

3 DSG to unknown, [12 February 1923].

4 Neutra, in *To Tell the Truth*. Dione Neutra, interviewed by Lawrence Weschler (1978). Completed under the Auspices of the Oral History Program, University of California, Los Angeles. Copyright © 1983 The Regents of the University of California, III, 129, 112; and SPG to "Mother," 30 July 1924.

5 EJG to "Mother" [Sarah Gibling], 14 December 1900; EJG to "Junior" [SPG], 25 November 1915; and Mark Schindler to author, 13 September 1998.

6 "Marriage of Miss Miriam [*sic*] Da Camara a Surprise to Her Many Friends," *The Palm Beach Post*, 27 December 1917, courtesy of The Historical Society of Palm Beach County.

7 The Hotel Woodward is at 421 West Eighth Street. In Highland Park, the Schindlers stayed at The Sycamore, 4938 Pasadena Avenue (now Figueroa Street) at Echo Street; the building has since been demolished. The Echo Park apartment was at 1719 Kane Street (now Clinton Street), apartment C; this building has been demolished as well. SPG to unknown, 3-6 December [1920]; SPG to SSG, 9 [December 1920]; and SPG to "Parents," 2 [March] 1921.

8 SPG to unknown, [13? December 1920]; and SPG to unknown, [19 December 1920].

9 SPG to unknown, 20 February 1921.

10 SPG to "People," n.d. [June 1921].

11 SPG to "Family," n.d. [October 1915]; SPG to "beloved people," 29 May 1921; and SPG to Emsa, 25 June 1921.

12 SPG to Ruth [Theberath], 12 February [1921]; SPG to SSG, 15 February 1922; SPG to Ruth Imogene [Theberath], 10 February 1921; SPG to "People," 5 February 1921; SPG to Emsa, 25 June 1921; and SPG to SSG, Monday, [9] January 1922.

13 SPG to SSG, [26 October 1922].

14 R. M. Schindler, "Who Will Save Hollywood?" *Holly Leaves* (3 November 1922). Schindler's speeches are noted in: "Hollywood Art Association," *Holly Leaves* (7 January 1922); "For a Hollywood Emblem," *Holly Leaves* (14 January 1922); "Hollywood Insignia," *Holly Leaves* (1 June 1923); "Art Association Session Enjoyed," *Hollywood Daily Citizen* (5 June 1923); and "Has 'Community Night'," *Holly Leaves* (8 June 1923). Discussing Los Angeles, Wright observed that "There they were with steam-shovels tearing down the hills to get to the top in order to blot out the top with a house...." In Frank Lloyd Wright, *An Autobiography* (London, New York: Longmans, Green and Company, 1932), 234.

15 The fiestas and the participation of Schindler, Viroque Baker and A. R. Brandner are discussed in: "By Art Association," *Holly Leaves* (10 June 1922); "Second Annual Fiesta," *Holly Leaves* (1 June 1923); "Art Association Session Enjoyed," *Hollywood Daily Citizen* (5 June 1923); "Second Fiesta in Bowl," *Holly Leaves* (8 June 1923); "Fiesta Plans Complete," *Holly Leaves* (6 July 1923); "Open Bowl Year with Big Parade," *Hollywood Daily Citizen* (7 July 1923); "Fiesta Recalls Old Spanish Days," *Hollywood Daily Citizen* (9 July 1923); and "Second Annual Fiesta," *Holly Leaves* (13 July 1923).

The Hollywood Art Association met variously at the Franklin Galleries and at the new Hollywood Public Library, a Spanish-inspired building designed by Dodd and Richards and located at 6357 Hollywood Boulevard (northwest corner, Hollywood Boulevard and Ivar Avenue). The library, opened in June 1923, included a Community Art Gallery. Schindler served on a committee to decorate the gallery. William Francis Vreeland, "Hollywood's Community Art Gallery," *Holly Leaves* (6 July 1923). Schindler's drawing for the skylight is in the ADC/UCSB. Whether the skylight was executed remains unclear. There is no archaeological evidence: the library building was moved from its original site to a location one block south on Ivar in 1939. It was remodeled out of existence at the time by John and Donald Parkinson and stood until 1982 when an arson fire destroyed it. Schindler's skylight screen is mentioned neither in *Annual Reports of the Hollywood Library, 1923-25*, nor in *Minutes, Board of Library Commissioners, 1923-24*. I thank Sally Dumaux, Special Collections Librarian, Goldwyn Hollywood Regional Branch, Los Angeles Public Library; and Susie Frierson, Commission Executive Assistant, Los Angeles Public Library, for their help.

16 RMS to unknown, October 1921. Copy in possession of author.

17 SPG to unknown, 22 May 1922.

18 SPG to unknown, 22 May 1922; and SPG to "Mother 'n Father 'n Dorothy," 16 July 1922.

19 SPG to "Mother 'n Father 'n Dorothy," 16 July 1922.

20 DSG to unknown, 12 November 1922; and SPG to unknown, 17 November 1922.

21 DSG to unknown, 30 July 1922; and DSG to unknown, 31 July 1922. I thank the Mosers' son, Lorenze, and grandson, Elias, for their help.

22 DSG to unknown, 10 August 1922; DSG to unknown, 11 August 1922; and DSG to unknown, 20 August 1922.

23 DSG to unknown, 5 August 1922; and DSG to unknown, 20 August [1922]. Dorothy commented that "There is even a cot in R.M.S.'s room;" and that the Schindlers might "graduate to the 'sleeping baskets'."

24 DSG to unknown, 22 [April 1923]. Helen Barr was Dorothy's friend from Wellesley College.

25 SPG to SSG, n.d. [12? April 1924].

26 Maurice Browne, *Too Late to Lament: An Autobiography* (London: Victor Gollancz, Ltd., 1955), 287; SPG to "Mother," n.d. [October 1925]; and SPG to "Father," n.d. [October 1925].

27 DSG to "Ye Editor of the Gazaboo," n.d. [c. November 1922]; DSG to SSG, n.d. [December 1923]; and RMS to unknown, [1 December 1923].

28 SPG to unknown, n.d. [28 December 1922].

29 DSG to unknown, 10 December 1922; and DSG to unknown, 6 December 1922.

30 SSG to SPG, 20 November 1923; and RMS to unknown, 3 June 1924 (copy in possession of author). In her personal life, Helena Rubenstein was Mrs. E. W. Titus; Schindler's drawings in the ADC/UCSB are so identified. The extent of work actually completed has not been ascertained; the house, though standing and recognizable, has been extensively remodeled. I thank Susan Richardson, Archivist, The Historical Society of the Town of Greenwich, for her help.

31 RMS to unknown, 20 April 1924; and Clyde Chace, in an interview with Kathryn Smith and the author, 28 July 1987, Friends of the Schindler House.

32 EJG to SSG, 15 January 1925; and SSG to EJG, 5 January 1926. The 5 January letter is the only known source of information about the Rankin house: "On Sunday R. M. came in, just as I was entertaining the Howenstein's [*sic*] at dinner, and said, Well, here are the plans for the Rankin house—(Just as I had suspected he would). When I told him he was precipitate, that I had told him I would not do it, he got quite angry and *nasty*, said I had promised, that the Rankins so understood, had moved into the guest studio to wait."

33 SPG to SSG, 9 January 1925.

34 "The Crossroads of New York," *Variety* (26 May 1922); "Fighting Blood," *Variety* (18 October 1923) ("Short Subject Releases," in *Film Year Book 1924*, 79, lists seven films with this title released between 18 February and 19 August 1923); "O'Hara in 'Listen Lester,'" *Morning Telegraph* (New York) (17 February 1924); and "George O'Hara," *Variety* (18 October 1966).

115 35 DSG to [EJG], 2 February [1925]; Weschler, *To Tell the Truth*, 106: "We were put up in a one-room apartment, which was vacant at that time, and that's where we lived for several months until a larger apartment became available."

36 Dione Neutra, *Richard Neutra, Promise and Fulfillment, 1919-1932. Selections from the Letters and Diaries of Richard and Dione Neutra.* Compiled and translated by Dione Neutra (Carbondale, Illinois: Southern Illinois University Press, 1986), 136, 144; and Weschler, *To Tell the Truth*, 109.

37 Weschler, *To Tell the Truth*, 110.

38 RMS to [SSG, EJG], December 1925.

39 Richard J. Neutra, *Wie Baut Amerika?* (Stuttgart: Julius Hoffmann, 1927), 24-47.

40 Weschler, *To Tell the Truth*, 114-115.

41 Dione Neutra, *Richard Neutra, Promise and Fulfillment*, 171.

42 Weschler, *To Tell the Truth*, 155; and Neutra, *Richard Neutra, Promise and Fulfillment*, 153-154.

43 SPG to EJG, 11 October 1932; and RMS to SPG, n.d. [envelope postmarked 2 December 1935].

44 SSG to EJG, 1 September 1926.

45 SSG to EJG, 16 December 1926; and SSG to EJG, 19 December 1926. Katz's exhibition was held 5–31 December 1926.

46 SSG to EJG, 16 December 1926; RMS to SSG, 10 April 1925 [copy in possession of author]; and SSG to EJG, 1 November 1926.

47 DSG to unknown, 10 [July 1927]; and Neutra, *Richard Neutra, Promise and Fulfillment*, 167.

48 "Temple Activities and Notices," *Temple Artisan* 27, nos. 11 and 12 (April-May 1927): 175; "Community Hall for Halcyon," *Pismo Beach News* (29 April 1927); and *Temple Artisan* 28, nos. 9 and 10 (February-March 1928): 150-151. *Temple Artisan*, the house organ of The Temple of the People, is housed in the William Quan Judge Library, Halcyon. I thank Eleanor L. Shumway, Guardian in Chief, Blue Star Memorial Temple, for sharing her intimate knowledge of Halcyon and the Temple with me on two occasions: 17 December 1998 and 15–17 January 1999.

49 P.G.S. [SPG], "Utopia Found," *The Carmelite* (6 March 1929).

50 SPG, "Carmel Hours," *Touring Topics* 23, no. 11 (November 1931): 39.

51 SPG to "Family," n.d. [18 December 1927]; and SPG to "Father," 19 April [1928]. "The Black Sheep" appeared in 1927 on 27 November; 2, 9, 16, and 30 December; and in 1928 on 6 and 27 January; 1, 10, and 24 February; and 2 March.

52 "We Cast Our Hat in the Ring," *The Carmelite* (15 February 1928); and "Rumor Says Another Newspaper," *Carmel Pine Cone* (3 February 1928).

53 "Swan Song of 'S.A.R.,'" *The Carmelite* (30 May 1928); and "Another Bubble Bursts," *Carmel Pine Cone* (1 June 1928).

54 "Editorials ...," *The Carmelite* (6 June 1928).

55 SPG to EJG, 7 May 1928.

56 "Editorials ...," *The Carmelite* (13 February 1929); A. Manus to Editor (8 August 1928); "Tooth-Gnashing over the Library Tax" (9 January 1929); "Our Road Hazard" (17 April 1929); "Off with Their Heads" (1 May 1929); "Correspondence," Dora Hagemeyer to Editor, and P.G.S. [SPG] to Dora Hagemeyer, 8 May 1929.

57 *The Carmelite* (23 January 1929).

58 SPG to "Father," 4 December 1928.

59 "Torn From the Arms of Its Mother, *Carmelite* Makes New Start," *Carmel Pine Cone* (20 September 1929); SPG to EJG, 4 October 1929; and SSG to RMS, 26 October 1929, R. M. Schindler Collection, ADC/UCSB (hereafter "RMS at ADC/UCSB").

60 *The Daybooks of Edward Weston*, ed. Nancy Newhall (New York: Aperture, 1990), 60. The announcements are in the RMS at ADC/UCSB.

61 Scheyer to RMS, 11 November 1930, RMS at ADC/UCSB; and Scheyer to Feininger, 21 June 1931, Galka Scheyer Collection, Norton Simon Museum, Pasadena.

62 "Outcast," *Variety* (8 December 1922).

63 MacLaren to SPG, 31 January 1933.

64 On 27 September, Schindler wrote to Pauline that he had "rented the apartment to Mr. E. Locke & two friends ... He is moving in immediatly [*sic*]." RMS to SPG, 27 September [1933]; and Eric Locke to SPG, 15 December 1933.

65 The drawings for the Locke house are in the ADC/UCSB.

66 Thomas S. Hines, "Then Not Yet 'Cage': The Los Angeles Years, 1912-1938," in Marjorie Perloff and Charles Junkerman, eds., *John Cage–Composed in America* (Chicago and London: The University of Chicago Press, 1994), 65, 84; and Cage to SPG, 15 April 1935, Collection 980027, The Getty Research Institute for the History of Art and the Humanities, Los Angeles.

67 Edward Weston to Betty Brandner, n.d., Center for Creative Photography, University of Arizona, Tucson, AG 6 Subgroup Seventeen, Edward Weston Letters to Betty Brandner, 1920s.

68 Betty Kopelanoff to SPG, n.d. [postmarked 5 January 1934]; SPG to Betty Kopelanoff (note on verso of page one of Kopelanoff to SPG, 5 January 1934); and Kopelanoff to SPG, 3 March 1934.

69 SSG to EJG, 19 November 1926; SPG to "Father," 31 October [1931]; and SPG to "Mother," [2 September 1936].

70 SPG to "Father," 31 October 1931; and SPG to "Father," 14 July 1932.

71 SPG to "Mother and Father," [4 October 1933]; SPG to "Mother and Father," 11 June [1933]; and SPG to "Mother," 2 September 1936.

72 SPG, "Oceano Dunes and Their Mystics," *Westways* 26, no. 2 (February 1934): 12, 13.

73 The best source of information about the Dunes at Oceano is Norm Hammond, *The Dunites* (Arroyo Grande, California: South County Historical Society, 1992). I thank Mr. Hammond for his assistance, and also for taking me to the site of Moy Mell on 17 January 1999.

74 "Editorial," *Dune Forum*, contributor's number (late 1933), unpaginated; SPG to EJG, [24] September 1933; SPG to "Mother," 28 September 1933; and *Dune Forum* (February 1934): 44-46.

75 SPG to "Mother," 13 December 1933; and SPG to "Mother," 30 August 1935.

76 *See* "Local News," *The Ojai* (11 June 1935) for mention of Pauline and Mark Schindler's departure for Commonwealth; John F. Wells, ed., *Time Bomb: The Faubus Revolt* (Little Rock, Arkansas: General Publishers, 1962), 4; Raymond and Charlotte Koch, *Educational Commune. The Story of Commonwealth College* (New York: Schocken Books, 1972), 2, 5, 6; Koch, *Educational Commune*, 3; and Wells, *Time Bomb*, 100.

77 Wells, *Time Bomb*, 101; SPG to "Mother," [27 May 1935]; and SPG to [Father], 20 June 1935.

78 SPG to "Father," 8 June 1935; SPG to DSG, 11 July 1935; and SPG to "Father," 13 July 1935.

79 SPG to "Mother," 28 July 1935.

80 "The Architecture Issue," *The Carmelite* 3, no. 5 (13 March 1929); Carol Aronovici to SPG, n.d. [1932]; and SPG to "Mother," 2 May 1936.

81 SPG to unknown, 28 January 1927; SPG to "Father," 16 January 1930; SPG to "Mother," 15 March 1930; SPG to "Mother," 11 February 1933; and SPG to "Father," 25 February 1933.

82 EJG to SSG, 18 October 1928; SPG to RMS, [6 or 7] November 1931; and RMS to [SPG], 9 November 1931.

83 SPG to "Mother," [November 1934]; Pauline G. Schindler v. Rudolph M. Schindler, D-171000 (February 13, 1940); and Rudolph M. Schindler v. Pauline G. Schindler, D-171397, in *Findings of Fact and Order*, Los Angeles County Archives, Superior Court Records.

84 SPG to RMS, 9 July 1953.

1 JOSÉ RODRIGUEZ RESIDENCE, Glendale, California, 1940–42. View
of living room. Photograph by Grant Mudford

RICHARD GUY WILSON

SCHINDLER'S METAPHYSICS: SPACE, THE MACHINE, AND MODERNISM

Using deformed planes, open trays, prows, triangular projections, slanted and curving surfaces, diagonal frames, deep voids, and transparent walls and windows of all forms, R. M. Schindler created a new spatial aesthetic. Schindler's architecture not only challenged traditional forms and styles, but also departed from the received opinion about what constituted modern architecture. Spatial complexity and ambiguity characterize his architecture; his buildings are unsettling, abstract, and non-referential. Space for Schindler encompassed not simply the open or free plan of other modern architects, but was an active moving presence, reaching outward to embrace the landscape and circling inward in complicated patterns that could be vertical, horizontal, diagonal, and oblique.

Schindler's work lacks the geometrical clarity, the air of fine-tuned, machine-honed rationalism, sought by many modernists of the first half of the twentieth century. In contrast to most of his contemporaries, Schindler questioned the machine. In a 1928 speech he cryptically explained: "Machine Age—not Human."[1] Instead of celebrating modern architecture as a machine-made product, Schindler believed that the modern architect's concern lay not with plastic materials but, as he described in a 1921 lecture, "with forms of space." In his notes for the lecture, Schindler sketched out a defining conclusion: the "arch.[itect] not a decorator—and not any more a sculptor—architecture a new and independent art—and its material is Space."[2] Although initially a proponent of the new machine and the construction possibilities offered by steel and concrete, Schindler's attitude toward the machine changed as he searched for a new spatial aesthetic.

Schindler stood so far apart from the identified mainstream of modernism and its competitors—whether Streamline Moderne, Art Deco, or Wrightian—that Henry-Russell Hitchcock (the critic and historian who helped define the American modernist orthodoxy) could observe in 1940: "The case of Schindler I do not profess to understand. There is certainly immense vitality ... But this vitality seems in general to lead to arbitrary and brutal effects." Hitchcock identified his work as "extreme Expressionist and Neo-Plasticist" and immature, envisioning it as "sets for a Wellsian 'film of the future.'"[3] This was not their first encounter: in 1930, Hitchcock told Schindler he hoped "to see [his] work in California—although frankly it would be [Richard] Neutra's which would draw me there."[4]

Hitchcock's dismissal reveals Schindler as an artist who practiced his own brand of modernism—a style rejected by the Eastern

Modernist establishment (a theme constantly reiterated by scholars). Schindler's exclusion from The Museum of Modern Art's (MOMA) "International Exposition of Modern Architecture" exhibition and catalogue of 1932, and the accompanying book, *The International Style: Architecture Since 1922*, is a mini-scandal in the annals of modern architectural history. The exhibition traveled for two years and, along with the book, gave the prominent name "International Style" to what most Americans would come to consider as modern architecture. Hitchcock co-authored the book and catalogue with Philip Johnson, the museum's "Director of Architectural Exhibition."[5] In 1931, Schindler learned (possibly through Neutra) of the impending exhibition and sent materials to Johnson. Johnson curtly replied that the exhibition's plans were "already completed and it would be absolutely impossible to include any more buildings."[6] In turn, Schindler questioned the very idea of a "so-called 'International Style.'" He wrote to Johnson, "my work has no place in it," explaining: "I am not a stylist, not a functionalist, nor any other sloganist. Each of my buildings deals with a different *architectural* problem, the existence of which has been entirely forgotten in this period of rational mechanization." Schindler attacked one of the central premises of modernism, the portrayal of the machine, with a caustic flourish: "The question of whether a house is really a house is more important to me, than the fact that it is made of steel, glass, putty, or hot air."[7] Johnson replied that the group of ten architects to be shown, which included Schindler's former partner Richard Neutra, was "very carefully selected" and confessed, "my real opinion is that your work would not belong in the Exhibition."[8]

Such negative criticism wounded Schindler and helped to cultivate his persona as a misunderstood genius living a lonely exile in the cultural outpost of Los Angeles. After his death in 1953, Esther McCoy and then David Gebhard, followed by many writers including Reyner Banham, Stefanos Polyzoides, Barbara Giella, August Sarnitz, Lionel March, Margaret Crawford, and Judith Sheine, have critically and historically repositioned Schindler within the modernist canon. The Schindler-studies industry has treated him sympathetically, raising his status from an ignored Los Angeles architect to one of a seminal modernist on par with his European contemporaries Le Corbusier, Ludwig Mies van der Rohe, and his fellow Angeleno, Neutra.[9] Interpretations have varied. Schindler's work has been viewed as an early version of Robert Venturi's concept of "Complexity and Contradiction," or as the precursor to the recent Neo-Deconstructivist Santa Monica wave of Frank O. Gehry and Thom Mayne. Influences ranging from De Stijl to the Wagnerschule to Frank Lloyd Wright have been cited, and his work has alternately been held up as an expression of California sybaritic living and, in some extreme cases, as true International Style architecture (implying that Hitchcock couldn't recognize it!).[10] All of these perceptions contain some validity, and the variety of interpretation suggests a difficulty inherent in the critical address of an avowed individualist or rebel (the image which Schindler worked hard to embody). They also reveal the problem of predetermined stylistic categories. Schindler's perceptions of the machine help to differentiate his architecture from that of others and provide an insight into his most important contribution and indeed his greatest concern: the creation of a new kind of space.

First, an observation should be made about the myth of Schindler as an unrecognized talent. From the later 1920s to the mid-1940s, Schindler was a known presence on the American architecture scene, even if MOMA cognoscenti refused their approbation in 1932. The oft-cited obscurity does not come until later, closer to his death in 1953. Prior to this Schindler actively promoted his work in a variety of ways, giving frequent lectures on his work throughout his career and teaching several courses on modern architecture in Los Angeles. His 1934 course at the University of California, Los Angeles, received a national notice as he explained, "the New architecture is not a mere style," and warned of "pseudo modernism."[11] He sought to show his work in museums and art galleries and, although he failed with MOMA in 1932, he participated in an exhibition that the museum sponsored in 1935 on California architects, in which his John J. Buck Residence (1934) and William E. Oliver Residence (1933–34) appeared, along with his remodeling of Sardi's Restaurant (1932–34).[12] He failed to gain admittance to MOMA's 1944 exhibition on architecture, but did have his work exhibited at the Berkeley Art Museum in 1929, the California Arts Club in Los Angeles in 1930, the Architectural League of New York's annual show in 1931, the M. H. de Young Memorial Museum in San Francisco in 1933, the San Francisco Forum in 1934, an American Institute of Architects-sponsored show in Paris in 1937, and several Southern California-based exhibitions. He avidly sought publicity, regularly sending photographs and drawings of his designs, manifestos, and writings to architectural and other editors. From the late 1920s until World War II, Schindler's work frequently appeared in books and magazines both at home and abroad; in 1937 alone it appeared in eleven different publications. From most points of view, Schindler's publication record would be considered significant, although other American architects such as Neutra appeared more frequently. After 1945, his appearances in printed materials decreased, and though they total nineteen, many of these were in regional publications. Certainly contributing to this low number was Schindler's illness with cancer, which also caused a decline in commissions.[13]

The "scandal" of Schindler's exclusion from the "International Exposition of Modern Architecture" exhibition becomes understandable when the catalogue, accompanying book, and illustrations are examined, for his work did not meet the dictates nor the appearance of the architecture that Hitchcock and Johnson promoted. MOMA's director Alfred Barr announced: "The present exhibition is an assertion that the confusion of the past 40 years, or rather of the past century, may shortly come to an end."[14] Barr, Hitchcock, and Johnson attacked the "Modernistic or half-modern decorative style" (now labeled Art Deco) and Expressionism, along with all of the traditional styles.[15] "Chaos" and the "American cult of individualism" reigned, according to the authors, but that would come to an end with the International Style.[16] The book advocated a recipe of three principles: "architecture as volume rather than as mass"; "regularity rather than axial symmetry serves as the chief means of ordering design"; and the proscription of "arbitrary applied decoration."[17] *The International Style* aspired to be a cookbook, a set of do's and don'ts: "Anyone who follows the rules, who accepts the implications ... can produce buildings which are at least aesthetically sound."[18] The rules were set forth: "Good modern architecture expresses in its design this characteristic orderliness of structure and this similarity of parts by an aesthetic ordering which empha-

sizes the underlying regularity. Bad modern design contradicts this regularity."[19] Schindler's designs, such as the well-known Philip Lovell Beach House in Newport Beach, California (1922–26) *(fig. 2),* incorporated most of these principles, but not within the orthodoxy MOMA demanded. The images shown in the exhibition and book were of tight white boxes that seemed to exude a machine-made air. All of the illustrations were in black and white, and while a close reading of the text revealed some color in the buildings, the overall impression was of thin, white, rectilinear volumes, very different from Schindler's variety of forms, colors, and textures.

The International Style's codifying of style by three principles came from Germanic formalist art history as enunciated by Heinrich Wölfflin and the very *au courant* Harvard University, which Hitchcock, Johnson, and Barr had all attended. *The International Style* also contained a contradictory thesis, for while claiming the aesthetic of the style did not depend on the machine, it also argued that "modern technics" had brought it into being.[20] Although Hitchcock and Johnson tried to distance their new "controlling style" from the European "functionalists" by claiming the style existed irrespective of its social and cultural origins, the images shown gave the overall impression that recent construction technology involving steel, concrete, and glass were the means of creating a new architecture devoted to function. They argued that the "simple forms of standardized detail suitable to mechanical production is thus an aesthetic as well as an economic desideratum."[21] Space in Hitchcock and Johnson's treatment came under "volume," and while "interiors that open up into one another without definite circumscribing partitions" were described, spatial flow was not a principle.[22] The images appeared to emphasize flat wall surfaces, large areas of glazing, thin

2 PHILIP LOVELL BEACH HOUSE, Newport Beach, California, 1922–26

steel or concrete supports, and steel-tube furniture. By and large, Schindler's work did not conform to the dictates laid down by Hitchcock and Johnson, nor to any of the other writers on modernism. The Lovell House in Los Angeles (1927–29) *(fig. 3)*, designed by Neutra, appeared in the "International Exposition of Modern Architecture" book and exhibition, whereas Schindler's Lovell Beach House did not.

Certainly similarities exist between Schindler's and Neutra's houses for Philip and Leah Lovell, but there are also major differences. Schindler's house interweaves space in a complex manner, whereas Neutra's "Health" house (as it was also known) creates surface volumes. This is not to say that space is not a concern in the Los Angeles house, for there is a dramatic stairwell with a vertical thrust that merges into the horizontal push of the library-living room which opens to the hills of Los Feliz *(fig. 4)*. However, the overall emphasis is elsewhere. The cagelike steel frame, supplied by Bethlehem Steel, becomes the ruling geometry of the design. Although there are projections, the frame's dimensions rule. Onto this geometrical order,

glazing, painted metal, and concrete gunite panels are affixed as flat **120** wall surfaces. The building emphasizes regularity, not variety. Neutra's Lovell House masterfully replays the new stylistic currents emanating from Europe, which he knew well from his time in Erich Mendelsohn's office in Berlin during the early 1920s.[23]

Schindler's Lovell Beach House contains some of the same elements, but they are employed differently.[24] Instead of the fine-tuned machine image of the Los Angeles house, the Lovell Beach House has a burly roughness. The shuttering marks of the concrete board work and the contrasting materials of concrete, wood, and stucco are prominent *(fig. 5)*. Schindler used an array of patterns and sizes for the windows and openings; instead of a regular, overall pattern as in the Los Angeles house, Schindler employed variously sized rectangles and long slit horizontals, and an assortment of scales. The five reinforced concrete piers of the frame dominate (especially now that they are painted white), but are counteracted at the upper levels by protruding surfaces of stucco boxes and deep voids (some now filled in). Spatially the mixture is complex; space is

3 Richard Neutra. Lovell House, Los Angeles, 1927–29

4 Richard Neutra. Lovell House, Los Angeles, 1927–29. View of living room

5 PHILIP LOVELL BEACH HOUSE, Newport Beach,
California, 1922–26. View of construction, 1926.
Photograph by R. M. Schindler

6 PHILIP LOVELL BEACH HOUSE, Newport Beach,
California, 1922–26. View of living room

channeled underneath through open-framing elements, and then on the interior with a multi-level space. The central space, the living room, is two stories in height; a balcony provides access to the bedrooms along one side. A partition containing a built-in sofa partially separates the dining area from the living room *(fig. 6)*. Surfaces vary from plaster walls and open-beamed ceilings to glazing. The windows, with their incessant mullions and patterns, create both opacity and transparency that funnel the space out towards the sand and ocean.

An Oldsmobile advertising campaign of 1936 unconsciously summed up the difference between Schindler's and Neutra's architecture. Schindler's John J. Buck Residence (1934) served as a backdrop for an April 1936 Oldsmobile advertisement *(fig. 7)*, while a February advertisement of the same year featured Neutra's VDL Research House (1931) *(fig. 8)*. The Neutra advertisement praised streamlining and styling; Neutra himself liked to incorporate the machine literally into his architecture by using auto headlamps as fixtures in staircases, and symbolically by coating wood with alu-

minum paint. Names such as "VDL Research" and "Health" implied that the buildings were prototypes rather than individual houses. The Schindler advertisement, on the other hand, emphasized the machine as providing modern, "mental" comfort and making life more bearable—the term "style" did not even appear.[25]

The disparities in the advertisements, whether intended or not, are important. Whereas recognition of the machine—or technology—as a new governing element unites most of those architects and designers labeled as twentieth-century modern, rejection of the machine implies a traditionalist's approach to design. There are, however, manifold distinctions between the ways in which the machine was used and represented in architecture. One of the reasons for Schindler's "non-compliance" with orthodox modernism is his view contrary to the machine as a form-giver and, instead, his insistence upon space as architecture's central focus. For Schindler, modern architecture was rooted not in a fixed set of stylistic parameters but, as he indicated to Johnson, in the investigation of different architectural problems. Because space, and not the

7 Advertisement in *Collier's*, 1936, featuring Schindler's John. J. Buck Residence, Los Angeles, 1934

8 Advertisement in *Collier's*, 1936, featuring Richard Neutra's VDL Research House, Los Angeles, 1931

machine, was his central concern, Schindler's architecture looked different from that of other modernists, whose primary consideration was form.

An indication of Schindler's departure from orthodox modernism (and a building that Hitchcock and Johnson would have found appalling because of its rough, primitive quality) is his own dwelling, the Kings Road House (1921–22) *(fig. 9)*. The house is a "machine-made" house in the sense that concrete was used as a flat slab directly on the ground and for the solid enclosing walls. The walls were erected by using a tilt-slab or, as he termed it, a "SLABTILT" construction system that he derived from the designs of Irving Gill. The concrete wall slabs inclined from eight inches at the bottom to four inches at the top to create a battered appearance. Filled with several types of glazing, the thin three-inch spaces between the concrete wall units increased the sense of fortification. Untreated redwood employed in the roof, fascia, and sleeping baskets added an improvisational air to the public front. In its massing, Schindler's house might invoke a close analogy to an adobe house he had drawn while in New Mexico in 1915. Schindler would return in his various writings to the idea of the house made out of rock or earth—a sculptural mass, like the cave. And in a sense that is what Kings Road House embodies: the creation of a primitive cave merged with Schindler's new concept of space as the controlling medium. Behind the house's concrete walls, its rooms extended out through wide openings glazed with redwood mullions or covered by moveable screens onto various patios and gardens. Spatial flow was continuous between interior and exterior. He explained, "The shape of the rooms, their relation to the patios and the alternating roof levels, create an entirely new spatial interlock between the interior and the garden." To further the sense of spatial interpenetration, Schindler placed clerestory windows over many of the openings to create diverse levels of spatial movement and light. He described the Kings Road house as a "theme ... for a camper's shelter: a protected back, an open front, a fireplace and a roof."[26]

Schindler's vision of the house as a primitive shelter was intensified by the rough concrete, the untreated redwood, and the exposed timberwork of the ceiling. Instead of the flat, parallel planes of floor and ceiling beloved by modernists such as Le Corbusier or Neutra, Schindler's wooden joists stand out in relief, and ceiling heights shift to emphasize the variety of scale and the interplay of space *(fig. 10)*. Large concrete fireplaces dominate one wall of most of the interior rooms, and two appear on the exterior patios. But instead of resembling typical raised hearths, where the fire is separated from the floor, Schindler's sit right on the slab or on the ground. Instead of the bright porcelain fixtures indicative of precise mechanical production, poured concrete appears in Schindler's bathroom to form the bathtub and countertop.

In its linear line and repeated geometrical motifs, the Kings Road house betrays the impact on Schindler of Frank Lloyd Wright, for whom he had worked. Some of its plain, unadorned quality might be traced to Irving Gill, whom Schindler admired. The blank frontage towards the street recalls Adolf Loos's dictum that anonymous character is appropriate to private dwellings. But other elements are purely Schindler's own. A few years after the construction of Kings Road, he explained in a newspaper column: "Our rooms will descend close to the ground and the garden will become an integral part of the house. The distinction between the indoors and the out-of-doors will disappear." He went on to claim that walls would be "few, thin, and removable," and "All rooms will become part of an organic unit, instead of being small separate boxes with peepholes."[27] The employment of modern technology with a rough edge was as Schindleresque as the harsh juxtaposition of parts. The inclined concrete walls of the entrance capped by wide redwood boards, the thin frame of the sleeping basket, and the thin slab of roof all allow for a variety of spatial inter-penetrations. Density contrasts with transparency, colors clash, and the forms appear additive, or even ad-hoc: a harsh resolution.

The Kings Road House was Schindler's manifesto about what the modern house should be. Ten years earlier he theorized that man's original home—the cave, a "timid retreat"—had, with the advent of mechanized civilization, given way to a new idea of a dwelling that conquered the elements. He wrote that the new power of the machine "has enabled him to return to nature."[28] The Kings Road House was an expression of this idea and also of how security and open space might be combined.

That Schindler took a non-conformist stance towards orthodox modernism can be seen as part of his self-created mythology, though some origins of Schindler's rebellion do exist in his training. Much has been made of the influence of *fin-de-siècle* Vienna, where he was born and trained as an architect. Barbara Giella has documented Schindler's involvement in avant-garde circles, where he

9 KINGS ROAD HOUSE, West Hollywood, California, 1921–22. Photograph by Grant Mudford

10 KINGS ROAD HOUSE, West Hollywood, California, 1921–22.
View of Pauline Schindler's studio. Photograph by Grant Mudford

127 met writers such as Karl Kraus, Peter Altenberg, and Adolf Loos. No evidence exists as to whether Schindler ever met Sigmund Freud, but in Vienna's café society he could not have escaped some discussion about the nature of human consciousness. From his training as a structural engineer, Schindler progressed to the Academy of Fine Arts and studied under Otto Wagner. Wagner was a reformer, not a rebel, and believed that "modern" architecture would be a product of new mechanics and structural systems. From Wagner and the Viennese Secessionists, Schindler learned structure, geometrical principles, and a degree of abstraction. From Loos he discovered the importance of space and the art of provocative overstatement, as when Loos described Germanic culture as "the culture of the pig," or made the claim: "The modern person who tattoos himself is either a criminal or a degenerate."[29]

The relation of Loos's ideas and architecture to Schindler's work is complex; not all of Loos's ideas were fully articulated when Schindler knew him, and even then Schindler did not accept them

totally. Schindler probably learned to celebrate primitive architecture from Loos, but disagreed with Loos's argument that the house should be designed with a plain exterior, only to reveal its richness on the interior.[30] Loos had a respect for tradition, and he frequently incorporated classical elements into his work. In contrast, Schindler never drew from classicism and always saw as his mission the creation of a modern architecture. It is doubtful that Loos fully articulated his *raumplan* (space plan) verbally while Schindler knew him in Vienna, though the beginnings of multi-level space could be seen in the interior of Loos's commercial building on the Michaelerplatz in Vienna (1909–10).[31] Loos's developed spatial complexity became evident later during the 1920s, in such works as the Tristan Tzara House (1925/26) or the Villa Müller (1928–30) (*fig. 11*). These houses, with their complicated interior passages and staircases, multi-level rooms, spatial inter-penetration, and sectional shifts, were built long after all known connections between Loos and Schindler had ceased. Loos also instilled in Schindler a new concept of ornament, not as isolated appliqué, but as wall surface, as in the marble sheathes of the Kärntner Bar (1908) or the oak paneling of the Knize Store (1910–13). And Loos provided the model for a combative stance towards Wagner's and the Secessionists's more orthodox modernism. Schindler described Loos as "the only serious opponent against the architectural atrocities of the 'Secession'."[32] Finally, Loos admired America, and encouraged him to look for employment there.

At Loos's urging, Schindler (whose father had worked in New York for ten months between 1880 and 1881) came to the United States in 1914 in part to experience firsthand the new mechanical Atlantis. He wrote of observing floors cantilevered twenty stories in the sky; of

11 Adolf Loos. Villa Müller, Prague, 1928–30.
View of living room. Photograph by Pavel Štecha

500,000 daily commuters in a single terminal; of slender steel frames; of "perfect" elevators.[33] In time, Schindler even proposed writing a book on the new American building technology, but did not—in the end, Neutra wrote it.[34] All the young, European modernists dreamed of coming to America, but Schindler came and stayed. He received his ideas about the machine age in America, not from newspaper photographs and the gossip of drafting rooms, but from actual experience.

Schindler also came to the United States with the hope of working for Frank Lloyd Wright, whom he viewed—as did most European modernists—as an architect who understood and utilized the machine. Schindler later claimed to have discovered Wright when a librarian in Vienna "handed me a portfolio," though Wright had visited Vienna in 1910, and Wagner acknowledged him in 1911.[35] In C. R. Ashbee's *Ausgeführte Bauten* (1911), Schindler could have read Wright quoted as saying, "The machine is the normal tool of our civilization," and "There is no more important work before the architect now than to use this normal tool of civilization."[36] Although recent scholarship questions the idea that Wright employed the machine as a form generator in his architecture and design, early twentieth-century critics—especially the Europeans—opined that Wright's architecture was inspired by the machine. After working for Wright for three years, Schindler wrote: "He is a complete and perfect master of any material—and modern machine techniques are at the base of his form-making."[37] Later, in 1934, Schindler claimed that what he initially found in Wright's Wasmuth portfolio back in Vienna was "a man who had taken hold of this new medium. Here was 'space architecture.'" Schindler explained that Wright had not dealt with moldings, caps, and finials; instead, "here was space forms in meaningful shapes and relations. Here was the first architect."[38]

Schindler worked for Frank Lloyd Wright for five years, and Wright's impact can be seen in several ways. The linear "L" is one example, as is the repetition of rectangular forms at various scales. Schindler's renderings and title-block signature would always betray a Wrightian influence. During the beginning of his tenure with Wright, Schindler kept a notebook entitled "Frank Lloyd Wright Utterances." Among Wright's thoughts on ornament and Japanese art, Schindler recorded Wright's observation: "See how all things grow—who can doubt that a divine mind is working behind all this." Schindler appended to this Wrightianism his own feeling: "I doubt it—the thing called 'mind' seems unable to understand life—to mispersonify

nature is a childish truism of men in order [to] help him grasp—'the mind' is part of man & not behind him—is part of nature & and not behind it."[39] In short, Schindler's cosmology lay rooted in the individual, not in some divine presence.

In spite of Schindler's admiration of Wright, he differed greatly in his architectural philosophy. In 1934, Schindler explained: "The timeless importance of Wright lies especially in these first houses," referring to designs such as the Ward W. Willits House (1902–03) and the Frederick C. Robie House (1908–10) *(fig. 12)*, and those in which Wright's shaping of interior space was the major element. In these houses, at least according to Schindler's interpretation, Wright created overlapping spatial systems whose enclosing walls operated as screens. But by the time Schindler went to work for Wright, the elder architect's focus had changed, and Schindler observed: "I feel that in his later work he has again become sculptural. He tries," Schindler continued skeptically, "to weave his buildings into the character of the locality through sculptural forms." Even though "far above most of his contemporaries" as an artist, for Schindler Wright's later work belonged to the "Modernistic School"

12 Frank Lloyd Wright. Frederick C. Robie House, Chicago, 1908–10.
Photograph by Jon Miller

129 and was not truly modern.[40] The heavy forms Wright employed during the late 1910s and 1920s were inherently traditional in the sense that they confined space; they lacked that essence of modern architecture that aimed to open the human mind to an expanding space in all directions.

Before coming to the United States, Schindler addressed the relationship of space and the machine to architecture in his manifesto of 1912–13, "Modern Architecture: A Program." A paean to the possibilities of a new architecture, Schindler's writing reflects to some degree the influence of Wagner, Loos, and other European theorists, but also his departure from them.[41] It also contains elements of what Reyner Banham labeled "café-Freudianism," a search for fundamentals, or the "oceanic" sensation, a bond of the individual with the universal.[42] Schindler opened with a concept derived from Gottfried Semper: "The cave was the original dwelling.... *To build meant—to gather and to pile material around empty cells for air-living rooms*," progressing to the observation: "*We no longer have plastically shaped material-mass.... The only idea is space and its organization*." Schindler argued that the steel skeleton and concrete frame freed the architect from designing the building as a mass, and that the architect was no longer bound by representing construction in architecture. He wrote: "Man has found a more mature symbol for the conquest of physical forces—the machine. The mathematical conquest of statics makes the structure's formula and artistic expression meaningless."[43] The machine is viewed as a liberator of modern architecture; the trammels of the old conception of architecture as confining sculptural mass disappears with the new building technology of the machine age. This is a direct refutation of Wagner. Instead of the disappearance of traditional structural stability or gravitational orientation, the building becomes a mind-expanding space open to the world.

While Schindler was obviously entranced by the machine, his manifesto is more focused on the new possibilities of space in the modern age of architecture. A new cosmology is apparent: "The new monumentality of space will presage the limitless power of the human mind. Man trembles at the expanse of the universe." The final section of the manifesto takes up the house and its transposition through history from the cave to the modern dwelling. The major issue for the modern home is no longer "formal development," but controlling "light, air, and temperature."[44]

Twenty years later, perhaps in response to the MOMA exhibition, Schindler returned to his manifesto, translating it and adding a few rhetorical flourishes, such as "Functionalism is a hollow slogan used to lead the conservative stylist to exploit contemporary techniques." He rephrased certain parts, such as: "The architectural design concerns itself with 'Space' as its raw material and with the articulated room as its product. Because of the lack of a plastic mass the shape of the inner room defines the exterior of the building." And then, "The architect has finally discovered the medium of his art: S P A C E." He claimed the machine as a "ripe symbol," but only as a means for creating the modern dwelling.[45]

The oceanic and cosmological underpinnings of Schindler's original manifesto become even more apparent in his 1934 article, "Space Architecture." In it, he explained: "In the summer of 1911, sitting in one of the earthbound peasant cottages on top of a mountain pass in Styria [a region in southeast Austria], a sudden realization of the meaning of space in architecture came to me." Sitting in the stone house that was "but an artificial reproduction of one of the many caverns in the mountain-side," he realized that all architecture of the past "was nothing but sculpture." And then "stooping through the doorway ... I looked up into the summer sky. Here I saw the real medium of architecture—*Space*."[46]

In other essays of the 1930s, Schindler attacked the idea of "machines for living," the International Style, and, of course, Le Corbusier and Buckminster Fuller. Machines, Schindler wrote, were only "crude 'contraptions'"; "the structure of our machine is still infantile."[47] In another article, he attacked "the modern 'functionalist,' who is not an architect at all, but an engineer who has taken to building houses." For Schindler the source of architectural form is "the spirit," and "architectural design concerns itself with space as its raw material and with the organized room as its product."[48] Schindler's study of Loos's tactical wit is obvious: "The man who brings such machines into his living room is on the same level of primitive development as the farmer who keeps cows and pigs in his house." He claimed that "instruments of production" can never frame life, and "the creaks and jags of our crude machine age must necessarily force us to protect our human qualities in homes contrasting most intensely with the factory."[49] The vehemence of Schindler's criticism of the machine is striking for the 1930s and, while some of the anger certainly stemmed from his rejection by Hitchcock and Johnson, he stood far apart from the machine veneration carried on by most modernists.

Schindler came to the machine-age Atlantis as a primitive European *naïf* seeking knowledge from the fountainhead. He arrived just after Henry Ford popularized mass production, and he witnessed the transformation of America: while only sixteen percent of homes used electricity in 1912, that number increased to nearly seventy percent by 1930; the number of automobiles owned by Americans increased from two million to twenty-seven million between 1914 and 1930; and the number of mechanical refrigerators owned increased from zero to seven million between 1920 and 1935.[50] His letters reveal that though he initially approved of the machine as a liberating force (it could free the architect through new construction technology), he was also aware of its capacity to facilitate the endless production of trivialities. He found that machine production could be brutal, skyscrapers inhuman, details crude, mechanical perfection difficult.[51]

Schindler's infatuation with new construction possibilities, however, was evident: he experimented with poured concrete at Kings Road House and Pueblo Ribera Courts (1923–25), and explored gunite structural enclosures at the John Cooper Packard Residence (1924). But there is also a sense of disillusionment: concrete was difficult to handle, made details crude, and proved to be far too costly. Schindler felt modern structural systems should not just imitate the older trabeated enclosures; instead, a dynamic structure should lead to a new space. The Lovell Beach House, with its separation between the structural frame and the space trays, demonstrates this. The mystique of efficient production intrigued Schindler; with the Lovell Beach House, he tried to fully utilize every element, including using the wood of the formwork to construct the house's furniture.

In contrast to Le Corbusier's and Neutra's strident mechanophilic tendencies, Schindler had, by the mid-1920s, come to understand the machine as a tool, a complex and fascinating one to be sure, but one whose expression was not the central issue of architecture. In 1926, for example, he wrote six newspaper columns for Dr. Philip Lovell that are striking in their non-advocacy of the machine as form-giver. In these articles he covered mundane issues such as ventilation, plumbing, tile sewers, radiators, and placement of electrical outlets. But to Schindler, not all mechanical advances were positive: "the advent of the modern metal weather strip [is] a real menace, provided no other means to obtain a constant and diversified ventilation is provided." In contrast to the practical elements he enumerates is the mystical new space he describes: the architect will "divine" a dwelling where the rooms are part of an "organic unit," nature is friend, and inside and out disappear, so that "the house will be a form-book with a song."[52]

Though Schindler never abandoned his experimental attitude towards materials and construction, his experiences and failures made him wary of untested practices. The materials that attracted him were standardized studs, tar paper, the recently economical plywood, and large plate glass. He approached the issue of standardization by machine as a way to foster individuality. Standardization, Schindler claimed, should not dictate design nor become an end in itself, but should be in the service of the new. Instead of the prohibitively expensive and uncomfortable all-metal house (the ideal of modernists on both continents), he proposed an open wood frame or "Schindler Frame." This "space house" was constructed of vertical wood studs cut to door height throughout the house, and a continuous belt of top plates that allowed a variety of planes in ceiling and walls.[53]

Schindler also took advantage of standardization in his furniture designs of the early 1930s. Employing a variety of basic shapes, his "Schindler Units" furniture *(fig. 13)* evoked standardized production in that they could be assembled in different configurations. But he explained: "Only by confining the machine to making parts (units) which, through the very fact of their precision, may be joined freely, can we subdue its mechanical ferocity to individual human expression." The furniture allowed for change and individuality while still maintaining the overall "fluidity and continuity of space in the house."[54] The "Schindler Units" could be prefabricated (though

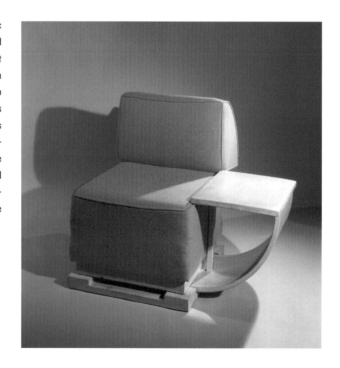

13 "SCHINDLER UNIT" CHAIR FOR ELIZABETH VAN PATTEN RESIDENCE, Los Angeles, 1934–36

14 GUY C. WILSON RESIDENCE, Los Angeles, 1935–38.
View of dining room

15 JOHN DEKEYSER DOUBLE RESIDENCE, Los Angeles, 1935.
View of living room. Photograph by Grant Mudford

apparently they never went into large-scale production), but their essence was their variability.

Most of Schindler's furniture design was site-specific, and he attempted to simplify it by using very basic shapes that the carpenter or home-craftsman could build out of plywood *(fig. 14)*. Primarily, Schindler advocated built-in furniture, and explained that a house so appointed "becomes a weave of a few basic materials used to define his space forms." Stationary furniture, he went on to observe: "becomes part of this weave until it is impossible to tell where the house ends and the furniture begins" *(fig. 15)*.[55] However, while his furniture designs—whether the built-in or moveable—followed from his overall spatial schemes, he was not adverse to comfort, designing over-stuffed chairs and advocating the use of throw pillows.

Thus the representation of the machine is absent in Schindler's design. Instead of bestowing ultimate status on the machine or a particular construction process, he viewed them simply as a means to a goal, which in 1934 he called "cosmic space." By way of explanation, he wrote: "Structural materials, walls, ceilings, floors, are only means to an end: the definition of space forms." Yet it would be wrong to say that the machine makes no impression upon his work. The repetitive note, for instance, which he claimed was a feature of the "new grammar" ranging from the monotone to "the tremor of the broken line," frequently emerges as detail and evokes the machine age in which he worked.[56]

Schindler's use of modern advancements such as lighting and electricity was always abdicated by his concern for space. Writing for Dr. Lovell's column in 1926, he attacked "the stupidity of furnishing electric light by means of a chandelier," stating that it can "only be surpassed by trying to make the bulbs look like candles." According to Schindler, light fixtures should not be hung in the middle of a ceiling, and electric light should not imitate natural light. While allowing for a few exceptions, Schindler argued for a diffused and softened artificial light employed for specific tasks such as reading and providing welcome: "The eye which emerges from the dark outside should be welcomed by meeting only the softest indirect rays possible." He especially abhorred "fixtures" and wanted the source of the light to be "as unobtrusive and glareless as possible"*(fig. 16)*.[57] Instead of using prominent ceiling fixtures, like those in the houses of Mies van der Rohe, Walter Gropius, and Le Corbusier, Schindler strove to integrate his fixtures into the overall architectural scheme as he did in the Lovell Beach House. By the mid-1930s, and after the advent of the International Style, he became even more outspoken on the topic: "This use of light in contemporary work is completely contradicted by any emphasis of the source: the 'light fixture.'" "Half-baked imaginations" focused on creating "light fixtures," he wrote, and missed the point that light should be understood "as an attribute of space." For Schindler, "The space architect uses the illumination of the room to shape it." Ultimately, Schindler sought more than mechanical representation. In the treatment of architectural lighting, for instance, the "primitive glass wall" becomes "the translucent light screen," and the character and color of light issuing from it will permeate space, giving it "body and make[ing] it ... palpably plastic." He even advocated colored lights, suggesting an almost Scriabinesque color poem.[58]

In 1952, he returned to the issue of color and translucency in an unpublished essay entitled "Visual Technique," in which he wrote:

16 GUY C. WILSON RESIDENCE, Los Angeles, 1935–38.
View of interior featuring recessed lighting.
Photograph by Grant Mudford

17 ADOLPH TISCHLER RESIDENCE, Los Angeles, 1949–50.
View of living room. Photograph by Grant Mudford

"The ultimate and revolutionary aim will be to create a feeling of color throughout the atmosphere of the room, rather than to be satisfied with static areas of color on the walls." Invoking natural colors, pointillist paintings, form-defining light, reflective surfaces to break up images, and overall transparency, Schindler conceived of rooms as a "power center of a color symphony." As he described it, the "space architect" would dramatize "space forms," creating in-depth color worlds and giving color to the void.[59] At times he came close to this ideal, as in the upper living spaces of the Adolph Tischler Residence (1949–50), where blue fiberglass panels changed according to the time of day and the color of the heavens (fig. 17).

Schindler attacked not only the modernists' fetishization of the light fixture, but also their emphasis on polished surfaces, whether mirrors or hardware. He acknowledged that mirrors could be employed profitably, but "not to cover up undigested members of the space design." Instead he argued for joining smaller pieces of mirror together slightly out of plane, "thereby breaking up the image." He advocated varnishing hardware to remove its reflective quality since "a shiny knob is as objectionable as an actual hole in the material."[60]

Above and beyond detailing, in general the shape of Schindler's houses is not machinelike, but rather reflects his intention to show variation. The seeming awkwardness of parts displays his attempt to create new space. A section of the Guy C. Wilson Residence (1935–38), for instance, is related to the reverse slope of the hillside (fig. 18).[61] The twist in the plan, the shift between the garage and living quarters on the first floor, and the lack of alignment between the bedrooms, is site-specific—inspired by the topography and view to the Silver Lake Reservoir below (figs. 19, 20, 21). These elements allowed Schindler to create a variety of room configurations, both horizontally and vertically. The staircase begins as a pentagonal opening, changes directions twice, and has no banisters (fig. 22). Indeed, negotiating a Schindler house takes fortitude. Roofs fly off at different angles. The space Schindler created here, and in other houses of the 1930s and 1940s, defies verbal description. Instead of a grid of rectilinear verticals and horizontals, different angles and

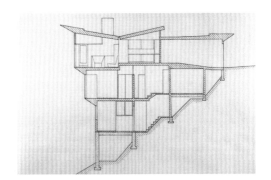 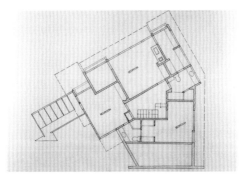 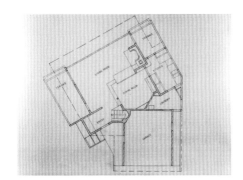

18 GUY C. WILSON RESIDENCE, Los Angeles, 1935–38.
Section looking north

19 GUY C. WILSON RESIDENCE, Los Angeles, 1935–38.
Floor plan, second level

20 GUY C. WILSON RESIDENCE, Los Angeles, 1935–38.
Floor plan, third level

Inside the drawing title block:
RESIDENCE FOR M. WILSON L A
R.M. SCHINDLER ARCHITECT 1/4/36
833 KINGS ROAD L A WY 9011

21 GUY C. WILSON RESIDENCE, Los Angeles, 1935–38

22 GUY C. WILSON RESIDENCE, Los Angeles, 1935–38.
View of interior stairwell. Photograph by Grant Mudford

23 GUY C. WILSON RESIDENCE, Los Angeles, 1935–38.
View of living room

ceiling and floor heights are used so that the main living space is divided into two levels, and the roof lifts upward in two directions from the center *(fig. 23)*. Entire walls oriented to a magnificent view of the reservoir below are translucent. As an enclosure it knows no limits; it pulsates, and the mind seeks to encompass it.

The José Rodriguez Residence (1940–42) utilizes five ceiling heights, and provides a contrast to man's memory of the cave. In this case, the entry level with its thick wall of fieldstone, and the upper floor with its exposed rafters and frame, appear as a tent support *(fig. 24)*. One penetrates the solid wall and ascends stairs that widen to a living room with a slanted ceiling and clerestory windows *(fig. 1)*. A large fireplace built out of the same fieldstone occupies one corner of the living room. Next to the solid fireplace, the space deepens and the entire wall is open to nature so that the main floor is an open space tray, with windows on all sides providing views and ventilation *(fig. 25)*. In a sense the Rodriguez Residence is a later variation of the Lovell Beach House, but reads more as a primitive hut than an artfully designed dwelling. There is a purposeful roughness to the wood details on the interior and the floors composed of plywood sheets. The projecting rafters and the

different depths and voids of the enclosing surfaces provide a vibrating new space that expands and contracts.

R. M. Schindler's architecture provides a revealing commentary on early- and mid-twentieth century modernism, for it stands apart from the general stampede to accept the machine. Modern architecture to Schindler involved not a search for a new style, but a higher goal: architecture born of a new consciousness of space. He acknowledged the potential of the machine in achieving a space architecture, but was wary of it becoming an end in itself and offering little room for human expression. Rather, his modernism was oriented toward using space as a medium, recognizing that comfort should be a goal and not a by-product. One might conclude that Schindler failed, or that his architecture is so individualistic that it could never be suited for a mass market. But the intrigue is still there, of really creating a new architecture—a modern architecture—based upon cosmic space.

24 JOSÉ RODRIGUEZ RESIDENCE, Glendale, California,
1940–42

Notes

This essay was originally presented as a paper,
"R. M. Schindler and the Machine," at the annual meeting
of the Society of Architectural Historians, April 1987, San
Francisco (Marion Dean Ross, chair of session). It has been
rewritten and expanded for this publication. For assistance I
am indebted to Kurt Helfrich, Curator, Architecture and
Design Collection, University of California, Santa Barbara.

1 R. M. Schindler (henceforth "RMS"), "The House You Want to Live In," 10 July 1928, Rudolph M. Schindler Collection, Architecture and Design Collection, University Art Museum, University of California, Santa Barbara (henceforth "RMS at ADC/UCSB").

2 RMS, "About Architecture," January 1921, 6 and 10, RMS at ADC/UCSB.

3 [Henry-]Russell Hitchcock, "An Eastern Critic Looks at Western Architecture," *California Arts and Architecture* 57 (December 1940): 21–23, 40–41.

4 Hitchcock to RMS, 2 [November] 1930, RMS at ADC/UCSB. Hitchcock's letter was written in response to a letter by RMS to Hitchcock (January 1930) that criticized Hitchcock's treatment of him in *Modern Architecture: Romanticism and Reintegration* (London: Payson and Clarke, 1929), 204–205, 213; and also Hitchcock's ignoring of Schindler's contribution to Frank Lloyd Wright's Imperial Hotel.

5 *See* Hitchcock and Philip Johnson, *The International Style: Architecture Since 1922* (New York: W. W. & Norton Co., 1932); and Hitchcock, Johnson, Alfred H. Barr, and Lewis Mumford, *Modern Architecture: International Exhibition* (New York: The Museum of Modern Art and W. W. Norton, Co., 1932). *See also* my "International Style: The MOMA Exhibition," *Progressive Architecture* 82, no. 2 (February 1982): 92–105. Although Johnson assumed the title "Director," the Department of Architecture was not formed until after the exhibition.

6 Telegram, RMS to MOMA, 5 January 1931 [1932], RMS at ADC/UCSB; and letter, Philip Johnson to RMS, 9 January 1932, RMS at ADC/UCSB, reprinted in August Sarnitz, ed., *R. M. Schindler, Architect: 1887–1953* (New York: Rizzoli, 1988), 208.

7 RMS to Johnson, 9 March 1932, RMS at ADC/UCSB; reprinted in Sarnitz, *Schindler*, 209.

8 Johnson to RMS, 17 March 1932, RMS at ADC/UCSB; reprinted in Sarnitz, *Schindler*, 209.

9 For a list of many of these studies, *see* the selected bibliography in this volume.

10 The best summary is in Margaret Crawford, "Forgetting and Remembering Schindler: The Social History of an Architectural Reputation," *2G*, no. 7 (1998): 131–143.

11 "Schindler's Warning," *Art Digest* 9 (1 October 1934): 8.

12 Letters and telegrams, Ernestine M. Fantl, MOMA, to RMS, 26 April 1935, 26 June 1935, 16 July 1935, and 19 September 1935, RMS at ADC/UCSB; and RMS to Fantl, 3 May 1935, 5 July 1935, 17 September 1935, 19 September 1935, and 21 September 1935, RMS at ADC/UCSB.

13 Sarnitz, *Schindler*, 210–220, contains a chronology and bibliography. *See also* David Gebhard, *Schindler*, 3rd ed. (1971; reprint San Francisco: W. Stout Publishers, 1997), 151–166.

14 Barr, "Foreword," in *Modern Architecture: International Exhibition*, 13.

15 *Ibid.*, 15.

16 Barr, "Preface," in *The International Style*, 13–14.

17 Hitchcock and Johnson, in *The International Style*, 20.

18 *Ibid.*, 68.

19 *Ibid.*, 57.

20 *Ibid.*, 95.

21 *Ibid.*, 71.

22 *Ibid.*, 86–87.

23 Thomas S. Hines, *Richard Neutra and the Search for Modern Architecture: A Biography and History* (New York: Oxford University Press, 1982).

24 RMS, "A Beach House for Dr. P. Lovell at Newport Beach, California," *Architectural Record* 66 (September 1929): 257–261.

25 The advertisements appeared in several magazines; for examples *see Collier's* 97 (15 February 1936 and 11 April 1936). *See also* Thomas S. Hines, "Designing for the Motor Age: Richard Neutra and the Automobile," *Oppositions* 21 (Summer 1980): 34–51.

26 RMS, "A Cooperative Dwelling," *T-Square* 2 (February 1932): 21.

27 RMS, "Shelter or Playground," in Dr. Philip Lovell's column, "Care of the Body," for the *Los Angeles Times,* 2 May 1926, 26–27, reprinted in Sarnitz, *Schindler*, 46.

28 RMS, "Modern Architecture: A Program" (1913), translated by Harry Francis Mallgrave, in Lionel March and Judith Sheine, eds., *R. M. Schindler: Composition and Construction* (London: Academy Editions, 1993), 12.

29 Adolf Loos, "Culture" and "Ornament and Crime," reprinted in Loos, *Ornament and Crime: Selected Essays*, ed. Adolf Opel (Riverside, Calif.: Ariadne Press, 1998), 160, 167; Barbara Giella, "R. M. Schindler's Thirties Style: Its Character (1931–1937) and International Sources (1906–1937)" (Ph.D. diss., Institute of Fine Arts, New York University, 1987), chapter 3; and Carl E. Schorske, *Fin-de-siècle Vienna: Politics and Culture* (New York: Vintage Books, 1981).

30 Loos, in Benedetto Gravagnuolo, *Adolf Loos, Theory and Works* (New York: Rizzoli, 1982), 22 and 139. *See also* Loos, quoted by Giella, "R. M. Schindler's Thirties Style," 136, from an article of 1910.

31 Harry Francis Mallgrave, "Schindler's Program of 1913," and August J. Sarnitz, "The Wagnerschule and Adolf Loos," in March and Sheine, *R. M. Schindler*, 15–19 and 21–31, respectively.

32 RMS to Louis Sullivan, 26 August 1920, quoted in Esther McCoy, *Vienna to Los Angeles: Two Journeys* (Santa Monica, Calif.: Arts + Architecture Press), 144.

33 RMS to Richard Neutra, March 1914, in McCoy, *Vienna to Los Angeles*, 104–106.

34 *Ibid.*, 25; Richard Neutra, *Wie Baut Amerika?* (Stuttgart: Hoffmann, 1927).

35 RMS, "Space Architecture," *Dune Forum* (February 1934): 45, reprinted in Sarnitz, *Schindler*, 50. On Wright in Vienna, *see* Anthony Alofsin, *Frank Lloyd Wright–The Lost Years, 1910–1922: A Study of Influence* (Chicago: The University of Chicago Press, 1993), although, strangely, Schindler is never mentioned in this study.

36 C. R. Ashbee, "Frank Lloyd Wright, A Study and an Appreciation," in *Frank Lloyd Wright: The Early Work* (originally published as *Frank Lloyd Wright: Ausgeführte Bauten*, Berlin: Ernst Wasmuth, 1911) (reprint, New York: Horizon Press, 1968), 4–5. Ashbee is quoting Wright's "In the Cause of Architecture," *Architectural Record* 23, no. 3 (March 1908): 155–222.

37 RMS to Neutra, December 1920 or January 1921, in McCoy, *Vienna to Los Angeles*, 130.

38 RMS, "Space Architecture," in Sarnitz, *Schindler*, 50.

39 RMS, "Frank Lloyd Wright Utterances" (c. 1918), Schindler-Wright Correspondence, Special Collections, The Getty Research Institute for the History of Art and the Humanities, Los Angeles.

40 RMS, "Space Architecture," in Sarnitz, *Schindler*, 50.

41 The dating of the manifesto, "Modern Architecture: A Program," has caused some comment. Schindler claimed both 1911 and 1912, but the only extant copy is written in German and dates "Juni 1913," RMS at ADC/UCSB. RMS, "Modern Architecture: A Program," in March and Sheine, *Schindler*, 10–13. For revised versions, *see* Sarnitz, *Schindler*, 42; or Gebhard, *Schindler*, 191–92.

42 Reyner Banham, "Ornament and Crime: The Decisive Contribution of Adolf Loos," *The Architectural Review* 121, no. 721 (February 1957): 85–88.

43 RMS, "Modern Architecture: A Program," in March and Sheine, *Schindler*, 10–13.

44 *Ibid.*, 12.

45 *Ibid.*

46 RMS, "Space Architecture," in Sarnitz, *Schindler*, 50. Schindler wrote a number of articles and essays (c. 1934) with a variety of similar titles that repeated similar ideas on space, architecture and furnishings. *See* RMS, "Furniture and the Modern House: A Theory of Interior Design," *Architect and Engineer* 123, no. 3 (December 1935): 22–25, and 124 (March 1936): 24–28, reprinted in Sarnitz, *Schindler*, 52–56; and RMS, "Space Architecture," *California Arts and Architecture* 47, no. 1 (January 1935): 18–19.

47 RMS, "Space Architecture," in Sarnitz, *Schindler*, 51.

48 RMS, "Contra," *Southwest Review* 17, no. 3 (Spring 1932): 353, 354.

49 RMS, "Space Architecture," in Sarnitz, *Schindler*, 51.

50 Richard Guy Wilson, Dianne H. Pilgrim, and Dickran Tashjian, *The Machine Age in America, 1918–1941* (New York: Brooklyn Museum and Abrams, 1986), chapter I.

51 Letters of RMS to Neutra, March 1914, 14 April 1920, and December 1920 or January 1921, reprinted in McCoy, *Vienna to Los Angeles*, 104–106, 121, and 129.

52 RMS, "Ventilation," in Dr. Philip Lovell's column "Care of the Body," *Los Angeles Times Sunday Magazine*, 14 March 1926, 25–26; and RMS, "Shelter or Playground," *Los Angeles Times Sunday Magazine*, 2 May 1926, 27–28. The other columns appeared on 21 March, and 4, 11, and 18 April; they are reprinted in *Oppositions* 18 (Fall 1979): 74–85, and in Sarnitz, *Schindler*, 43–47.

53 RMS, "The Schindler Frame," *Architectural Record* 101, no. 5 (May 1947): 143–146. This essay's topic had been predisposed in his 1932 essay, "Reference Frames in Space," *Architect and Engineer* 165 (April 1946): 10, 40, 44–45; and also in RMS, "A Prefabrication Vocabulary: The Panel-Post Construction," *California Arts and Architecture* 60, no. 5 (June 1943): 25–28. Both are reprinted in Sarnitz, *Schindler*, 59–60 and 56–57, respectively.

54 RMS, "Furniture and the Modern House: A Theory of Interior Design," in Sarnitz, *Schindler*, 55.

55 *Ibid.*, 54.

56 *Ibid.*, 53, 54.

57 RMS, "About Lighting," in "Care of the Body" column for *Los Angeles Times Sunday Magazine*, 11 April 1926, 30. Reprinted in Sarnitz, *Schindler*, 45–46.

58 RMS, "Furniture and the Modern House," 56.

59 RMS, "Visual Technique," unpublished manuscript, RMS at ADC/UCSB, printed in Sarnitz, *Schindler*, 66–67.

60 *Ibid.*

61 According to E. Richard Lind, a Schindler draftsman and later an architect, courtesy of Barbara Giella.

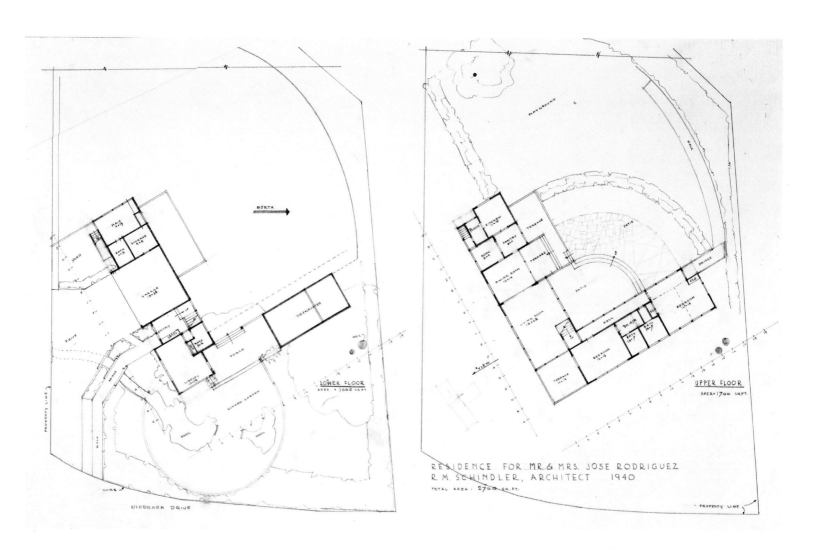

25 JOSÉ RODRIGUEZ RESIDENCE, Glendale, California, 1940–42. Lower- and upper-level plans

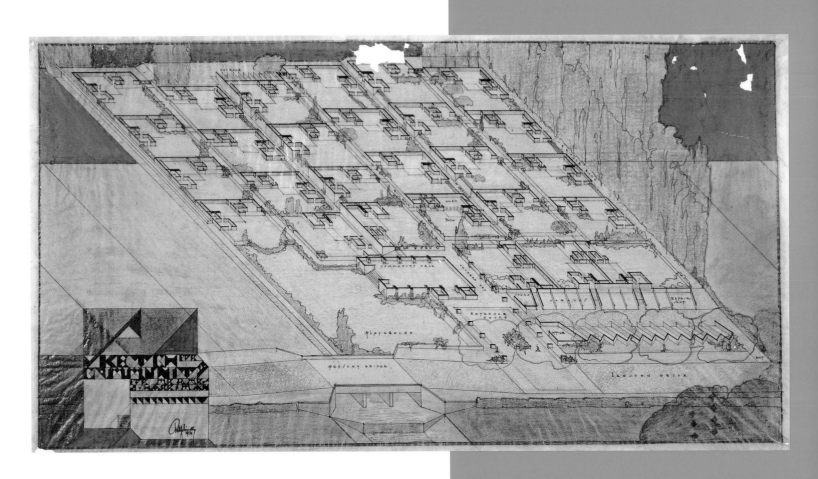

1 HARRIMAN'S COLONY (project), San Gabriel, California, 1924-25.
Aerial cutaway perspective

KURT G. F. HELFRICH

CONTEXTUALIZING "SPACE ARCHITECTURE": WHAT THE SCHINDLER ARCHIVE REVEALS

In a review of the 1967 catalogue which accompanied the major retrospective of Rudolph Michael Schindler's architectural work, the London-based *Architectural Review* noted: "Many other questions about Schindler still remain to be answered, and it is good news that his son, Mr. Mark Schindler, now intends to make all the drawings accessible by presenting them to the University of California."[1] The gift to the architectural archives, established by David Gebhard as part of the University Art Gallery (now the University Art Museum) at the University of California, Santa Barbara (UCSB), included much more than Schindler's architectural drawings.[2] A rough survey of the material made by Gebhard in November 1967 estimated over 7,000 drawings, as well as manuscript material including specifications, financial records, business correspondence, historic photographs, and a series of figure and nature studies made by Schindler as a young man in Vienna and Chicago.

Mark Schindler's choice of UCSB as the repository for the Schindler archives came after consideration of other institutions. His options included the University of California, Los Angeles (UCLA), where Richard Neutra, while ill at the same hospital where Schindler lay dying, had promised his archives in 1953; and the University of Southern California (USC), where Schindler had actively lectured during the late 1940s.[3] The accomplishment and persuasive vision of David Gebhard directly influenced Mark Schindler's ultimate decision. As director of the University Art Gallery, Gebhard organized a series of specialized exhibitions and publications dealing with California's contribution to contemporary architecture.[4]

Gebhard's initial plans for the gift included a retrospective exhibition that would be devoted solely to Schindler's work. In 1963, Gebhard wrote to the architectural writer and promoter of Schindler's legacy, Esther McCoy: "What I have in mind is a rather large show of just his work.... This would of course be an enlargement of your earlier exhibition of the mid-1950s.... In talking to people both here on the coast and out East I sense that we are now at a stage to far better appreciate his work than was the case even ten years ago."[5] Gebhard organized a small exhibition of Schindler's work in May 1964 for the University Art Gallery consisting of original drawings and photographs meant to demonstrate Schindler's importance as a pioneer in the development of modern American architecture.[6] In early 1965, he published a short article on Schindler's 1915 design for the unbuilt Dr. Thomas Paul Martin Residence in Taos, New Mexico.[7] That same year in his *A Guide to Architecture in Southern California (fig. 2),*

Gebhard singled out Schindler's importance: "[He] established his own practice in Los Angeles and in 1926 created at Newport Beach the Lovell Beach House, certainly one of the marvels of architecture in America. And Schindler continued to produce masterpieces of great ingenuity until his death in 1953, all of them characterized by a multitude of ideas not always fully carried out but certainly stimulating."[8] It was roughly at this time that Gebhard (fig. 3) began to actively collaborate with Esther McCoy on a comprehensive retrospective exhibition devoted to the work of R. M. Schindler.

Gebhard's and McCoy's plans for the exhibition were ambitious. In a letter of May 1965 to Viennese architect and Schindler advocate Hans Hollein, Gebhard described the intended exhibition as "a group of space-enclosures made up of photomurals of about eight of his major buildings. There will also be other four-by-five foot photos, enlargement of plans and presentation drawings. We are also starting this summer to produce (from his original working drawings) a small representative selection of his furniture, and a few other details." Initial plans called for the show to travel to Berkeley, Chicago, Yale, and if "all works out well at the Museum of Modern Art in New York" (MOMA), where McCoy and Gebhard had approached Arthur Drexler. Despite the personal enthusiasm of Philip Johnson, plans to travel the show to MOMA fell through due to Drexler's concern that a large-scale exhibition of Schindler's work would not be of interest to New York and eastern audiences.[9]

Gebhard and McCoy's exhibition was ultimately divided into two parts. The first (fig. 4) opened at the University Art Gallery, UCSB, in late March 1967, and consisted of Schindler's figure studies and architectural drawings for unrealized projects, as well as models and furniture.[10] The second, larger component (fig. 5) opened at the Los Angeles County Museum of Art in September and consisted of materials relating to Schindler's executed buildings.[11] The combined show traveled to the Yale University Art Gallery then, under the auspices of the United States Information Agency, on to Darmstadt, Berlin, Vienna, London, Amsterdam, Brussels, Zurich, and Bern. The exhibition's critical acclaim and positive reception helped to promote an interest among European architects in Schindler's work.[12] Gebhard followed up with a monograph on Schindler's career, published in 1972. Schindler's former wife, Pauline, singled out Gebhard and McCoy's efforts to reawaken interest in Schindler's career in December 1969: "it is you and Esther who have caused this to happen; this remembering and cherishing, enhancing; this placement in history."[13]

The archive of Rudolph Schindler's work at UCSB is the single largest research collection relating to his work and consists of drawings and manuscript material including historic photographs, business and personal correspondence, lectures and writings, books, and a clippings file of newspaper and magazine articles dating from his student years in Vienna until his death in 1953.[14] The surviving drawings represent over 600 projects that Schindler designed between 1910 and 1953, including a number of his early student compositions. They range in format from multi-colored presentation drawings (usually rendered by Schindler himself); to gridded, dimensioned working drawings done on tracing paper; as well as a number of free-hand initial studies whose fugitive, temporary nature is embodied in their very media—often done by the ever-thrifty Schindler on the verso side of duplicate blueprints made for other projects to save paper. Schindler was also an avid photographer, and his own photo album of

A Guide to

Architecture
in Southern California

Los
Angeles
County
Museum
of Art

2 Cover, *A Guide to Architecture in Southern California* by David Gebhard and Robert Winter, 1965

3 David Gebhard, c. 1967

prints dating from his early days in Chicago to the late 1920s includes over 1,000 images of landscapes, figures, American street scenes, Frank Lloyd Wright's studio at Taliesin West, and Schindler's own projects in Chicago and Los Angeles.[15]

Schindler's architectural approach reflects the impact of his Central European background, specifically the Art-and-Crafts training he received as a student of Otto Wagner at the Imperial Academy of Fine Arts in Vienna, and the theoretical writings and personality of his mentor, Adolf Loos.[16] Thankfully, Schindler's drafting abilities were wedded from his youth to writings and the desire to persuade through lectures. Wagner himself published a series of key books, including *Moderne Architektur* (1896), that clearly stated the principles he wished to instill in his students in their search for an appropriate modern design. For Wagner, every structure was to be designed to meet contemporary needs and local conditions. This meant that each architectural endeavor was to be approached as a problem requiring a completely new solution. Thus the designer had to take into account regional variations of landscape and setting, sound construction based on modern practices incorporating a thorough mastery of engineering, new materials, and the broader "demands of the present," which for Wagner meant social concerns including hygiene and low-cost housing.[17] As he stated in the 1902 edition of *Moderne Architektur*, "All modern creations must correspond to the new materials and demands of the present if they are to suit modern man; they must illustrate our own better, democratic, self-confident, ideal nature and take into account man's colossal technical and scientific achievements, as well as his thoroughly practical tendency."[18]

While the outward architectural expression of Wagner's Viennese structures often incorporated highly decorative elements, the basis of their design solution was always very serious—a rigorous experiment in reforming people's lives. Schindler combined Wagner's concerns with the theoretical writings of Loos to come up with his own solution, centered around man's creative conquest of the medium of his art: "Space." His own manifesto, first drawn up in 1912 while a student in Vienna, noted: "Today a different power is asking for its monument.... The machine has become the ripe symbol for

4 "The Architectural Projects of R. M. Schindler (1887–1953)" exhibition at the University Art Gallery, UCSB, installation view, 30 March–30 April 1967

5 "The Architecture of R. M. Schindler (1887–1953)" exhibition at the Los Angeles County Museum of Art, installation view, 29 September–19 November 1967

man's control over nature's forces. Our mathematical victory over structural stresses eliminates them as a source of art forms. The new monumentality of space will symbolize the limitless power of the human mind. Man trembles facing the universe."[19] Schindler's architecture revolved around the design of a structure as an outer skin or envelope shaped by and in turn shaping its interior space. His mastery of this concept of space architecture would allow him, at his most creative, to simultaneously conceive a building's structure as both interior and exterior space, breaking down the traditional division of inside and outside.

Schindler's success, or failure, at creating space architecture in Southern California continues to intrigue and mystify observers of his work. David Gebhard stressed the importance of "ambiguity" in Schindler's design during the late 1960s, a time when the tenets of modernism had come under fire. Gebhard saw Schindler's ambiguity as a vital quality arising from an ability to synthesize complex and seemingly contradictory design ideals—including Viennese Secessionist principles, the work of Frank Lloyd Wright, and De Stijl tendencies—in a unified personal vision. His appreciation of this quality in Schindler owed a debt to Robert Venturi's *Complexity and Contradiction in Architecture* (1966), as well as to the philosophy and writings of Charles W. Moore, who had completed UCSB's Faculty Club in 1968.[20] Reyner Banham explained the widespread contemporary appeal of the 1967 Schindler exhibition, noting: "The Schindler boom isn't deafening yet, but it is getting good and loud ... Schindler's architecture has been an unsettling revelation, undermining their long-held preconceptions about the nature and history of the Modern Movement."[21] Charles Moore, in reviewing Gebhard's monograph on Schindler in 1973, saw Schindler's career in Los Angeles as

part of the exotic development of Southern California—unusual at the time but later the model for the rest of the world. For Moore, the work was powerful because of its creator's vulnerability. Moore defined this vulnerability as "caring about the specific things you find and find out about so much that you will change your position to accommodate them: invulnerable architects see and learn things too, but they have a position, or a sense of mission, early arrived at, to which the learned and seen things contribute, without the power to change it."[22] Schindler's vulnerability was in sharp contrast to that of his contemporary, the archly invulnerable Walter Gropius, and the International Style at large, called by Moore "the temple of invulnerability."[23] Moore's understanding of Schindler was boldly self-referential and helped to outline the way that a whole international generation during the late 1960s came to treasure Schindler's work as that of the unrepentant outsider.

Moore's appraisal—as well as Gebhard's monograph—have in turn left us with an image of Schindler as an impractical artist-architect whose career was ultimately doomed by a small and wildly erratic output, as well as a self-propelled oblivion (compounded by his untimely death) within American architectural circles after 1945. However, the traditional characterization of the demise of Schindler's professional standing, while a moving story, is not entirely accurate.[24] Schindler's contribution to Southern California's growing importance in the field of residential modern architecture was pointed out for the general public in 1941, when a Works Progress Administration-sponsored guidebook to the Los Angeles area singled out his work. The book noted that Schindler's exteriors "display decks stressing the horizontal line and contrasting vertical surfaces of concrete and glass, which are especially striking when the house projects from the side or top of a hill."[25] While Schindler's post-1945 work was not featured as heavily in national architectural journals like *Architectural Record, Architectural Forum*, or *Progressive Architecture*, it was covered by John Entenza in his *Arts and Architecture*—a magazine then garnering national attention among younger proponents of the modern movement. Most of Schindler's late work was also prominently featured in Frank Harris and Weston Bonenberger's 1951 *A Guide to Contemporary Architecture in Southern California (fig. 6)*, which was elegantly designed by Alvin Lustig. Schindler himself, as the guidebook noted, was ready and willing to arrange site inspections for interested parties. His 1953 obituary in the *Los Angeles Times* described Schindler as a "noted architect" and exponent of modern design who had studied under Wagner in Vienna and had worked for Frank Lloyd Wright, designing over 500 homes in Southern California.[26] Arthur B. Gallion, dean of USC's School of Architecture, noted in his introduction to the American Institute of Architects-sponsored guide, *Southern California Architecture, 1769-1956*: "Though confined to the residential field, R. M. Schindler's poetic treatment of form and space is represented in a remarkable

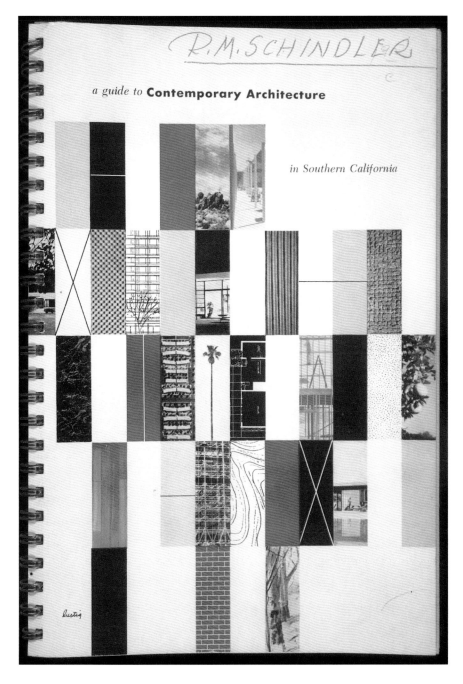

number of buildings in Southern California. The termination of his career in 1952 [*sic*] was a tragic loss to architecture."[27]

Schindler's overriding design tenet encompassed a need to meet contemporary conditions without a set formula in a quest to develop a modern Californian architecture centered around space as a creative medium. While the archive richly documents Schindler's ongoing search for an appropriate, modern Californian residence, the architect's assessment of his own career is equally revealing. Three representative projects spanning Schindler's career are particularly illuminating: the commercial hotel, Pueblo Ribera Courts, for Dr. W. Llewellyn Lloyd (1923–25); the unbuilt designs for prototypical, reinforced-concrete subsistence homesteads, termed Schindler Shelters (1933-39); and finally, the aerie-like residence hovering on a hillside built for Ellen Janson (1948–49). Surviving manuscript materials in the Schindler archive provide new perspectives on the formal concepts and intentions behind the development of these projects. The archival evidence highlights previously unexamined factors behind decisions about form, structure, and living patterns, ranging from client/designer interaction to the impact of new building technologies. Contrary to the popular conception of Schindler—as the isolated artistic designer unwilling to actively promote himself within the existing Southern California cultural establishment—the Schindler archive documents his sustained and often fierce dialogue with clients, contractors, and the larger architectural community in developing his concept of space architecture. Schindler's letters, writings, and lectures help to contextualize these specific designs and document his engagement with—rather than rejection of—contemporary cultural developments in Southern California.

6 Cover, *A Guide to Contemporary Architecture in Southern California* edited by Frank Harris and Weston Bonenberger, 1951

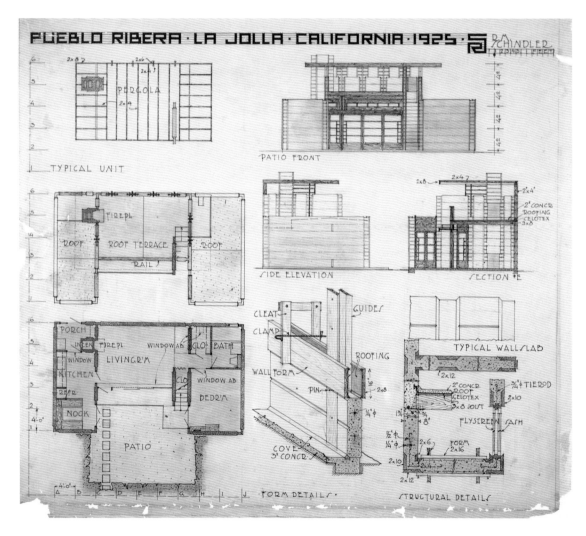

7 PUEBLO RIBERA COURTS FOR W. LLEWELLYN LLOYD, La Jolla, California, 1923-25.
Plans, elevations, and section of individual unit

8 PUEBLO RIBERA COURTS FOR W. LLEWELLYN LLOYD, La Jolla, California, 1923-25.
Plan of the complex

Schindler's 1923 design for the Pueblo Ribera Courts *(figs. 7, 8)* allowed him to apply on a larger scale those principles for communal indoor/outdoor living he had first developed for his own studio on Kings Road in West Hollywood (1921-22), and to continue his experimentation with poured concrete-slab construction. Schindler designed the twelve-unit complex for Dr. W. Llewellyn Lloyd and his wife, Lucy Lafayette Lloyd, on a slightly sloped site in La Jolla one block from the ocean. Lloyd, a transplanted dentist from Westfield, New Jersey, then living in Redlands, California, had met Schindler in late 1922.[28] Impressed by his work, Lloyd asked Schindler to design in a Southwestern manner what he later termed "bungalow apartments of distinction," adjacent to the ocean in the fashionable resort town north of San Diego.[29] Schindler's meticulous account card for the project notes that he first visited the site in mid-April 1923, and drew up the final plans for the complex by July.[30] Clyde R. Chace, Schindler's business associate and co-owner of the Kings Road House, served as the contractor for the project, which was substantially completed by March 1924.[31] Because of the physical distance between Schindler's studio in West Hollywood, Lloyd's residence in Redlands, and the project site, most of the communication between the architect and client was carried out through letters.[32] Lloyd's initial stipulation for the complex's design was that, in keeping with the economic status of the guests he hoped to attract, each unit should have its own garage.[33] He also asked Schindler to keep the total cost of the project to an absolute minimum in order to "meet the competition of the customary primitive wooden beach shack."[34]

Before visiting the site in early April 1923, Schindler sent Lloyd an initial sketch of a prototypical unit in the complex. He outlined his idea for the project:

I propose to treat the whole in true California style, the middle of the house being the garden, the rooms spreading wide into it, the floors of concrete, close to the ground. The roof is to be used as a porch, either for living or for sleeping [connected to the ground floor by an outdoor staircase], and should be one of the features of the place, with its ocean view. This will also make it possible for larger families to occupy the house. The unit is planned in such a way that it can be closely joined and combined with other units, without sacrificing privacy of rooms, gardens, or roof.[35]

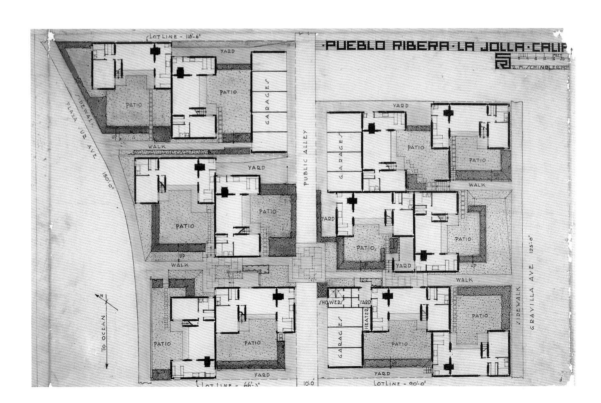

Dr. Lloyd approved the layout of the units, but immediately questioned Schindler's use of exposed concrete for the walls and floors. He was skeptical of its waterproofing properties and its hard, inelastic quality as flooring. Schindler was able to persuade Lloyd to use the concrete, writing with an almost Wrightian disdain: "Your banker's apprehension lest concrete walls be not waterproof is utterly unfounded. A well-mixed concrete of proper proportions is in itself waterproof.... The many swimming-tanks, silos, etc. successfully constructed in concrete, are ample proof that their material is waterproof when properly applied."[36] For the floors, Schindler was able to persuade Lloyd that his method of staining and waxing them and then covering portions with rugs would mitigate their inelasticity.

Lloyd's major stumbling block was obtaining the money to finance construction of the complex. Negotiations dragged on with the local building and loan company, who questioned Schindler's unorthodox design, materials, cost estimates, specifications, and work schedule.[37] Meanwhile, Lloyd became concerned about the lack of windows in the bedroom, kitchen, and bathroom, as well as the safety of his potential guests with such an open indoor/outdoor lifestyle. Schindler indicated that transom windows would be used in these areas to let in light and air, but Lloyd was adamant that conventional windows had to be included in the design so the occupants would not only have a view, but could also get air into the rooms if the sliding sash doors were closed. Lloyd argued:

You assure us there will be plenty of ventilation from the transom windows and there would be if the wind came from the right quarter and everything were open, but not one person out of ten will leave their bedroom door open. Women alone would be especially timid.... There must be a window in each bedroom and should be one in the kitchen when possible. Ladies like to look out when they are working.[38]

By early July 1923, Lloyd's loan had come through and construction of the Pueblo Ribera Courts began. Excavation work and the pouring of the concrete pads and walls began in August under Clyde Chace's supervision *(figs. 9, 10)*. By mid-October, the roofers had arrived to cover the first unit. Lloyd then requested that Schindler design an office area (ultimately not built) for him as an addition to the north end of Unit II. Schindler complied, drawing the initial sketch of the office addition on Lloyd's letter *(fig. 11)*. Lloyd, however, continued to experience problems financing the construction of the complex. In late January 1924, he wrote to Schindler that, while construction was almost finished, "my great worry is that the funds will not even now stretch far enough to finish the buildings and furniture.... The mistakes you two boys have made have run to twenty-five percent over the estimate, and the end is not yet in sight."[39] He had sunk all of his capital into the venture, and breaking even required that the complex be fully rented, continuously. The first guests arrived at the complex in mid-February, only to discover that their Hudson and Cadillac automobiles would not fit into the garages Schindler had designed. By late March the rains arrived, and a number

9 PUEBLO RIBERA COURTS FOR W. LLEWELLYN LLOYD, La Jolla, California, 1923–25.
View of construction, c. 1923. Photograph by R. M. Schindler

10 PUEBLO RIBERA COURTS FOR W. LLEWELLYN LLOYD, La Jolla, California, 1923–25.
Photograph by R. M. Schindler, c. 1924

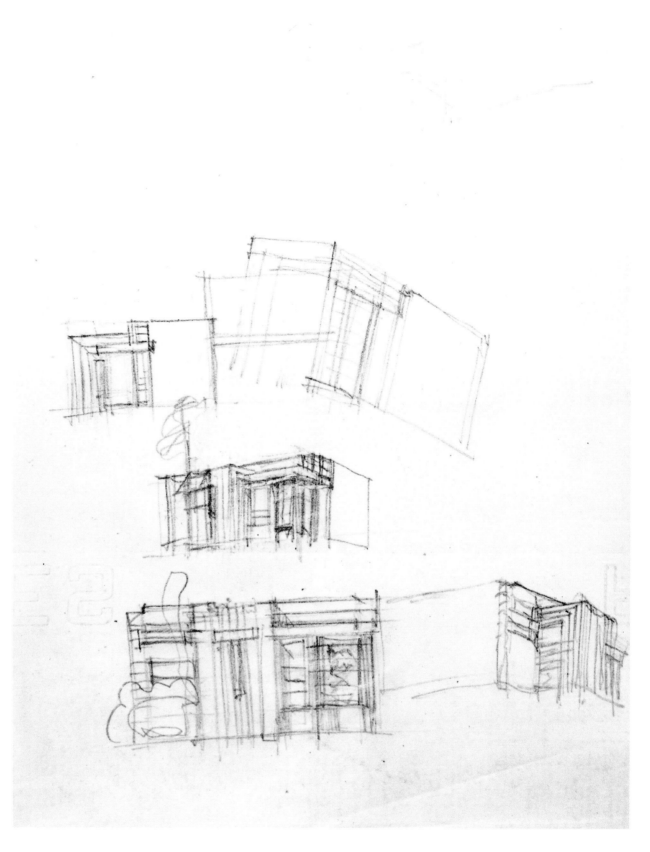

11 PUEBLO RIBERA COURTS FOR W. LLEWELLYN LLOYD,
La Jolla, California, 1923-25.
Sketch for office addition to unit eleven, 1924

12 PUEBLO RIBERA COURTS FOR W. LLEWELLYN LLOYD, La Jolla, California, 1923-25

of the units flooded due to faulty grading of the sloping site, as well as the settling and cracking of the concrete floors and walls. Water also poured in through the sliding sash doors (which warped from the rains) and from the rooftop sleeping cribs, causing Lloyd to describe the units as "practically uninhabitable."[40] Lloyd struggled as best he could, with roofers patching the composition roof and following Schindler's advice to caulk the holes in the concrete with grout.

Despite the problems, Schindler's unusual design for the Pueblo Ribera cottages attracted the attention of visitors to La Jolla. Lloyd was anxious to capitalize on this by affixing a sign, "El Pueblo Ribera—Visitors Welcome," directing visitors to the first unit in the complex where he and his wife lived. As Lloyd noted, however, one problem with Schindler's asymmetrical grouping was locating the main office: "People wander around and around trying to find someone to show them around or to find something definite regarding them. As it is now, there is no head to the group, so I must in some way direct visitors to our house where they will get attention."[41] By August 1924, all of the units were rented and Lloyd wrote that, "the houses are making a great hit with everybody. Everyone likes them, most of the tenants are so enthusiastic that they become real boosters when they leave."[42] To help advertise the cottages and attract visitors, Lloyd created two brochures for the "El Pueblo Ribera" complex. He asked Schindler to send him a pen-and-ink sketch of one of the cottages to be reproduced on the first leaflet. Schindler's drawing (*fig. 12*) is not only an outstanding example of his rendering technique, but also visually communicates the flexible indoor/outdoor lifestyle he wished to promote through his design. Though unable to use Schindler's drawing, Lloyd did include a drawing of the façade of one of the units similar to Schindler's sketch.[43]

The brochures are important archival documents that show how Lloyd both capitalized on Schindler's design objectives for Pueblo Ribera and modified them to attract the more conventional well-heeled visitors to La Jolla. In the first pamphlet (*fig. 13*), Lloyd described the twelve "artistic" concrete bungalows as having unusual privacy because of their overall layout—each with its own patio and a pergola roof garden with an outdoor fireplace and rustic

EL PUEBLO RIBERA
The Bungalow Apartments of Distinction

A GROUP of 12 new concrete bungalows situated on the finest beach in La Jolla.

¶ Best place for bathing, most even climate in the world.

¶ Showers for use of bathers.

¶ Each bungalow has a splendid view of the ocean.

¶ Each having unusual privacy.

¶ Each having a patio.

¶ Each having a pergola roof-garden, an out-door fireplace and rustic seat in each pergola.

¶ Garage for each bungalow.

¶ Interiors comfortable, cozy and completely furnished, with fireplace in each living room.

¶ Entire bungalow heated by gas if desired.

¶ Furniture hand-made and especially designed for these bungalows.

¶ Kitchen has many built-in features: ice box in the cooler, incinerator for burning trash and garbage, ironing board cunningly hidden under the breakfast-nook table.

¶ Each bungalow an all the year around home.

¶ Visitors always welcome, we consider it a privilege to show these artistic bungalows.—Or write for further information and rates.

¶ If possible, tourists wishing to stay only a short time will be accommodated at the following rates:

For 1 or 2 persons $6.00 per day.

3 persons $1.00 per day extra

For 1 or 2 persons per week $25.00 (Except during July, August and September.)

3 persons per week $7.00 extra.

These rates include hot and cold water, gas and electricity.

Garage $2.00 ℗ week, $5.00 ℗ month.

¶ The Windansea Hotel, across the street, has the distinction of serving the finest meals in La Jolla. Tenants wishing a vacation from the cares of cooking or desiring an occasional meal will find excellent accommodations there. It is worth a trip of many miles to have one of Mrs. Snell's meals in the artistic dining room of the Windansea Hotel.

13 Brochure text for Pueblo Ribera Courts, c. 1924

seat. Grounded in language reminiscent of Arts-and-Crafts bungalows popular during the first two decades of the century (deliberately used by Lloyd to appeal to the burgeoning middle-class visitors to California, who were satirized by Sinclair Lewis in *Main Street* and *Babbitt*), the description characterized the Interiors as comfortable, "cozy," and completely furnished with handmade pieces specially designed for the units. Modern amenities were stressed: each unit had its own private garage and each kitchen had built-in features including ice boxes, incinerators, and an "ironing board cunningly hidden under the breakfast-nook table."[44]

The second leaflet included a series of contemporary photographs *(fig. 14)* showing the complex, an aerial view of its location within La Jolla, and the lifestyle its design and proximity to the ocean provided. Guests are shown lounging in one of its interiors, dressed in bathing suits on their way to the beach, playing sports, sunbathing, and resting on one of the rooftop terraces. Physical and spiritual improvement were stressed in describing the complex's unique cottages with their "solid stone walls opening to sunshine and secluded patios ... each with genuine privacy and quiet, impossible in hotels, bungalow courts, etc."[45] Despite the two brochures, which sought to mitigate the unconventional nature of Schindler's design by stressing its "artistic" as well as physical and spiritual health-giving properties, Lloyd was unable to attract the necessary steady stream of guests. By April 1925 he wrote Schindler with some irony, "I am making one more desperate attempt to get the thing on its feet this summer and if I fail all my money and all I could borrow will be used up and I must stop. Everybody praises the places to the skies, but only a few have the courage, apparently, to live in them."[46]

SCHINDLER SHELTERS, 1933-39

During the twenties and thirties, Schindler constructed a series of impressive residences in the Los Angeles area, most notably the John Cooper Packard Residence (1924), the James Eads How Residence (1925–26), a beach house for Dr. Philip Lovell (1922-26), the Manola (Manolita) Court Apartments for Herman Sachs (1926-40), a summer house for Charles H. Wolfe (1928-31), as well as residences for Robert F. Elliot (1930; 1939) and Hans N. Von Koerber (1931-32). Between 1926 and 1931, Schindler's collaboration with fellow Viennese-trained architect Richard J. Neutra and the Romanian-born urban planner Carol Aronovici, under the name AGIC (Architectural Group for Industry and Commerce), had given

him firsthand knowledge of the new possibilities for modern design then developing in Europe. David Gebhard has characterized Schindler's work of the 1930s as having a "cleaned-up machine-like quality" with an increased use of "hard, non-tactile materials" and a rejection of "'warm' materials, especially wood" that owed much to Neutra's influence.[47] Competition with Neutra, whose work was included—while Schindler's was excluded—by Philip Johnson and Henry-Russell Hitchcock in their 1932 "International Exposition of Modern Architecture" at The Museum of Modern Art served, no doubt, as a further impetus to Schindler's creative efforts.[48]

In 1933, Schindler began work on his "Schindler Shelters," a series of prototypical houses of three, four, and four-and-a-half room units *(fig. 15)*, employing a special form of hollow concrete-shell construction patented by Glendale structural engineer Neal Garrett.[49] Schindler's interest in the problem of prefabricated, low-cost workers' housing went back to his early years in Chicago.[50] While working

14 Brochure for Pueblo Ribera Courts, c. 1927

15 SCHINDLER SHELTERS (project), Los Angeles, 1933-39.
Drawing for a four-room unit on embossed paper plate
used for printing

THE
MONOLITH
HOME

R M Schindler

FIRST SKETCH
OAK PARK 1919

16 MONOLITH HOME (project for Frank Lloyd Wright),
location unknown, 1919

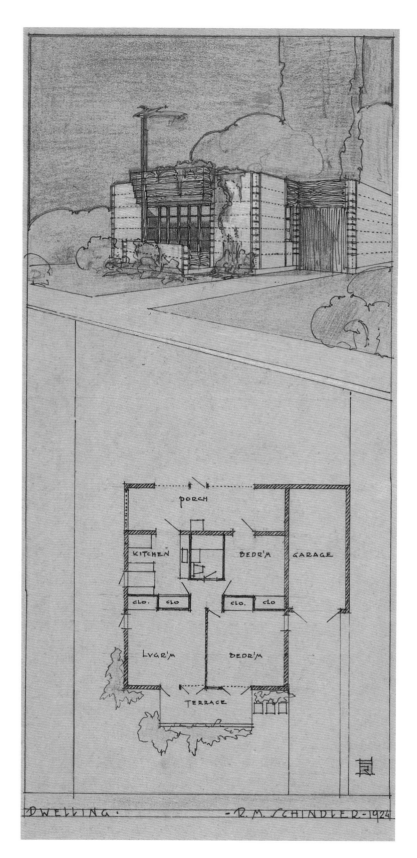

17 GOULD & BANDINI WORKMEN'S COLONY (project),
Los Angeles, 1924

for Frank Lloyd Wright, he had produced designs for workmen's housing, including the Monolith Home (project) (1919) *(fig. 16)*. This was followed in 1924 by two unexecuted designs of workers' housing for Gould & Bandini in Los Angeles *(fig. 17)* and Job Harriman in San Gabriel, California *(fig. 1)*.[51] Between 1929 and 1938 Schindler also designed two prefabricated cabins for William Lingenbrink of the American Holding Corporation at its Park Moderne development in Calabasas *(fig. 18)*. Schindler's first cabin at the Park Moderne was similar in form to the Pueblo Ribera units, but differed from them through his use of a standardized four-foot module as the organizing principle for its design. This module governed the cabin's horizontal plan as well as its vertical space, but Schindler eschewed slavish adherence to the module system, later arguing: "It is not necessary that the designer be completely enslaved by the grid. I have found that occasionally a space-form may be improved by deviating slightly from the unit. Such sparing deviation does not invalidate the system as a whole but merely reveals the limits inherent in all mechanical schemes."[52]

Schindler's work on the Schindler Shelters was directly motivated by the Federal government's efforts to improve the nation's housing crisis for low-income and unemployed workers under Franklin D. Roosevelt's New Deal. Schindler became interested in the newly created Subsistence Homestead program, a part of the National Recovery Administration. A favorite program of Eleanor Roosevelt's, it was funded by a special appropriation of $25 million, and was administered by the Department of the Interior. An undated *Los Angeles Times* newspaper clipping, which Schindler saved from the early days of Roosevelt's presidency, described the type of settlements being promoted: "A subsistence homestead, broadly described, is a parcel of ground on which a man may produce part, at least, of what he requires for his table while engaged in work outside."[53] During a visit to Los Angeles, the Division's director, W. A. Hartman, singled out Southern California's small home-farm movement as a model for future subsistence homesteads: "The small farm home of this section, on which the worker lives and produces much of what the his family eats, while employed in industry or in business or professional lines elsewhere, serves as a real guide to all interested in the program."[54] Schindler organized his Schindler Shelters around these goals.

Spurred by the prospect of government funding, Schindler sought to make his structures cost effective by standardizing the units around the four-foot module, while allowing for adaptation to individual

requirements in size, plan, and elevation to avoid what he termed a "rabbit hutch" effect.[55] Schindler developed his units in a pinwheel fashion around a central hall space ventilated and lit by clerestory lighting. The only fixed design elements in the Schindler Shelter were the kitchen, bathroom, and laundry, which were contiguous and grouped around a central core utility wall containing plumbing—allowing it to become a factory-made unit *(fig. 19)*. In addition, Schindler also included prefabricated closets that served as flexible wall dividers to break up the spaces. The living room itself could be expanded to any size without affecting the overall plan because it was joined to the body of the house on only two sides. Similarly, the central hall could be enlarged in various directions to allow for additional bedrooms. The houses would employ specially designed sliding horizontal "track-sash" windows made from stamped sheetmetal (at half the cost of the usual steel sash windows) to admit light and sunshine freely, making the rooms as much a part of the outdoors as possible. As a further health feature, Schindler planned enclosed sunbathing decks over the garages. All the rooms were planned to have at least two exposures, while the living room

PARK MODERNE

HOLLYWOODS' MOST UNIQUE SUBURBAN SUBDIVISION

Ideal climatic conditions. Raise your own garden products and live independently away from congestion. No lot under 5000 square feet in size. Restrictions are reasonable and protective.

BIG LOTS $100 TO $350

Garden soil, water, electricity, roads, some trees. Improvements in and paid for. Charming location in foothills with views. Suitable for small estates, week end or suburban residence. 21 miles or ½ hour drive to center of Hollywood over broad highway with 30 ft. of cement paving.

How To Go

From Hollywood over Cahuenga Pass follow the Ventura Highway to a mile beyond Girard (where the Mulholland Drive meets the Ventura Highway), go south one mile to PARK MODERNE.

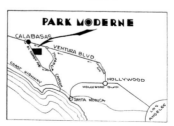

PARK MODERNE

PARK MODERNE is owned by the American Holding Corporation.

Wm. Lingenbrink, General Manager

C. Henry Taylor, Tract Manager

OFFICE

Room 500, Hollywood Security Building, Hollywood Blvd. at Cahuenga Blvd.

Phone HE 0244

18 Brochure for Park Moderne Model Cabins, Calabasas, California, 1929–38. Schindler-designed unit at top left

SCHINDLER-SHELTER TYPE 3-RMS. © R.M SCHINDLER · ARCHITECT

SCHINDLER-SHELTER A-TYPE 4-RMS. © R.M SCHINDLER · ARCHITECT

SCHINDLER-SHELTER B-TYPE 4 RMS © R.M SCHINDLER · ARCHITECT

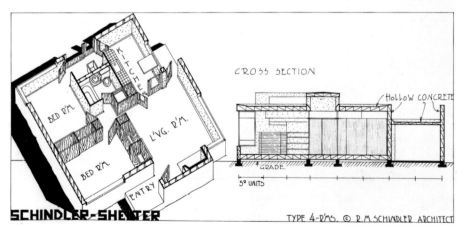

SCHINDLER-SHELTER

TYPE 4-RMS. © R.M SCHINDLER ARCHITECT

19 SCHINDLER SHELTERS (project), Los Angeles, 1933-39

had four. Special design features included the central location of the kitchen to facilitate the monitoring of small children at play in their rooms and the living room. The kitchen itself could open out into the living room and its dining table could be wheeled into that main space, so the family would not be forced to "partake their evening meal, which has social importance, among greasy dishes and wet linens."[56] Each house, set in its own garden with room for a vegetable patch, also had an attached garage that was slightly wider than normal to provide space for a work bench.

While their flexible, pinwheel-like plans were a great asset, it was the Shelter's method of fabrication that Schindler felt would be their most effective selling point as low-cost housing units. In his program for the units, Schindler argued that the monolithic buildings composed of one material easily erected by unskilled workers (making use of Neal Garrett's patented hollow concrete-slab system of construction) would reduce construction costs as well as the physical weight of the supporting walls and ceilings.[57] The Garrett method (*fig. 20*) involved building the walls, floors, and roof with continuous, prefabricated standard-sized blocks consisting of rigid, stamped, sheetmetal plates sixteen inches wide by six feet in height.[58] The two panels were then braced by a weblike system of metal "fingers" forming a truss, sixteen inches in depth. A layer of fine wire mesh supported by thin metal tubing surrounded the panels, which could be dimensioned to any length. These were then sprayed with Portland cement and allowed to dry, hardening into a solid mass. Floors were constructed first, laid directly on grade with walls set into them at the ends. Roofs were similarly constructed and then hoisted into position. Interior partitions of more light-weight materials were added once the shell had hardened. Schindler

advertised the structures as fire-, water-, and vermin-proof, with its seamless double walls, ceilings, and floors providing insulation in winter and summer.

Schindler believed that the Garrett system solved the problem of making concrete construction a viable system for low-cost housing as it avoided expensive form work and the need for skilled labor. Garrett's method of construction took concrete out of the class of bulky mass materials through the use of thin slabs. Schindler felt that it was perfectly adapted to the problems of modern architecture and asserted that the Garrett system established concrete as a: *thoroughbred material for the "Space Architect." It eliminates the conventional sculptural treatment of a building material mass and allows the Architect to concentrate on his new medium, Space. It further humanizes concrete by providing a construction which has the resiliency of the wood frame construction, eliminating the present popular prejudice against concrete in dwelling construction.*[59]

Schindler passionately believed in the potential of his Schindler Shelter design to help relieve the housing crisis of the early 1930s. He had the design patented under the name "Schindler Shelter," and his drawings were exhibited in December 1933 as part of the Architects Exhibit, Inc., held at the Los Angeles department store Barker Brothers. In its first illustrated coverage of Schindler's work, the *Los Angeles Times* featured the Schindler Shelter design in their Home Builder's Department in December 1933.[60] Schindler sent the plans to a number of Federal agencies, including the Interior Department's Subsistence Homesteads Division in Washington, D.C. In their response, the division found fault with Schindler's design, not in terms of cost, but because of its small kitchens. They noted: "We

The GARRETT Plastered HOUSE– A FRAMELESS, Reinforced UNIT

By LEWIS GOSS

EARTHQUAKE resistant, fireproof and vermin proof, a new type of patented double-wall concrete construction for residences and commercial structures is claimed to effect a great saving in both material and labor costs.

Weighing considerably less than buildings of conventional design, this unit construction is achieved by building the walls, floors and roof of continuous units, consisting of two thin layers of reinforced Portland cement mortar, rigidly joined together by steel truss-like construction. The reinforcing in the floors is continued into the walls, and into the roof; thus making no structural distinction between the various parts.

A cross-section of a floor, wall or roof will show the following construction: Two layers of hardened concrete approximately one-inch thick in which are embedded

reinforcing consisting of 18 gauge, 1-inch mesh, wire netting.

The slabs are rigidly connected and braced by a series of steel truss-like systems of the Pratt type, spaced 16 inches apart. These systems of webbing are formed by vertical and diagonal, half-tubular, steel members which

have their end portions thoroughly embedded in the concrete and connected to the wire mesh.

The inventor, Neal Garrett, registered civil engineer of Glendale, Calif., has developed a system of light, portable forms which are particularly adaptable to this type of construction. The forms consist of rigid, stamped, sheet-metal panels, 16 inches wide, 6 feet long, and weighing 12 pounds each. Garrett has also developed a pipe scaffolding with easily adjustable connections which make possible rapid setting of the forms. *(Turn page.)*

163 believe it very important that the kitchen in subsistence homesteads should be the largest room in the house, as this becomes the workshop for the entire family."[61] The real problem lay in the cost of construction and the architectural vocabulary Schindler proposed for his Schindler Shelters. In his letter to the Subsistence Homesteads Division, Schindler argued that the true value of his designs lay in their use of concrete and metal, both fireproof and durable materials. He noted:

scarcity of cash will make extensive [future] repairs impossible. The wooden house of the past is unfit through its excessive depreciation—a few years and the neighborhood becomes a slum. The Schindler Shelter reduces maintenance to a minimum. Metal and concrete are used for its execution. These materials allow a treatment which will reduce the contrast between housekeeping in the town and country.[62]

The aim of the Subsistence Homesteads Division was to provide low-cost housing for workers in rural areas, while the reality of the Schindler Shelters was that their construction costs were higher than those of conventional, wood-framed structures. Wedded to this was the Federal Government's uneasiness with using the architectural vocabulary of the modern movement in its public housing projects. Indeed, the house designs for the most famous of Subsistence Homestead communities, such as the development in Reedsville, West Virginia (known as Arthursdale), employed conventional construction techniques and traditional architectural details based on the colonial revival *(fig. 21)*. The Schindler Shelters were too modern for bureaucratic taste, more at home on the pages of *Popular Mechanics* than in actual built form.[63] Schindler himself grudgingly conceded this as early as 1935 when he began reworking the Schindler Shelter scheme using a more conventional wood-frame construction, which he would rename his Panel-Post Method in the late 1930s.

ELLEN JANSON RESIDENCE, 1948–49

Schindler's postwar residential designs have always been regarded as his most problematic, tainted by contemporary dismissal as too removed from post-1945 mainstream modernism and therefore not "serious" design—exemplified by his exclusion from John Entenza's Case Study House program—and for us by their sense of incompleteness, due to Schindler's unexpected death from cancer in August 1953.[64] Esther McCoy and David Gebhard both have noted the improvisational nature of Schindler's late designs, which often changed as the buildings themselves were being constructed. Gebhard characterized Schindler's late drawings as "more and more cursory, even sloppy; they were just enough to meet the requirements of the building departments;" while McCoy observed: "It was the daylight [meaning the construction site, itself] rather than the drafting light that illuminated the 'image.'"[65] Writing in the late 1960s, Gebhard, despite his championing of Schindler's ambiguity in relation to mainstream postwar American modernism, confessed to being mystified by Schindler's late houses, suggesting that they went too far, their "atmosphere of dissonance and ambiguity, instead of being one of several means to an end, now became for him the end in itself."[66] Twenty years later, he had modified his thinking somewhat to appreciate Schindler's ability through these last structures to "manoeuvre all of this complex and at times contradictory vocabulary into products which are in fact calm and self-assured."[67] Esther McCoy believed that Schindler's late work reflected his renewed struggle with space: "his deepening insights

Right: a re-fabricated house, one of 49 just erected in the subsistence homestead green near Reedsville, West Va. Architect Eric Gugler added a sun porch and some lattice work to the factory-built house, painting it white with green roof and shutters. Below: Mrs. Roosevelt inspects.

Gibson

20 Advertisement in *Progressive Contractor*, July 1933

21 From an article in *The Architectural Forum*, 4 May 1934

into human nuances were reflected in nuances of form ... [Schindler's late] houses were a kind of intimate portraiture in structure."[68] Of all of Schindler's late residences, none reflected these personal nuances more closely than the house he constructed for Ellen Janson between 1948 and 1949 *(fig. 22)*.

Ellen Margaret Janson *(fig. 23)*, a poet and writer of children's books, was the last—and perhaps, the most serious—in a series of romantic friendships in Schindler's life following his separation and subsequent divorce from Pauline Gibling Schindler.[69] Janson and Schindler met sometime during the late 1930s, most likely through Pauline at one of the many social/cultural events she organized at the Kings Road House. In 1939, Janson compiled the first major biographical sketch of Schindler, outlining his architectural philosophy and describing his work. In 1948, Janson asked Schindler to build a house in the Hollywood Hills on a steep slope in a ravine facing the San Fernando Valley. Their joint nickname for the new house was "Skyhooks," and its design and construction was of vital and personal interest to Schindler. Ellen Janson, recalling the playful

dialogue between herself and Schindler in arriving at a design for the house, explained: "I had always wanted to live in the sky. Then I came to know a space architect. The architect asked me, 'how would you like a house made of cobwebs?' Yes, I should love it, for they wouldn't shut away the sky at all. But how would you hang up the cobwebs? 'On sky-hooks,' he said."[70] Schindler's initial sketches in 1948 *(fig. 24)* called for a one-story, platform-like structure containing a central core with bathroom and kitchen separating a living room and bedroom, anchored to the hillside by a base at its center. A lower story with its own separate entrance was added the following year, incorporating a study with a bathroom and kitchen. Schindler most likely added this story at Janson's urging to create a self-contained unit for his own personal use. By the last year of his illness, Janson was urging Schindler to live full-time at "Skyhooks," where she promised to take care of him without stifling his creativity: "*Be* Robinson Crusoe on your wild solitary island. Let me be-not your man Friday!—but an enchantress who walks on your sands so lightly ... that you would not know she was there except for the soft wing-brush on your cheek in the wind."[71]

22 ELLEN JANSON RESIDENCE, Los Angeles, 1948-49

23 Ellen Janson at construction site, c. 1949

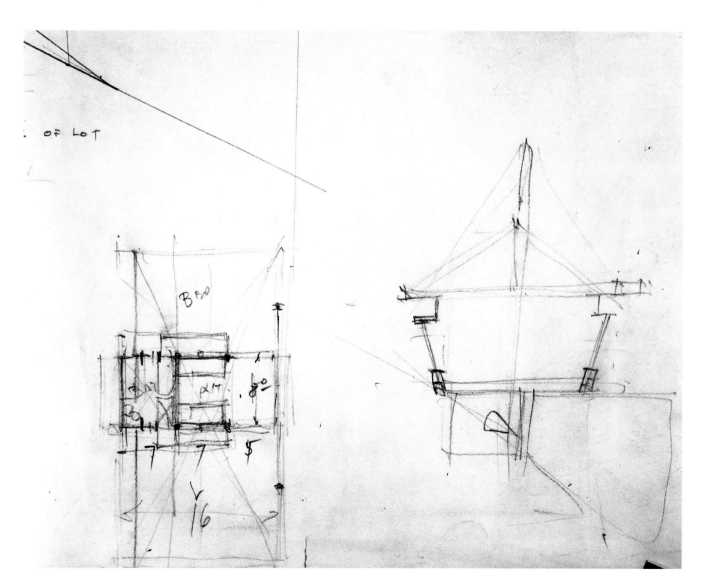

OF LOT

24 ELLEN JANSON RESIDENCE, Los Angeles,
1948-49. Initial sketches of floor plans (left) and
section plan (right)

The design of the Janson Residence embodies Schindler's principles of space architecture—using wood construction—that he had outlined in his 1944 article "Reference Frames in Space." In the article Schindler reasserted his use of the four-foot module as the organizing principle for his sense of scale and rhythm, but argued that true space forms could only be created by their designer mentally: [T]he only way to really perceive a "space-form" is by being inside of it and therefore no perspective or model, even though it were sectional or transparent, could help much in designing space. In order to succeed with this difficult feat the architect ... must establish a unit system which he can easily carry in his mind and which will give him the size values of his forms directly without having to resort to mathematical computations.[72]

Schindler argued that such a system had innumerable advantages over conventional methods of dimensioned design, the foremost being that "room walls used to create space forms do not rise straight and boxlike from floor to ceiling, but may project or recess in between."[73] Schindler's design for the Ellen Janson Residence shows his mastery of this formula, using a central, enclosed rectangular core as the base rooted in the earth for a platform of intersecting planes whose skin was clothed on the outside by a series of wooden decks and vinelike, trellised structures. His initial sketches show the organizing design principles behind the plan—a series of intersecting rectangles forming a cross, its center the base of the structure anchored to the hillside. The structure's wood-framing support system was completed by August 1949. Surviving photographs documenting the process of erection (figs. 25, 26, 27) are among the best and most extensive in the Schindler archives, and show the complicated system of bracing Schindler devised for this platform house.

While the Janson Residence's site, on the ridge of a steep slope, was chosen because of its reasonable cost, it also allowed Schindler to return to one of his earliest principles in the development of a uniquely Southern Californian residence—the sympathetically sited hillside house. Schindler had first outlined his hopes for such structures in an October 1922 essay, titled "Who Will Save Hollywood?". Describing the conventional builder's methods of dealing with these hillside sites, Schindler noted: A large slice is cut off the doomed ridge ... a steep breakneck bluff is thrown up by excavator and upon this ungainly platform, the house is set ... perching on an artificial platter between earth and sky ... staring wide-eyed over the edge of the rim into nothing ... innocently unaware of the abyss in front, and of the threatening triangular breaker of clay behind it.[74]

For Schindler, these hillside sites, if respected, would become the setting for a truly Californian house. He described their proper siting in the following terms: "the building must never be placed straddling the ridge, but should hug the flank of it, becoming part of its surroundings, and leaving the main lines of the mountain untouched."[75] Schindler's two-story Janson Residence adheres closely to these early principles. The stacked quality of its two floors set on an unexcavated bottom-story base recalls his designs for earlier hillside houses, particularly the Guy C. Wilson Residence (1935-38) in Silver Lake, but it is the exterior deck (fig. 28) that Schindler designed for the top story which moves the Janson design in a new direction. By visually breaking down the solidity of the structure behind, the deck creates a visual tension for the viewer, and gives the Janson Residence a treehouse-like quality, noted by Gebhard, that is Schindler's ultimate gesture towards simultaneously respecting and imposing his own dynamic vision of the California hillside house.

Besides its site, the design of the Janson Residence also reflected Schindler's reawakened fascination with the concept of structural

25 ELLEN JANSON RESIDENCE, Los Angeles, 1948-49. Photograph by Charles R. Sullivan

26 ELLEN JANSON RESIDENCE, Los Angeles, 1948-49.
Detail of deck under construction.
Photograph by Charles R. Sullivan

27 ELLEN JANSON RESIDENCE, Los Angeles, 1948-49.
Photograph by Charles R. Sullivan

28 ELLEN JANSON RESIDENCE, Los Angeles, 1948-49.
Photograph by Charles R. Sullivan

translucence and the new possibility, based on the use of modern corrugated colored plastics like alsynite, to transform the appearance of interior and exterior space. Schindler had first experimented with this concept in his unbuilt Translucent House project for Aline Barnsdall of 1927-28. His U-shaped structure included an upper-roof zone composed of translucent glass folded over at the top to meet the flat, concrete roofs, the effect from inside being of a horizontal roof area floating over a glass zone. In the Janson Residence, Schindler's intention was to explore the possibilities of translucence by using colored alsynite in continuous areas without bars to serve as the main walls of the structure.[76] In one of his last essays, "Visual Technique," Schindler defined "translucency" as the ability of the modern architect to:

transfuse the very space he is shaping with color, forcing all objects in it to become active parts of his palate, while reflecting individually the rays of his color medium. A "translighted" room as a group not only changes by contrast the colors of adjoining rooms, but also of the out-of-doors. It becomes the power center of a color symphony as far as the eye can reach.[77]

The Janson Residence, with its combination of colored alsynite that Schindler originally intended to use to visually anchor its four cor-

ners and in the clerestory windows, was meant by Schindler to be appreciated as a color symphony both from the inside and outside. From inside, these areas lit the interior spaces with a diffused, colored light that still allowed for spectacular views of the then sparsely populated canyon—making the relatively small living room and bedrooms large by their unrestricted views. From outside, the combination of the clear glass and blue alsynite helped to enhance Schindler's complicated design of intersecting planes *(fig. 29)*. But it was at night that the colored alsynite was meant by Schindler to be most dramatic; lit from the outside, the panels were meant to "release color into the air."[78] Here, then, was Schindler at the end of his career playing with color to "dramatize his space-forms, change their apparent proportions, heighten their three-dimensional qualities, soften their outline, and give color to the void."[79]

IN EARLY 1949, SCHINDLER WAS SENT A QUESTIONNAIRE by the University of Southern California's School of Architecture to provide information for a guidebook the school was planning to publish on

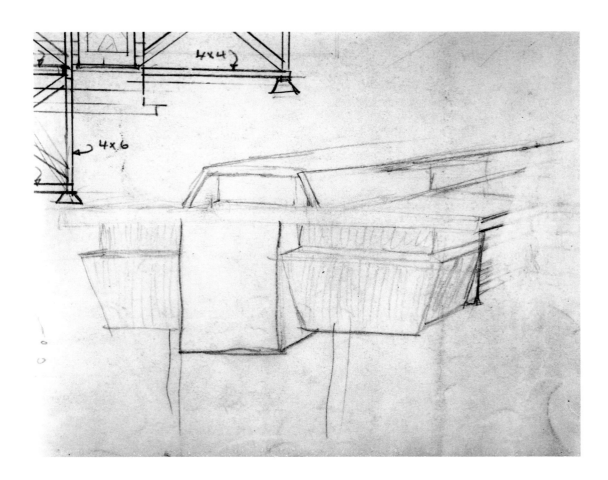

29 ELLEN JANSON RESIDENCE, Los Angeles, 1948-49.
Perspective sketch showing proposed corner treatment

169 contemporary architecture in Southern California. The publication, meant to identify and locate key buildings in Southern California's contribution to the development of the modern movement, was a means of redressing the lack of any published architectural guidebooks to the region, and took as its model John McAndrew's *Guide to Modern Architecture, Northeast States*, published by The Museum of Modern Art in 1940. Schindler was excited by the USC project and planned to use his questionnaire as a means of organizing a larger publication on his own career and architectural philosophy. The pamphlet Schindler compiled included typed copies of his published writings, Ellen Janson's biographical portrait, and a program for modern architecture. The pages were enclosed within a specially designed, folded cover sheet with Schindler's distinctive signature/logo *(fig. 30)*. Schindler sent copies to architecture schools throughout the United States, as well as to a wide range of key players within the contemporary American architectural establishment, including Douglas Haskell, editor of *Architectural Record*; Talbot Hamlin at Columbia University; Peter Blake, then a curator in the Department of Architecture and Design at The Museum of Modern Art; and Bruce Goff at the University of Oklahoma. Blake responded positively to Schindler's pamphlet, noting: "in view of the many controversies in contemporary architecture, I think it is always useful and exciting to find one direction such as yours, so clearly and articulately confirmed."[80]

The fact remains, however, that in any assessment of Schindler's work, we are hindered by his early death in 1953. Esther McCoy, trying to make sense of his career, divided it into segments: the concrete period; the cubistic period; and the period of the roof. A new emerging period, embodied for her in the Samuel Skolnik Residence (1950-52), she termed the "screen wall period." For McCoy, these last houses—including the Kallis, Lechner, and Tischler Houses—represent Schindler's final break with his European past, and a period whose potential and ultimate direction we are left to guess at, as she noted in her final appreciation of him in 1988: "If he had been allowed to continue work for several years, I am sure he would have sifted through the houses of the 1950s to select the very few he considered germinal. He was a good self-critic."[81] Trying to sum up Schindler's significance in 1954, Talbot Hamlin characterized him as the least understood and appreciated of all the American pioneers of modern architecture. For future generations, Hamlin felt that Schindler's "imaginative cubism, his daring creation of dynamic architectural forms, and his many writings will, I believe, be more and more seen as the truly important contributions to twentieth-century architecture that they are."[82] Fortunately, for researchers in the twenty-first century, the Schindler archive serves as a ready instrument in our continuing search to understand the full meaning of what Rudolph M. Schindler termed the true development of space architecture—one that he passionately believed would make Southern California the cradle of a new architectural expression.

30 Pamphlet cover sheet with Schindler logo, c. 1949

My thanks to the staff of the University Art Museum, University of California, Santa Barbara (hereafter "UCSB")— including Marla Berns, Elizabeth Brown, Paul Prince, Sandra Rushing, Rollin Fortier, and Peggy Dahl—who have helped make my 1997 transition to Santa Barbara and work as Curator of the Architecture and Design Collection immensely rewarding and enjoyable. I would also like to thank UCSB graduate students Cristina Carbone, Eileen Everett, Eric J. Lutz, Elizabeth Mitchell, Pamela Post, and staff member Anne Renaud, who have processed, re-housed, and cata- logued the Schindler archives over the past three years. Their work helps ensure that this rich archival collection survives into the twenty-first century with greater accessibility to those interested in Schindler's creative legacy. In addition, I would also like to thank Michael Darling of The Museum of Contemporary Art, Los Angeles, and Judith Throm of the Archives of American Art, Smithsonian Institution, Washington, D.C., for their research assistance.

1 On David Gebhard's catalogue for the 1967 Schindler exhibition at UCSB, *see* Sherban Cantacuzino's somewhat waspish review, "Schindler Shortcomings," *Architectural Review* 143 (March 1968): 177. Schindler's first name was originally spelled Rudolf, but was Anglicized by others to Rudolph after his arrival in Chicago in 1914. Schindler's family and close Austrian friends called him "Rudi," while he asked his new American friends to call him "Michael" (because it was less German sounding). Schindler used "R. M. Schindler" as his professional name and a number of his appren- tices, including Esther McCoy, affectionately called him "RM" or "RMS."

2 The gift of the Schindler archives to UCSB was publicly announced in March 1968. *See* "R. M. Schindler Drawings, Photos Given UCSB Gallery," *Santa Barbara News-Press*, 17 March 1968, C-3. In a May 1967 memorandum to Chancellor Vernon Cheadle, Professor Alfred Moir, dean of the art department at UCSB, noted: "the pro- posed gift is of … inestimable historic value. Together with other collections of architectural material already belonging or promised to our campus, it will provide the nucleus of an important research archive in American architecture, which would attract international attention." Alfred Moir to Vernon I. Cheadle, 31 May 1967, Donor File, Rudolph M. Schindler Collection, Architecture and Design Collection, University Art Museum, UCSB (hereafter "RMS at ADC/UCSB").

3 In an interview conducted for the ADC oral history program, Mark Schindler recounted the subsequent history of the Schindler archives. It was stored in a number of garages and even a former chicken coop, during which some materials were damaged. Interview with Mark Schindler, UCSB, September 1998.

4 These included "Four Santa Barbara Houses, 1904-1917: Charles and Henry Greene, Bernard Maybeck, Francis Underhill, and Frank Lloyd Wright," held in 1963; and "George Washington Smith, 1876- 1930: The Spanish Colonial Revival in Southern California," held in 1964. *See* David Gebhard, "The UCSB Art Gallery," *Artforum* 2, no. 12 (Summer 1964): 31.

5 David Gebhard to Esther McCoy, 28 May 1963, General Correspondence (1962-1963), Esther McCoy Collection, Archives of American Art, Smithsonian Institution, Washington, D.C. (here- after "EMC at AAASI"). The Schindler Memorial Exhibit was organ- ized by McCoy and held at the Felix Landau Gallery in Los Angeles from 14 May to 5 June 1954. At the exhibition's opening, Gregory Ain, who had worked briefly for Schindler in the 1930s, gave a lec- ture on Schindler's importance in the development of a Southern California architecture. *See* "Tribute Paid Pioneer, R. M. Schindler Memorial Show Now on View," *Los Angeles Times*, 23 May 1954, IV- 7. Interestingly, Gebhard first contacted McCoy about Schindler in May 1954 when he wrote her from the Fine Arts Gallery at the University of New Mexico in Albuquerque, asking to take the Memorial exhibition. *See* Gebhard to McCoy, 28 May 1954, in "McCoy, Esther" correspondence file, David Gebhard Collection, Architecture and Design Collection, University Art Museum, UCSB (hereafter "DGC at ADC/UCSB").

6 Gebhard used Schindler materials gathered for Esther McCoy's 1956 exhibition, "Roots of California Contemporary Architecture." *See* exhibition list for "Exhibit of R. M. Schindler, Architect, held in the Front Gallery, Fine Arts Building, 1-20 May [1964]," Schindler Research Files, DGC at ADC/UCSB.

7 David Gebhard, "R. M. Schindler in New Mexico—1915," *New Mexico Architecture* 7 (January-February 1965): 15-21.

8 David Gebhard and Robert Winter, "Architecture in Southern California," in *A Guide to Architecture in Southern California* (Los Angeles: Los Angeles County Museum of Art, 1965), 14.

9 David Gebhard to Hans Hollein (Vienna), 26 May 1965, Schindler Research Files, DGC at ADC/UCSB. Gebhard and McCoy initially approached Philip Johnson about MOMA's interest in a Schindler retrospective. In late February 1965, Johnson replied, "I don't have much to do with the Museum of Modern Art these days, but I shall pass your letter on to Arthur Drexler, who is the director of the Department of Architecture there and I am sure he will be interested." Johnson to Gebhard, 26 February 1965, General Correspondence (1965), EMC at AAASI. Drexler responded to Gebhard in late May 1965 with hesitation: "We are still interested in an exhibition of the work of R. M. Schindler, but we have second thoughts … At this point, I am not certain that we want to give Schindler's work a full- scale presentation in our exhibition form—I certainly think there ought to be a comprehensive book, but I suspect that an exhibition here would best concentrate on a handful of buildings, probably the earliest ones." Drexler to Gebhard, 27 May 1965, Schindler Research Files, DGC at ADC/UCSB.

10 "The Architectural Projects of R. M. Schindler (1887–1953)," pre- sented at the University Art Gallery, UCSB, 30 March – 30 April 1967. *See* the exhibition announcement designed by David Gebhard, Exhibition Files, ADC/UCSB.

11 "The Architecture of R. M. Schindler (1887–1953)" was held in the Special Exhibitions Gallery of the Los Angeles County Museum of Art from 29 September through 19 November 1967. Schindler Research File, DGC at ADC/UCSB. For a review of the show, *See* Esther McCoy, "Renewed Interest in Popularity of Schindler's Architecture," *Los Angeles Times*, 22 October 1967, Calendar-46.

12 *See* Harriette von Breton, "First Exhibition of Noted Architect," *Santa Barbara News-Press*, 9 April 1967, C-10. For the list of USIA-sponsored exhibition venues, *see* the letter from Eugene D. Corkery to Sonja Olsen, 9 October 1969, Schindler Exhibition Files, ADC/UCSB.

171

13 Pauline Gibling Schindler to David Gebhard, December 1969, Schindler Research Files, DGC at ADC/UCSB.

14 The Getty Research Institute for the History of Art and Humanities in Los Angeles owns the correspondence between Schindler and Wright dating from his years under Wright's employ (1918-23). There is also a small amount of original Schindler archival material, mostly photographs, in the EMC at AAASI.

15 Eric J. Lutz, a doctoral candidate in the Department of the History of Art and Architecture, UCSB, has recently catalogued Schindler's photograph album, and is presently working on a dissertation that will critically assess Schindler's work as a photographer during the 1910s and 1920s.

16 In a 1929 lecture, "Famous Architects I Knew," Schindler summed up Wagner's philosophy as one of "classic form seen through the engineering eye." Loos's philosophy, Schindler argued, was formed in reaction to Wagner's and stressed the importance of America as a nation representing the future. In the same lecture, he described Frank Lloyd Wright as leaving the tyranny of the drafting board, "not for reality as [for] Loos, but for Space—3rd dimension." For Schindler, Wright's ultimate importance was in starting a new architectural development, "Spatial Architecture." *See* "Famous Architects I Knew," 18 January 1929, Manuscript Files, Lectures and Essays, RMS at ADC/UCSB.

17 *See* Otto Wagner, *Modern Architecture: A Guidebook for His Students to This Field of Art*, trans. Harry Francis Mallgrave (1896; reprint, Santa Monica, Calif.: The Getty Center for the History of Art and the Humanities, 1988), 86, 97.

18 *Ibid.*, 78.

19 *See* Schindler, "A Manifesto—1912," in David Gebhard, *Schindler* (1972; reprint, San Francisco: William Stout, 1997), 147-48. There is some discrepancy as to the actual dating of the manifesto, as Schindler's own handwritten manuscript is dated June 1913. The English translation used with the subsequent 1912 dating is part of a self-published collection of his work and writings that Schindler put together in the late 1940s.

20 David Gebhard, "Ambiguity in the Work of R. M. Schindler," *Lotus* 5 (1968): 106-121. Margaret Crawford also assesses Gebhard's concept of ambiguity in her essay "Forgetting and Remembering Schindler: The Social History of an Architectural Reputation," in the special issue, "R. M. Schindler: 10 Casas/10 Houses," *2G*, no. 7 (1998): 136-137. On Gebhard's appreciation of Charles Moore, *see* David Gebhard, "The Bay Tradition in Architecture," *Art in America* 52 , no. 3 (March 1964): 60-63; "Charles Moore: Architecture and the New Vernacular," *Artforum* 3, no. 8 (May 1965): 52-53; and "Pop Scene for Profs," *The Architectural Forum* 130, no. 2 (March 1969): 78-85. For an exploration of Moore's appreciation of ambiguity, *see* his "Plug It In, Ramses, and See If It Lights Up," *Perspecta* 11 (1967): 33-43.

21 Reyner Banham, "Rudolph Schindler: Pioneering Without Tears," *Architectural Design* 37 (December 1967): 578.

22 Charles Moore, "Schindler: Vulnerable and Powerful," *Progressive Architecture* 54 (January 1973): 136.

23 *Ibid.*

24 Esther McCoy was fond of comparing Schindler's final years to those of Irving J. Gill, noting Schindler's own fear of fading into architectural oblivion as Gill had done by the late 1920s. In her *Five California Architects*, she movingly wrote: "Several times during his last years Schindler spoke of Gill's interrupted career. Gill's decline in popularity was like a cold wind that had blown too close to Schindler's own door. He once said that what he feared most was to end his life 'puttering in architecture as Gill did.'" In McCoy, *Five California Architects* (1960; reprint, New York: Praeger Publishers, Inc., 1975), 192.

25 Writers' Program, Works Progress Administration, *Los Angeles: A Guide to the City and Its Environs* (New York: Hastings House, 1941), 108.

26 *See* "Rudolph M. Schindler, Noted Architect, Dies," *Los Angeles Times*, 15 August 1953, 1-12.

27 Arthur B. Gallion, "Introduction," in Douglas Honnold, *Southern California Architecture, 1769-1956* (New York: Reinhold Publishing Corporation, 1956), 21.

28 Llewellyn and Lucy Lloyd may have been introduced to the Schindlers by Karl Howenstein and his wife, Edith Gutterson. Howenstein had been connected with the Church School of Art in Chicago where Schindler gave a lecture series on architecture and design in 1916. His wife Edith had been a friend of Schindler's from his time in Chicago. Edith Gutterson first designed the distinctive open-necked tunic shirts that Schindler wore until his death. *See* "Gutterson, Edith" correspondence file, RMS at ADC/UCSB.

29 Gebhard, *Schindler*, 48.

30 *See* the account card for "Lloyd, W. Llewellyn, Route A, Box 223, Redlands, Cal. For Court-La Jolla," RMS at ADC/UCSB.

31 Schindler proposed that Clyde Chace serve as general contractor for the project in May 1923. *See* RMS to W. Llewellyn Lloyd, 23 May 1923, Project Files, "Pueblo Ribera Court," RMS at ADC/UCSB.

32 The letters between Lloyd and Schindler are among the largest single concentration of surviving project-related correspondence in the Schindler archives. Similar letters between client and architect exist for the Carlton Park Residence in Fallbrook, California (1925–26); the Philip Lovell Beach House in Newport Beach, California (1922-26); and the Hans N. Von Koerber Residence in Torrance, California (1931-32). With some exceptions, after the early 1930s most of Schindler's projects were within easy commuting distance from his Kings Road studio, so most of the communication concerning design and construction was conducted verbally.

33 Schindler had also initially suggested a larger main house in the complex for Lloyd's personal use. Lloyd to RMS, 5 April 1923, Project Files, "Pueblo Ribera Court," RMS at ADC/UCSB.

34 *See* "Houses for Outdoor Life: A Vacation Settlement on the Pueblo Ribera, La Jolla, California, R. M. Schindler, Architect," *Architectural Record* 68, no. 1 (July 1930): 17-21.

35 RMS to Lloyd, 9 April 1923, Project Files, "Pueblo Ribera Court," RMS at ADC/UCSB.

36 RMS to Lloyd, 14 May 1923, Project Files, "Pueblo Ribera Court," RMS at ADC/UCSB.

37 Lloyd, describing the stiff opposition he encountered and his basic sympathy for Schindler's ideas, wrote: "Everyone here tells me concrete houses cannot be made water-tight in the manner you have planned. I hope soon to be able to prove them in error." Lloyd to RMS, 13 June 1923, Project Files, "Pueblo Ribera Court," RMS at ADC/UCSB.

38 Lloyd to RMS, 8 June 1923, Project Files, "Pueblo Ribera Court," RMS at ADC/UCSB.

39 Lloyd to RMS, 25 January 1924, Project Files, "Pueblo Ribera Court," RMS at ADC/UCSB.

40 Lloyd to RMS, 30 March 1924, Project Files, "Pueblo Ribera Court," RMS at ADC/UCSB.

41 Lloyd to RMS, 26 April 1924, Project Files, "Pueblo Ribera Court," RMS at ADC/UCSB.

42 Lloyd to RMS, 8 August 1924, Project Files, "Pueblo Ribera Court," RMS at ADC/UCSB.

43 Lloyd to RMS, 9 March and 21 March 1924, Project Files, "Pueblo Ribera Court," RMS at ADC/UCSB.

44 "El Pueblo Ribera, La Jolla, California," undated brochure, Project Files, "Pueblo Ribera Court," RMS at ADC/UCSB.

45 "La Jolla, California, El Pueblo Ribera, Village by the Sea," undated brochure, Project Files, "Pueblo Ribera Court," RMS at ADC/UCSB.

46 Lloyd to RMS, 3 April 1925, Project Files, "Pueblo Ribera Court," RMS at ADC/UCSB. Lloyd was unable to pay Schindler the remaining balance of $150 on the project until April 1930. In spite of this, the two remained on good terms. Lloyd provided Schindler with photographs of the complex for publication in a number of architectural journals in 1928. In 1941, following Lloyd's death, his widow, Lucy Lafayette Lloyd, asked Schindler to prepare plans to renovate one of the units in the complex by enclosing the rooftop porch as a permanent bedroom and adding a second-story addition over the bedroom area. Schindler complied with a set of drawings, but nothing came of the project due to financial problems. See Lucy Lloyd to RMS, 2 July and 21 August 1941, and RMS to Lucy Lloyd, 6 July and 21 August 1941, Project Files, "Pueblo Ribera Court," RMS at ADC/UCSB.

47 Gebhard, Schindler, 62.

48 Schindler's push to publicize his own work in the American architectural press began to accelerate during the early 1930s with the shift towards coverage of the modern movement in journals like Architectural Record and Architectural Forum. In a letter of January 1931 to Maxwell Levinson, editor of the Philadelphia journal T-Square, Schindler enclosed photographs of his Kings Road studio in West Hollywood, noting that "although the house was built ten years ago, it is of special interest just now. It initiates a development in residence building, which was recently furthered by Mies van der Rohe in his model residence at the German Building Exposition [Stuttgart, 1927]. Although my house is speaking in different materials different language, it says essentially the same thing." The house was featured in the February 1932 issue of T-Square along with a biographical sketch of Richard Neutra. See "A Cooperative Dwelling, R. M. Schindler," T-Square 2 (February 1932): 20-21; and RMS to Maxwell Levinson, 20 January 1931, Business Letters, "T-Square Journal," RMS at ADC/UCSB.

49 Schindler first became aware of Neal Garrett's work through a May 1933 Los Angeles Times Sunday Magazine article on the Garrett method of cement plaster construction, which he saved. See Ransome Sutton, "What's New In Science: One-Piece Houses," Los Angeles Times Sunday Magazine, 7 May 1933, 15. In Project Files, "Schindler-Shelters," RMS at ADC/UCSB.

50 See Schindler's copious notes on the April 1918 issue of Architectural Forum devoted to "Workingmen's Housing," in "Notes on Workingmen's Housing," Manuscript Files, RMS at ADC/UCSB.

51 See the April 1924 specifications for a typical unit of an Industrial Housing Scheme, "Detached dwelling," part of a workers' colony for Gould & Bandini planned for Bandini Square, Los Angeles County. In Project Files, "Gould and Bandini," RMS at ADC/UCSB. Schindler's plans for Job Harriman (who lived in New Llano outside of Leesville, Louisiana) included housing and a college. See Project Files, "Harriman, Job," RMS at ADC/UCSB.

52 Schindler, "Reference Frames in Space" (1932), Architect & Engineer 165, no. 1 (April 1946): 10, 40, 44-45.

53 See "Farm Home Experiment Head Here. 'Subsistence Homestead' Director in City to Pick Site for Colony," Los Angeles Times, n.d. In Project Files, "Schindler Shelters," RMS at ADC/UCSB.

54 Ibid.

55 See "The 'Schindler-Shelter' Plan," Project Files, "Schindler Shelters," RMS at ADC/UCSB.

56 See the manuscript by E. Kanaril, "Schindler-Shelters," 1933, 4. In Project Files, "Schindler Shelters," RMS at ADC/UCSB.

57 See "Schindler-Shelter, Garrett Construction," Project Files, "Schindler Shelters," RMS at ADC/UCSB.

58 See the brochure, "The Garrett Plastered House Offering a New Field of Opportunity in the Business," 1933, Project Files, "Schindler Shelters," RMS at ADC/UCSB.

59 Kanaril, "Schindler-Shelters," 5-6.

60 See "New Dwelling Details Told. Reinforced Concrete Slabs Utilized for House. Changes Easily Made, Says Description of It. Partitions May Be Placed Anywhere Desired," Los Angeles Times, 31 December 1933, 1-17. In Project Files, "Schindler Shelters," RMS at ADC/UCSB. Aspects of Schindler's architectural philosophy had been featured by the Los Angeles Times Sunday Magazine in a series of six articles between March and April 1926 as part of Dr. Philip Lovell's "Care of the Body" column.

61 L. Brandt (Washington, D.C.) to RMS, 10 January 1934, Project Files, "Schindler Shelters," RMS at ADC/UCSB.

62 RMS to Committee for Subsistence Farms, 11 January 1934, Project Files, "Schindler Shelters," RMS at ADC/UCSB.

173 63 The Schindler-Shelters were featured in the May 1935 issue of *American Architect* along with Schindler's design for the William E. Oliver Residence. *See* "News of Planning and Construction: Schindler Shelters," *American Architect* 146 (May 1935): 70-71. Schindler sent to *Kokusai Kenchiku* editor, M. Koyama, drawings and text about the Schindler Shelters in May 1935. RMS to M. Koyama (Tokyo), 20 May 1935, Project Files, "Schindler Shelters," RMS at ADC/UCSB. Koyama included the material in the July 1935 issue. *See* "Schindler-Shelters," *Kokusai Kenchiku* 11 (July 1935): 252-258. My thanks to Professor Mari Nakahara for providing me with a copy of the article.

64 For a discussion of the possible reasons behind Schindler's exclusion from the Case Study House program, *see* Elizabeth A. T. Smith, ed., *Blueprints for Modern Living: History and Legacy of the Case Study Houses* (Los Angeles, Calif.: The Museum of Contemporary Art; and Cambridge, Mass.: The MIT Press, 1989), 19, 39 n. 2, 85-86.

65 Gebhard, *Schindler*, 145; and McCoy, *Five California Architects*, 150.

66 Gebhard, *Schindler*, 135.

67 Gebhard, "Late Designs, 1944-1953," in Lionel March and Judith Sheine, eds., *R. M. Schindler: Composition and Construction* (London: Academy Editions, 1993), 255.

68 McCoy, *Five California Architects*, 182.

69 On Ellen Margaret Janson, *see* her entry in *Who's Who in California*, vol. 1 (Los Angeles: Who's Who Publications Company, 1943), 451. *See also* her *Poems, 1920-1949* (Hollywood, Calif.: E. Janson, 1952), which is dedicated to R. M. Schindler: "For Michael, Who Makes All Things Possible."

70 Ellen Janson, from an interview with Barbara Giella, quoted in Judith Sheine, "Construction and the Schindler Frame," in March and Sheine, *R. M. Schindler: Composition and Construction*, 245.

71 Ellen Janson to RMS, n.d. [1952/1953], Personal Correspondence, "Janson, Ellen," RMS at ADC/UCSB.

72 Schindler, "Reference Frames in Space," 1944, 3. In Essays and Lectures, Manuscript Files, RMS at ADC/UCSB.

73 *Ibid.*, 5.

74 Schindler's essay was published under the auspices of the Hollywood Art Association as "Who Will Save Hollywood? A Plea for the Proper Respect and Treatment of Our Wonderful Endowment of Nature," *Holly Leaves* 11 (3 November 1922): 36.

75 *Ibid.*

76 *See* Schindler's answer to the Questionnaire for the Directory of Contemporary Architecture, collected by School of Architecture, University of Southern California (1949). In Essays and Lectures, Manuscript Files, RMS at ADC/UCSB.

77 Schindler, "Visual Technique," 1952, 8. In Essays and Lectures, Manuscript Files, RMS at ADC/UCSB.

78 McCoy, *Five California Architects*, 191.

79 Schindler, "Visual Technique," 6.

80 Peter Blake to RMS, 24 March 1949, "Modern Architecture Book" Manuscript Files, RMS at ADC/UCSB.

81 Esther McCoy, "Schindler at Work: An Appreciation," in Sheine and March, *R. M. Schindler: Composition and Construction*, 259.

82 Talbot Hamlin on R. M. Schindler, compiled for the R. M. Schindler Memorial Exhibition at the Felix Landau Gallery, 1954. Original in the EMC at AAASI.

1 KINGS ROAD HOUSE, West Hollywood, California, 1921–22.
Photograph by Grant Mudford

MICHAEL DARLING

THE VULNER-ABLE ARCHI-TECTURE

OF R.M. SCHINDLER

In 1921, with the impact of California fresh on my mind, I built my own house, trying to meet the character of the locale.... I introduced features which seemed to be necessary for life in California; an open plan, flat on the ground; living patios; glass walls; translucent walls; wide sliding doors; clerestory windows; shed roofs with wide shading overhangs. These features have now been accepted generally and form the basis of the contemporary California house.

—R. M. Schindler, 1952 [1]

At the end of his career, R. M. Schindler knew full well the magnitude of his contribution to modern architecture. For him, the prolific and varied body of work he was to leave behind was held together by a consistent and indeed rigorous ethos, one that was often overlooked by superficial appraisals. As the quote above suggests, his design decisions were based on a specific, programmatic rationale as fully articulated as that of any leading modernist of his day. How was it then, given a highly conceptualized approach to architecture so strongly expressed through buildings and a large body of writings, that twenty years after his death Schindler could still be considered a "vulnerable" and "derivative" architect?

In a 1973 review of David Gebhard's monograph on Schindler, the architect and academician Charles Moore used just these terms to thematize Schindler's work as it was then seen within the continuum of modern architecture.[2] Reading between the lines, however, Moore's use of "vulnerability" in this context was not necessarily pejorative, but indicative of the paradigm shift that had recently occurred within the field of architecture. If hurled from the tower of canonical modernism, the "vulnerable" epithet would intimate that the accused lacked faith in his (most certainly a man) own ideas, possessed a weakly developed architectural rationale and, perhaps worst of all, was susceptible to shifts in style. That Schindler was viewed by the East Coast architectural establishment as a vulnerable architect of this sort led to his exclusion from the epochal "International Exposition of Modern Architecture" exhibition of 1932 at The Museum of Modern Art in New York, among other professional injustices. Coming from Moore, however, an established postmodernist and architectural ironist, it was another sort of vulnerability that he, along with architect Hans Hollein before him and historians such as Gebhard, Esther McCoy, and Reyner Banham, found so compelling and exemplary.

For Moore, "Bona fide vulnerability ... involves caring about the specific things you find and find out about so much that you will change your position to accommodate them: invulnerable architects see and learn things too, but they have a position, or a sense of mission, early arrived at, to which the learned and seen things contribute, without the power to change it."[3] Schindler undoubtedly had positions, but they were by definition dynamic, permeable, and alive, allowing all manner of external factors to guide his design solutions. His architecture changed each time he learned about its site, climate, culture, and client needs; the resulting buildings ranged from adobe compounds to log houses, Spanish-style haciendas to fantastical desert huts. As critiques of canonical modernism began to mount during the 1950s and 1960s (too late for Schindler to appreciate the sea change), Schindler's prolific and widely varied work offered a historical alternative to the International Style ("the temple of invulnerability"[4]), and defectors from Moore to Hollein to Frank O. Gehry found in it a non-dogmatic, highly flexible approach to design that took cues from real life as much as from abstract ideals. So-called "vulnerability" could be an aspiration.

Indeed, Schindler's vulnerability was not passive but active, and can be seen in many ways as a prescient form of contextualism, whereby everything from local materials, building practices, architectural styles, landscape formations, climate types, emotional responses, and clients' habits were pointedly assimilated into the overall design. An enormously eclectic body of work resulted from such an aggressively attuned approach; each structure can be seen as a unique solution to the problems offered by a given commission. Judged by the standards set forth by the dominant architectural community of his day, quirky inconsistency riddles Schindler's work. Yet, when examined on a case-by-case basis, one realizes that his buildings responded socially to their respective settings without ever compromising the vigorous spatial and tectonic concerns that were part of his overarching goal of developing a truly modern architecture. For Schindler, modern architecture was about constant, fluent adaptation to our collective surroundings, not the creation of haughty abstractions.

In his writings and lectures, he often employed biological metaphors to discuss the ways in which architects could adaptively address architectural problems. Rather than relying on lofty invocations of the machine, as was common during the first half of the century, Schindler focused on decidedly unpretentious images to bring home his humanistic approach to building: "We want to build to have live contact with our neighbors. We have come down to earth ... Modern architecture lies down flat on the ground like a kitten who suns itself."[5] While sunbathing cats might seem more the province of conservative Victorian sensibilities than avant-garde architecture, Schindler's work proves that open-minded observation of adjacent nature and culture, rather than blind faith in the salvation of the machine, could yield some of the most exciting and progressive buildings of the century. And if a zoological metaphor might better describe Schindler's proclivities than a mechanistic one, his work

might be best viewed as chameleon-like—constantly changing to **176** match environmental conditions while maintaining a core identity.

Since almost all of Schindler's built work was realized in the United States, it is most instructive to look at examples of his contextual susceptibility through the lens of his American experiences.[6] Prior to arriving in the States in 1914, however, he did document and experiment with vernacular Austrian building types; Schindler's loose-leaf pocketbook (c. 1910) *(fig. 2)* is a testament to the architect's interests and influences, as is the Summer Residence (project), Vienna (1914) *(fig. 3)*. Judging from the respect he accorded his later discoveries in America, one can assume that he appreciated certain aspects of their Alpine regional character. Pitched roofs still make sense in snow country, and half-timber construction arguably takes good advantage of abundantly available materials, even though the resulting imagery is still suffused with traditional trappings. Once in the States, his camera and sketchpad became favored tools for recording and understanding the whys and wherefores of American architecture, as he amassed a catalogue of building types that

2 Pocketbook sketch, c. 1910. Drawing by R. M. Schindler

3 SUMMER RESIDENCE (project), Vienna, 1914

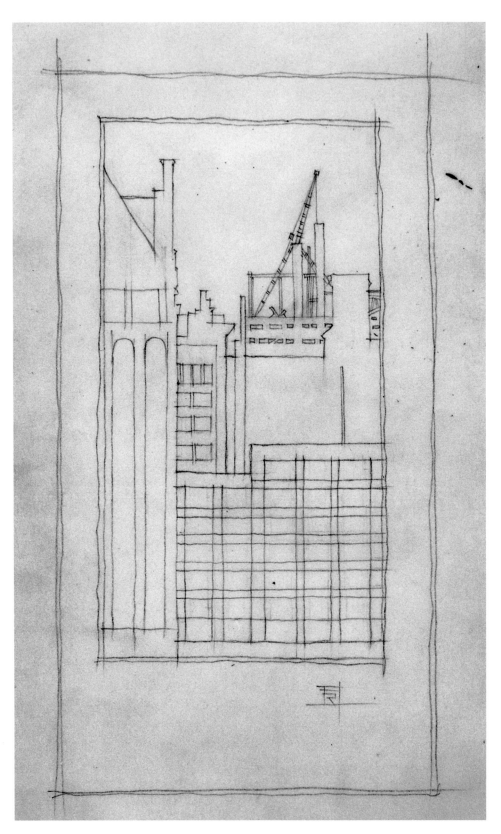

4   Sketch of Chicago skyline under construction,
date unknown. Drawing by R. M. Schindler

179 seemed attuned to the particularities of their time and place. In Chicago, the budding skyline was a repeated subject for both pencil and lens (*figs. 4, 5*), but it was during a trip to the West and Southwest in 1915 when Schindler encountered structures that would have lasting influence on his own practice.

In Santa Fe and Taos, New Mexico, Schindler made numerous photographs and sketches of adobe buildings, and he would develop certain recurring features of this indigenous style in later projects. In some cases, he made drawings and photographs of similar artifacts as if to better understand the nuances and logic of their design and construction (*figs. 6, 7*). Schindler surely appreciated the direct connection of building to earth in these structures, where wall meets ground and tamped dirt serves as simple flooring. Such continuity between indoor and outdoor planes and surfaces was famously explored in his own house on Kings Road in West Hollywood six years later. Also of interest in terms of its influence on the Kings Road House (1921-22) is the gentle inward slant of battered adobe walls, where each progressive layer of adobe is reduced

in order to mitigate against excessive weight at the top (*fig. 8*). Schindler took a similar approach in this later work, substituting poured concrete slabs for adobe, but with related effect in the distribution of load. The expression of roof support, both in the interiors of Pueblo-style adobes and by the protrusion of vigas on exterior walls, also found its way into many subsequent Schindler buildings, albeit with mechanically milled lumber instead of stripped logs. The Log House (project) of 1916–18 took this concept to another extreme, and will be discussed later for its expressive, but not gratuitous, display of this rustic building material.

Still another feature of traditional, native Southwestern architecture is the corner fireplace, which usually creates the focal point of a room and is almost always placed at floor level. Schindler was extremely fond of the fireplace for its symbolic, functional, and organizational potential, and it is hard to imagine a Schindler house without one. Doubtless his thinking about the architectural use of the hearth was influenced by the equally smitten Frank Lloyd Wright, but Schindler's even earlier exposure to the adobe fireplace, with its

5 Chicago skyline, c. 1915.
Photograph by R. M. Schindler

6   Governor's Palace, Santa Fe, New Mexico, 1915.
Photograph by R. M. Schindler

7   Adobe building, Taos, New Mexico, 1915.
Drawing by R. M. Schindler

8   Rear façade of a church, Taos, New Mexico, 1915.
Photograph by R. M. Schindler

9 Former chapel of Victor Higgin's studio, Taos,
New Mexico, 1915. Photograph by R. M. Schindler

10 RICHARD LECHNER RESIDENCE, Studio City, California,
1946–48. View of living room. Photograph by
Robert C. Cleveland

sculptural, integrated hood *(fig. 9)*, goes a long way toward explaining the presence of this favorite feature in countless homes *(fig. 10)*. The rectilinear massing of volumes in the adobe complexes captured by Schindler, often of irregularly stepped boxes *(fig. 11)*, recurs in the plaster-skinned houses of the 1930s [such as the Robert F. Elliot (1930), Hans N. Von Koerber (1931-32), and John J. Buck (1934) *(fig. 12)* residences]. Likewise, the Southwestern builder's predilection for covered outdoor patios became a common component of Schindler's architecture, allowing for both open-air rooms and shelter from omnipresent sunshine. Even the exterior ladders favored by Southwestern builders for roof access found their way into Schindler's work. Evidence can be found in a photograph of his Popenoe Cabin of 1922 *(fig. 13)*, an image that is strikingly similar to those the architect took in Taos and Santa Fe in 1915.

While all of the above-mentioned features of adobe architecture were eventually assimilated into Schindler's practice in less-immediately recognizable forms, the country house he designed for Dr. Thomas Paul Martin in 1915 made more spontaneous use of the idiom.

Presumably engaged by Martin during his travels in New Mexico, Schindler's scheme for a Taos getaway borders on pastiche in its close approximation of the adobe style *(fig. 14)*. Closer examination, however, reveals a complex orchestration of architectural concepts. The plan *(fig. 15)* is a strict exercise in *beaux-arts* symmetry, reminiscent of other work with which he was then engaged in Chicago, such as the Neighborhood Center Project of 1914 *(fig. 16)* or the Unidentified Residence Project, c. 1917 *(fig. 17)*. However, the inward-facing courtyard rimmed with over-hanging roofs, as well as the deep porch on the south end, are features extensively used in Southwestern architecture and wholly appropriate to the harsh climate *(figs. 18, 20)*. So, too, are the unadorned, monolithic walls of adobe that gently peek above the wide, horizontal expanse of the desert, an effort by Schindler to approximate the scale of the surrounding landscape.[7] On the other hand, the architect's use of the projecting viga to circumscribe an outsized courtyard is a departure from the local norm, allowing the exposed logs to cantilever far beyond the supporting walls of adobe and run in long, precise rows of almost mechanical clarity. This not only achieves a pleasing visual rhythm and shows an

11 Adobe building, Taos, New Mexico, 1915.
Photograph by R. M. Schindler

12 JOHN J. BUCK RESIDENCE, Los Angeles, 1934.
Photograph by Grant Mudford

13 PAUL POPENOE CABIN, Coachella, California, 1922

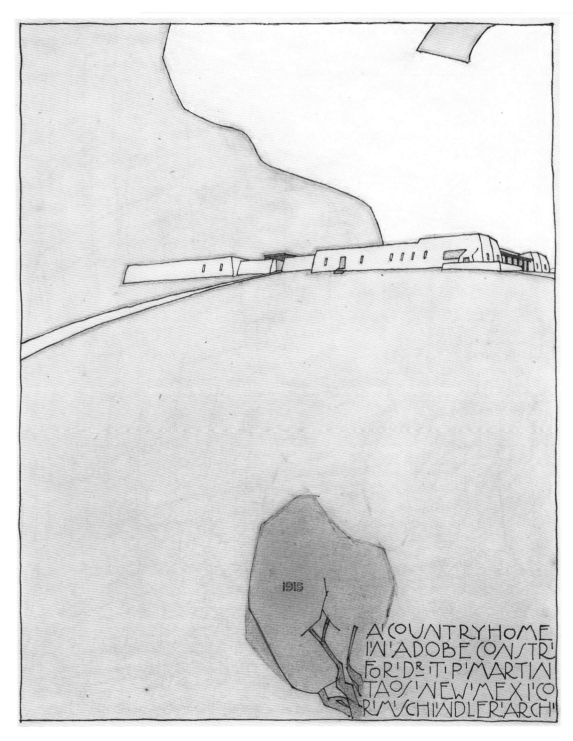

A·COUNTRY·HOME
IN·ADOBE·CONSTR·
FOR·DR·T·P·MARTIN
TAOS·NEW·MEXICO
R·M·SCHINDLER·ARCH·

1915

14   THOMAS PAUL MARTIN RESIDENCE (project),
Taos, New Mexico, 1915. Presentation drawing

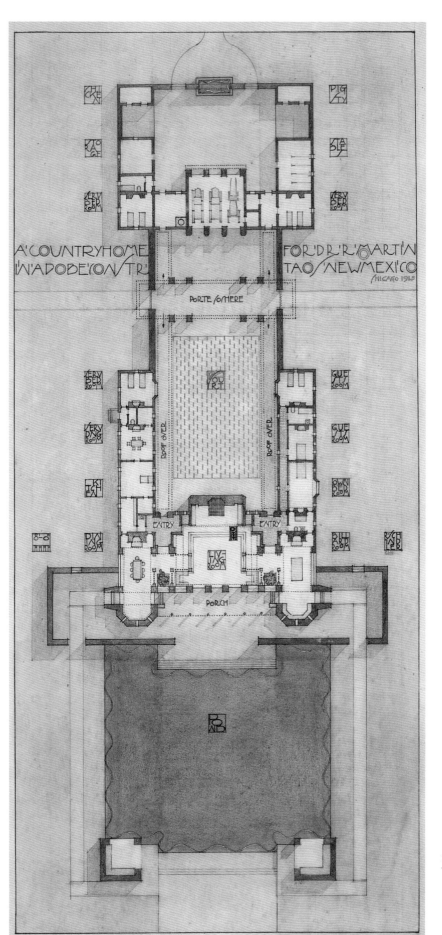

A·COUNTRY·HOME·IN·ADOBE·CONSTR· FOR·DR·R·MARTIN TAOS·NEW·MEXICO CHICAGO·1915

15 THOMAS PAUL MARTIN RESIDENCE (project),
Taos, New Mexico, 1915. Plan

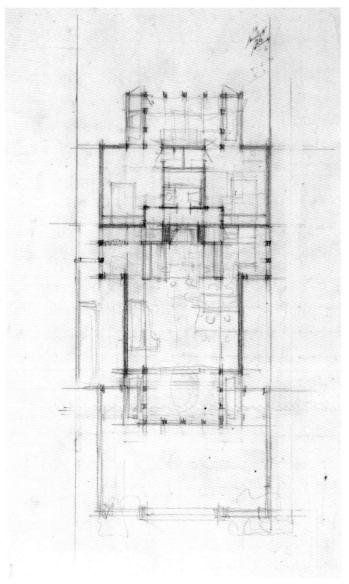

16 NEIGHBORHOOD CENTER (project), Chicago, 1914.
Presentation drawing

17 UNIDENTIFIED RESIDENCE (project), Oak Park,
Illinois, c. 1917. Floor plan

A COUNTRY HOME
IN ADOBE CONSTR
FOR DR T P MARTIN
TAOS NEW MEXICO
R M SCHINDLER ARCH

18 THOMAS PAUL MARTIN RESIDENCE (project),
Taos, New Mexico, 1915. Presentation drawing

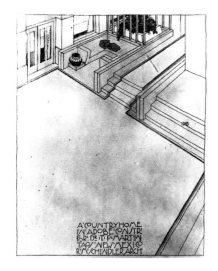

19 THOMAS PAUL MARTIN RESIDENCE (project),
Taos, New Mexico, 1915. View of stairs and living room

20 THOMAS PAUL MARTIN RESIDENCE (project),
Taos, New Mexico, 1915. Presentation drawing

embrace of vernacular traditions, but also suggests a marriage of modern engineering and "rustic" technique. The vast open spaces of the living room, with its Loosian changes of floor level, is a further example of modern planning and construction married to traditional form *(fig. 19)*. In a letter to Dr. Martin, which accompanied a set of five drawings of the house, Schindler clearly delineated his intentions for a building that mediated old and new:

The whole building is to be carried out with the most expressive materials Taos can furnish, to give it the deepest possible rooting in the soil which has to bear it, but I will avoid with all means to copy a few ornamental forms of any old imported style even if formerly used on the place. The building has to show that it is conceived by a head of the twentieth century and that it has to serve a man which is not dressed in an old Spanish uniform. [8]

For Schindler, the regionalist trappings were a way for the inhabitant to engage his surroundings (and provide a compatible setting for Martin's collection of Indian artifacts) without sacrificing the amenities offered by then-current architectural know-how. In a statement that approaches universal relevance for all of Schindler's work, although addressed to this particular commission, the architect wrote: "This house is not a mere shelter, but the frame for a man in which to enjoy life through his culture." [9]

The adobe house was the perfect vehicle for a New Mexican experiment in active contextualism. However, Schindler's adaptation of the log cabin, the most mythical and clichéd of building types from the Wild West, showed both a fearless disregard of accepted architectural taste and a curious continuation of ideas he first encountered in Vienna. Schindler scholar Lionel March has pointed out that, before coming to the States, Schindler may very well have seen Adolf Loos's 1913 design for a log house for the janitor of the Schwarzwald School *(fig. 21)*. [10] As Loos possessed respect for vernacular types and would go on to design other rustic mountain houses, this bit of architectural arcana is not entirely unusual. Yet, Schindler's infusion of modernity into such a loaded, archaic, and representational architectural image is revelatory. Schindler's Log House (project) (1916–18) *(fig. 22)* explores advanced ideas about modular construction that would have interested his mentor, while maintaining an unmistakable connection to vernacular precedents on American soil and elsewhere. The language of typical log construction, characterized by horizontal rows of lumber joined at the corner by notched intersections, is unabashedly reiterated by Schindler—albeit complicated by the introduction of secondary volumes, stonework piers, and uncharacteristic glass inserts. The flat roofs of the building signal another break with tradition, belying its modern proclivities and taking the design to a level of formal purity that Loos, presumably because of climate, could not achieve. In the Log House, as with the Martin Residence, Schindler exaggerated the projection of structural beams beyond the walls to signify a contemporary adaptation of the material, exploited here to dramatize

PLAN ZVR ERRICHTVNG
EINER BAVLEITVNGSHVTTE
FVR DIE SEMMERINGSCHVLE

MASSTAB 1:100

21 Adolf Loos. Project for the janitor's house of the
Schwarzwald School, Semmering, Austria, 1913

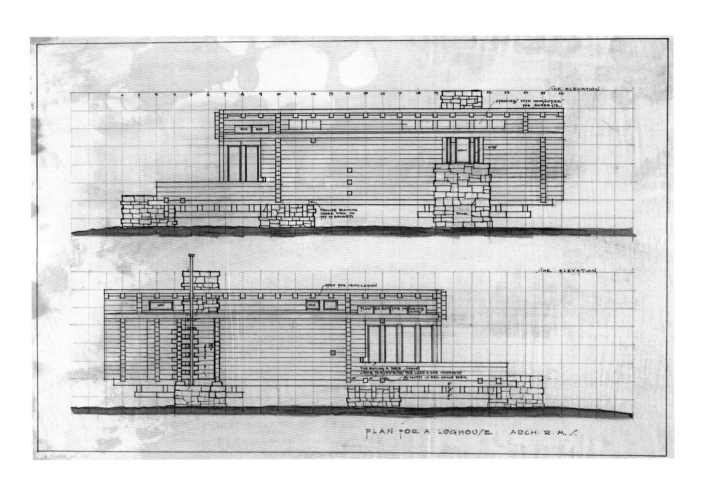

22 LOG HOUSE (project), location unknown, 1916–18.
Side elevations

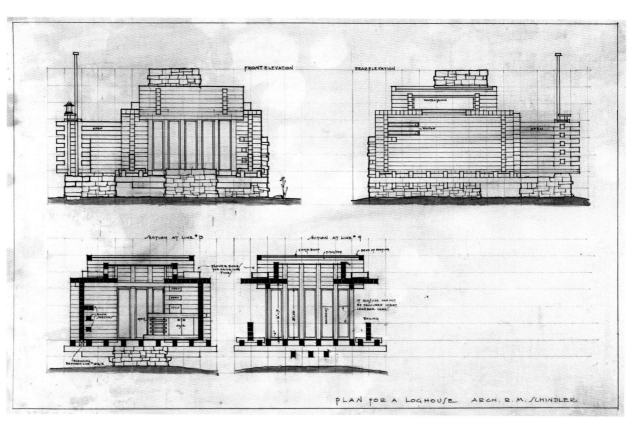

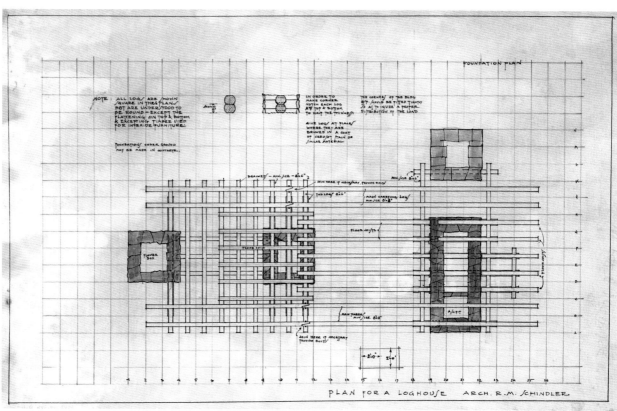

23 LOG HOUSE (project), location unknown, 1916–18.
Front and rear elevations with sections

24 LOG HOUSE (project), location unknown, 1916–18.
Foundation plan

the planar qualities of the intersecting walls, as March previously noted *(fig. 23)*.[11]

Perhaps the most important design element of the Log House is the overriding modularity of the concept. Not only does the design prefigure Schindler's later work in the development of prefabricated, standardized units (not to mention the legions of other architects obsessed with the concept later in the century), but it is one of his earliest explorations of a proportional system that integrates plan, elevation, and construction. The house is strictly organized on a grid, based on modules of two feet that would accommodate four six-inch-diameter logs per module in the upper elevations of the structure, and three eight-inch logs in the substructure *(fig. 24)*. Variations within this proportional system, from single log protrusions to complex transitions between volumes, are thus visually harmonized, and dimensions for clerestory windows and other fenestration are easily and rationally derived. Later, Schindler would come to rely on the four-foot module in much of his work, and landmark houses such as the James Eads How Residence (1925–26), with its elegant transitions from concrete to wood to glass all orchestrated by geometric principles and tightly conceptualized construction systems, are direct beneficiaries of this early project.[12]

That Schindler could perceive in the American log cabin an opportunity, to both address the cultural history of vernacular architecture and explore a modular approach to composition and construction with far-reaching practical application, should be surprising. The fact that such an un-dismissive and boundlessly permeable sensibility led him to similarly unusual and brilliant architectural solutions throughout his career makes it less so, but remarkable nonetheless.

Schindler's relocation to California in 1920 (to supervise the Barnsdall project for Wright) signaled the commencement of his truly mature work, for it was in California that he found his muse. The range of micro-climates, varied geography, and legendary light led him to innumerable experiments in tailoring design to site, none more celebrated than his first solo effort in Los Angeles: his own house on Kings Road (1921–22) *(fig. 1)*. The house is rich in social history, pioneering ideas about collective habitation, and innovative construction techniques, but it is its derivation from Schindler's favorable experiences in the California wilderness that align it with his previous experiments in site-specificity. Rather than a direct response to the site, however, the Kings Road House is the result of the application of an idealized notion about the Californian environment.

Photographs taken before and after construction show that the immediate surroundings consisted of flat, featureless bean fields bordered in the distance by unpopulated hills *(fig. 25)*. The elegant urbanity of Irving Gill's Dodge House (1916), also located on the street, was at least one local exception. The architectural imagery Schindler adopted for this rather forlorn site in some ways matched the humility of its locale, yet it was also a projection of an exotic mountain experience. In the fall of 1921, the architect and his wife, Pauline, drove up to Yosemite in a convertible car as a brief respite from his work with Wright. Unsurprisingly, Schindler was smitten with the beauty of the Sierras and wrote a rhapsodic letter to his friend Richard Neutra, describing the scene: "I received your letter high up in the mountains where I am having a vacation for which I have waited a long time. It is one of the most marvelous places in America. I camp at the shore of the Tenaya, sleep on a bed of spruce needles under a free sky and bathe in the ice-cold waterfall."[13]

25 Kings Road House site before construction, West Hollywood, California, 1921. Photograph by R. M. Schindler

26 "Our Tent," Yosemite National Park, Camp 9, October-November 1921. Photograph by R. M. Schindler

27 Schindler bathing at Illiluette Falls, Yosemite National Park, October-November 1921. Photograph by Pauline Schindler

Photographs from the trip show the tent in which they camped *(fig. 26)* and verify Schindler's bathing habits *(fig. 27)*. Yosemite had a profound effect on the Schindlers, leading in part to an unpublished story by Pauline titled "Joys of Tent Life in California," and directly influenced the design of the house Schindler was to build for himself and another couple on Kings Road. He took the idyllic conditions of Yosemite to be general conditions for California at large and constructed a house that offered, in his words: "the basic requirements for a camper's shelter: a protected back, an open front, a fireplace, and a roof."[14] Tilt-up concrete walls enclosed rooms on three sides, while the glass and sliding light-weight doors of the fourth opened onto outdoor spaces contiguous with the floor planes of the interiors *(fig. 29)*. Each room was equipped with a floor-level hearth, and fireplaces heated the outdoor spaces as well. Sleeping was to be done in rooftop "sleeping baskets" to take advantage of the "favorable" climate. While such indoor/outdoor living is indeed possible for good portions of the year, rain and cold temperatures beset even Southern California. Schindler's captivation with the general characteristics of the region's weather, however, overrode such inconsistencies.

The fact that Schindler romanticized the rather banal site of his house can be seen in an elevation sketch that shows it as if viewed from the bottom of a (non-existent) hill *(fig. 28)*, yet the casual layout of the house and its indoor/outdoor orientation did pioneer concepts that later became commonplace in Southern Californian domestic architecture. Wide sliding doors, walls of glass oriented toward garden patios, clerestory windows, and shade-providing overhangs all appear here in 1921, and throughout California for decades thereafter. The Kings Road House is in many ways Schindler's manifesto for site-sensitive (if not wholly site-specific) Californian architecture, not dissimilar to the earlier attempts of the Thomas Paul Martin Residence and Log House, and forms the conceptual basis from which his subsequent buildings would spring.

Even when he had to follow the stylistic dictates set forth by local planning organizations, he was able to intuit design schemes that took their cues from the context while also advancing his own design language. The Hans N. Von Koerber Residence of 1931-32 presented such a situation. The Hollywood Riviera subdivision stipulated the

194

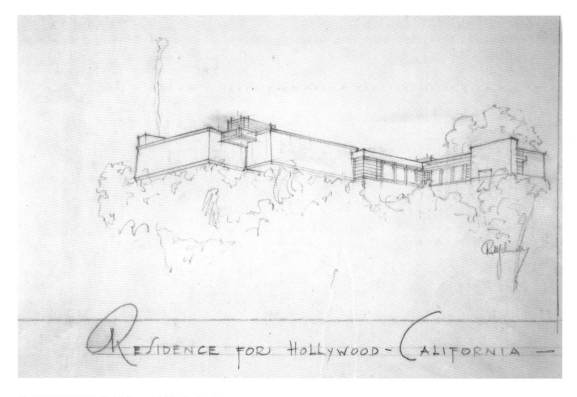

28 KINGS ROAD HOUSE, West Hollywood, California, 1921-22.
Detail, perspective view

29 KINGS ROAD HOUSE, West Hollywood, California, 1921–22.
View of Schindler's studio with Schindler-designed furniture.
Photograph by Grant Mudford

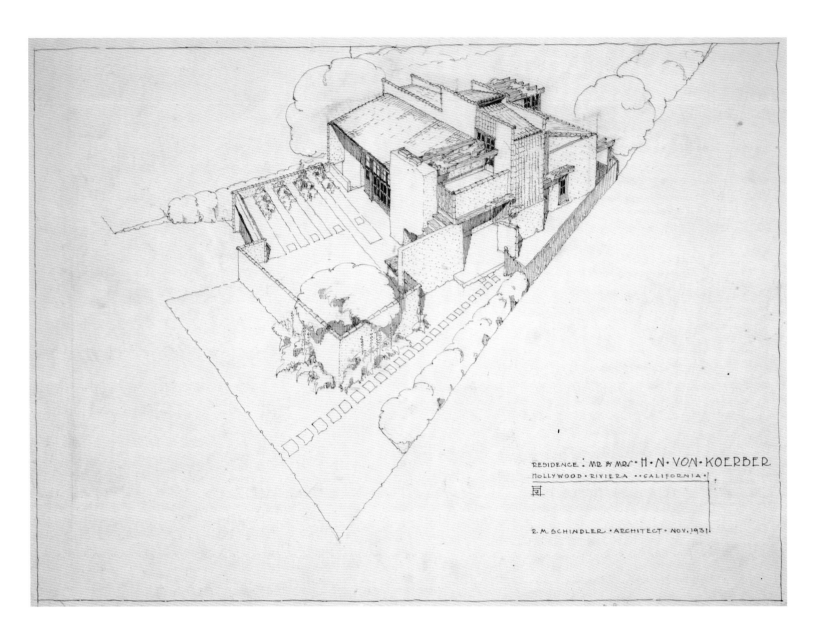

RESIDENCE : MR & MRS · H · N · VON · KOERBER
HOLLYWOOD · RIVIERA · CALIFORNIA ·

R. M. SCHINDLER · ARCHITECT · NOV. 1931

30 HANS N. VON KOERBER RESIDENCE, Torrance, California, 1931-32

use of the Spanish Style idiom *(fig. 30)*. Despite David Gebhard's suggestion that Schindler's use of Spanish Colonial Revival motifs (not only here, but in the Anne M. Burrell projects of the early 1920s, for example) amounted to an ironic incorporation of a "low art" (popular) style, it is possible to believe that Schindler found contextual value in the mode. For someone interested in achieving a local character, the Spanish style had its merits. After all, Irving Gill, Schindler pointed out in an undated letter to Esther McCoy, "was the first one to bend the Spanish into Californian," and in the same letter wrote that "Spanish architecture which although still foreign was much closer to the landscape [than the Craftsman style]."[15] From letters between Schindler and Mr. and Mrs. Von Koerber, it appears as if Schindler himself selected the site, presumably with full knowledge of the stylistic restrictions of the area.[16] In the Von Koerbers he found clients who deeply appreciated the regional aspirations of his Kings Road home ("You can hardly imagine what it means to me to have found somebody who fully senses the character of my house, even more, somebody who—like me—desires to live in such a surrounding."[17]), and who went so far as to give him a design mandate that could almost be scripted by the architect himself:

We are interested—even apart from the expense issue—in showing that even with extreme modesty and by using the least expensive materials in standard sizes a beautiful appearance can be achieved. Please do completely leave behind which professional circle we belong to. Just consider us solely as human beings feeling a strong affection for nature and for a life in and with nature and who would like to express this affection under consideration of the local climate and the most uncomplicated way of life.[18]

At this time, Schindler had begun to wholeheartedly adopt the typical Southern Californian building method of wood-frame construction covered in stucco, and with his "Schindler-Frame" process endeavored to simplify homebuilding by using standard-sized lumber. This method dovetailed perfectly with the stucco-skinned Spanish style, yet Schindler pushed the conventions of the mode to unusual extremes, assembling a dynamic composition of asymmetrical volumes and planes that breathed new life into the tradition *(figs. 31, 32)*. Tiled shed roofs did not only end at the eaves, but spilled down the wall plane, confusing the boundaries between horizontal and vertical in a similar manner as the John Cooper Packard Residence (1924), and in later projects such as the A. Gisela Bennati Cabin (1934-37) and Adolph Tischler Residence (1949-50). The tiles playfully led indoors as well, cascading down either side of the fireplace while also lining the floor of the hearth. Unlike the often dark and confined spaces of Spanish Colonial Revival houses, the Von Koerber house is boldly opened up by clerestory windows, sectional diversity, and ample fenestration to take advantage of ocean and garden views *(fig. 33)*. The daring with which Schindler treated the Spanish style in this project could be seen as a precedent-setting challenge to other architects to experiment within the mode, where a conciliatory aesthetic gesture to the surrounding neighborhood is matched by a bold departure from convention. In the seventy years since, however, few if any have taken it so far.

The mountain cabin Schindler designed for olive oil merchant A. Gisela Bennati in 1934 exhibits a similar vivacity in working within constraints. The tract in Lake Arrowhead stipulated the use of "Normandy style" and, in response, Schindler introduced to the neighborhood a vacation house that was almost nothing but roof *(fig. 34)*. The dramatic A-frame carries a shingled roof all the way to the ground on both sides, while each gabled end is at least partially glazed *(fig. 35)*. The triangular form and resulting merging of roof and wall is not merely a reactionary retort to the local planning board, but both an extension of preexisting formal repertoire and a distinctly contextual gesture. The aforementioned Packard, Von Koerber, and Tischler houses explore a similar dissolution of the rectilinear section, and the projected houses for Mrs. Laura Davies (1922-24) and Mrs. M. Davis Baker (1923) are even earlier explorations of the steeply gabled roof *(fig. 36)*. Neither of the latter two projects, however, seem to make use of the triangulated space under the sloping roof as Schindler did in the Bennati cabin, where an entirely functional second story with two bedrooms and a bunkroom was created. The exposed beams throughout the house reiterate the unrelenting geometry of the structure while also modulating the space and providing formal cues for the extensive built-in furnishings *(fig. 38)*.

Schindler also turned to the triangular A-frame design in an effort to tie the structure to its site. The essentialized form of the pine tree, with its peaked distribution of foliage, is mimicked in the shape of the cabin and made explicit in the presentation drawing *(fig. 37)*. The fireplace, chimney, and base of the house are constructed from native stone in another effort at achieving "local character." Additionally, outdoor floodlights aimed into the trees at either gabled end provide some of the artificial lighting indoors and maintain the connection to the surrounding pine forest even at night.[19] The Museum of Modern Art recognized the topographical qualities of the Bennati cabin and in 1941 asked to include it in a traveling exhibition

31 HANS N. VON KOERBER RESIDENCE, Torrance, California, 1931-32

32, 33 HANS N. VON KOERBER RESIDENCE, Torrance, California, 1931–32

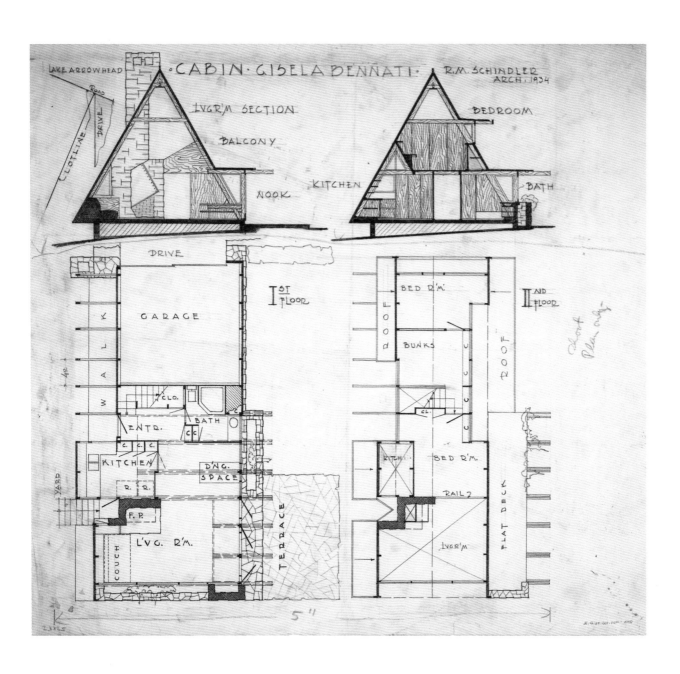

CABIN · GISELA BENNATI · R.M. SCHINDLER ARCH. 1934

LAKE ARROWHEAD

LIVGR'M SECTION

BALCONY

NOOK   KITCHEN

BEDROOM

BATH

DRIVE

GARAGE

I ST FLOOR

WALK

CLO.

ENTR.

BATH

C. C. C.

KITCHEN

R. R.

F.P.

D'NG. SPACE

L'VG. R'M.

COUCH

TERRACE

YARD

BED R'M.

FOOD

BUNKS

ROOF

II ND FLOOR

CL.

KITCH.

BED R'M.

RAIL?

L'VG'M

FLAT DECK

5'1

34 A. GISELA BENNATI CABIN, Lake Arrowhead, California, 1934-37.
Plan and sections

35 A. GISELA BENNATI CABIN, Lake Arrowhead, California, 1934-37.
Photograph by W. P. Woodcock

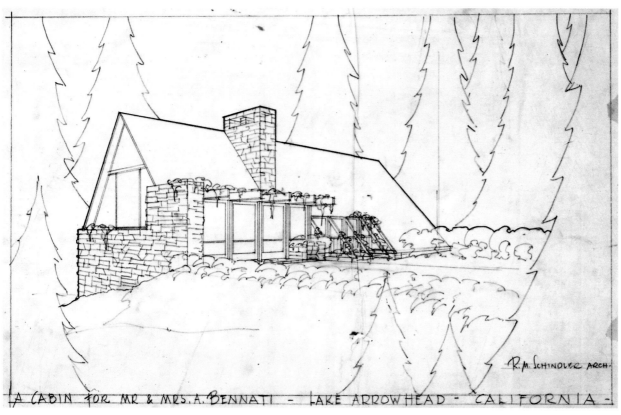

R.M. Schindler Arch.

A CABIN FOR MR & MRS. A. BENNATI - LAKE ARROWHEAD - CALIFORNIA -

203 dedicated to "Regional Building." Elizabeth Mock, then an assistant in MOMA's Department of Architecture, wrote that she "had always been fascinated by the idea of an all-roof house," and was interested in how the construction and materials related to the site and climate.[20] The house was perhaps a little too vernacular or too representational for Mock's taste, however, and in subsequent correspondence she referred to it derisively as a "scherzo," taken as a joke or folly.[21]

Although by the time of this interchange an interest in vernacular building methods and materials, in addition to a growing awareness of site-specificity, had crept into the purview of the modern movement, many of the leading practitioners relied on surface effects to achieve their "new look." The houses on American soil of Bauhaus émigré Marcel Breuer, for instance, incorporated stone and sloping roofs as an attempt to integrate modernist sensibilities with East Coast traditionalism, though still guided by elegant abstraction. Le Corbusier, perhaps the most well-known adventurer in vernacular modes, used local materials to camouflage his machines for living, but sometimes with negligible understanding of the actual conditions of the site. His house at Les Mathes (1935), while incorporating rubble walls and a timber roof to acknowledge local building practices, was built without the architect ever having visited the remote locale.[22] His earlier vacation house for Hélène de Mandrot in Le Pradet (1929-31), as historian Colin St. John Wilson has noted, also incorporated local stone masonry walls, but Le Corbusier was chiefly preoccupied with formal distinctions between load-bearing elements and glazed panels *(fig. 39)*.[23] The house was a stunningly refined sculptural statement, but failed miserably to satisfy the desire of the client for a hospitable dwelling (despite her criticism of an early scheme for not taking into account the presence of strong wind and sun on the site). De Mandrot quit the house after half a year of habitation.[24] For St. John Wilson, the de Mandrot house:

illustrates an aspect of Le Corbusier's mind that was both its strength and its weakness: the attempt to raise every project to the level of a general issue of which it would then become a model demonstration. The intellectual force behind this aspiration is what gives all of his work a certain loftiness that, at the time, reinforced his role as both pacemaker and law-giver.

Its inadequacy lay in the fact that it operated solely in the field of ideas which furthermore were ideas exclusively dedicated to the marriage of form and technology. Its role seems to have been concerned more with the justification of a system than with the quality of life in Le Pradet.[25]

Schindler's work, too, embodied the ideal that each project could be seen as a model demonstration. His "Schindler-Frame" construction method, for instance, was tested in building after building, yielding a wide range of expression that underlined its varied applicability. As consistently as his architectural imagery was inconsistent, Schindler's demonstrations of form and technology were deeply rooted in a concern for negotiating harmony between client and site, opting for vulnerability over predetermination to achieve that goal.

36 LAURA DAVIES RESIDENCE (project), Los Angeles, 1922-24

37 A. GISELA BENNATI CABIN, Lake Arrowhead, California, 1934-37.
Presentation drawing

38 A. GISELA BENNATI CABIN, Lake Arrowhead, California, 1934-37.
View of dining room

His house for Maryon E. Toole (1946–48), located in the desert town of Palm Springs, serves as a worthy illustration of this tendency and an instructive contrast to the Corbusian example cited above. Like the de Mandrot house, it incorporates local stone masonry to tie the structure to the rocky, barren landscape, but here the site is truly a muse, inspiring Schindler to follow metaphor and fantasy as much as the vicissitudes of nature in the design. The reddish-brown granite of the walls is put into direct contrast with light cement mortar suggesting, in the architect's words, "the patterns of a panther's skin," while the house as a whole "is shaded by an ample but lightly poised roof reminiscent of a giant leaf" *(fig. 40)*.[26] Casting aside zoomorphic inaccuracy (the spotted walls recall a cheetah or leopard more than a panther), as well as the fact that none of these animals are indigenous to the area, Schindler's detour into African fantasy leads to a design with a decidedly exotic, even primitive, look to it, while not appearing entirely out of character. The spotted rock walls, for instance, alternatively blend in with the landscape and call attention to themselves. Low-slung (seven feet or less in height) and firmly connected to the earth, the walls create sheltering enclosures that militate against the desert heat and wind, while the broadly fanning, overlapping roof structure provides deep shade. The area between the low walls and soaring roof is extensively glazed, maintaining views of the surrounding landscape and San Jacinto Mountains, while the high open-beamed ceiling prevents the small house from feeling cave-like or cramped *(fig. 41)*. Distinctions between indoors and out are continually blurred, with exterior walls playfully intruding on the interior, and floor and roof planes maintaining continuity on either side of the enclosure *(fig. 42)*.

The plan is equally compelling, as Schindler has devised an ostensibly symmetrical footprint that could be read as a geometricized leaf whose axial roof structure mimics foliar organization *(fig. 43)*. The architect willfully subverts this symmetry in the actual spatial arrangement of the plan as the rooms are laid out independently of the axis. Closer inspection reveals still more complexity, where the placement of load-bearing walls in plan suggests the internal collapse of a T-shaped form split lengthwise and cranked in opposing directions at thirty degrees. The linear apex of the roof

39 Le Corbusier. Villa de Mandrot, Le Pradet, France, 1929–31

40 MARYON E. TOOLE RESIDENCE, Palm Springs, California, 1946–48

41 MARYON E. TOOLE RESIDENCE, Palm Springs, California, 1946–48.
View of living room

42 MARYON E. TOOLE RESIDENCE, Palm Springs,
California, 1946–48. Detail of bedroom.
Photograph by Shirley C. Burden

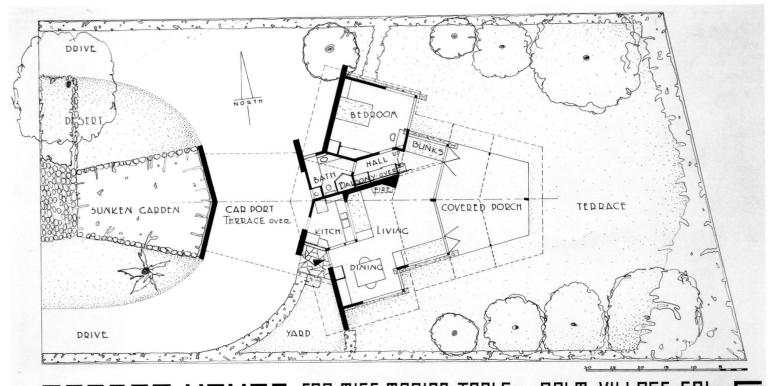

DESERT HOUSE FOR MISS MARIAN TOOLE   PALM VILLAGE CAL.
R.M. SCHINDLER ARCH. 1946 LOS ANGELES CAL. 5

43 MARYON E. TOOLE RESIDENCE, Palm Springs, California, 1946–48

never completely disappears, however, but serves as a constant reminder of the house's distinctive setting, directing one's eyes toward the covered porch and out onto the terrace beyond. The richness of the Toole house shows an architect in full command of his medium, orchestrating a range of architectural concerns toward a fully integrated whole. In this project, Schindler simultaneously addresses site conditions, the evocative power of metaphor and fantasy, and the organizational potential of geometric gamesmanship, not to mention material expression and client taste (Miss Toole had a penchant for non-Western aesthetics) *(fig. 44)* to achieve an exuberantly multi-lingual structure.

By the time of the Toole house, Schindler had explored a wide range of architectural imagery not, it would seem, as practice for gratuitous exoticism or sloppy pastiche, but in an effort to engineer thoughtful harmonies between a building and its environment without regard for prevailing architectural taste. In early works such as the projected Thomas Paul Martin Residence and Log House, he drew upon local, yet widely divergent, traditions for houses in the Southwest and Midwest, respectively. Once in California, he dedicated himself to addressing its enormously varied topography. During this quest he built such idiosyncratic structures as the Kings Road, Von Koerber, Bennati, and Toole houses in suburban, mountain, and desert locales, in addition to beach houses, hillside homes, and numerous urban buildings. Schindler tried his hand at such Californian typologies as the bungalow court [Jacob Korsen Bungalow Court (project), 1921–22] *(fig. 45)*, motor hotel [Highway Bungalow Hotels (project), 1931] *(fig. 46)*, beach club [A. E. Rose Beach Colony (project), 1937], and auto trailer (Trailer Project, 1941–46) *(figs. 47, 48)*, even going tropical with the projected Aloha Hotel (1944–46). His vulnerability to regional exigencies led him far afield to find appropriate architectural solutions, and because of his purposeful meandering his oeuvre can appear erratic. Closer study of some of his most stylistically disparate buildings shows just the opposite: a determined and sustained effort to understand and respond to given conditions. Schindler knew full well that what he had accomplished ran against the grain of the most celebrated movements of contemporary architectural practice, but also that he had created a uniquely regional body of work that could be considered the paradigmatic, classical type for California. While in the hospital being treated for the cancer that would kill him one year later, Schindler reflected on his peculiar relationship to his adopted region, as compared to such peers as Neutra and Wright:

I came to live and work in California. I camped under the open sky, in the redwoods, on the beach, the foothills and the desert. I tested its adobe its granite and its sky. And out of a carefully built up conception of how the human being could grow roots in this soil—unique and delightful—I built my house.

And unless I failed it should be as Californian as the Parthenon is Greek and the Forum Roman. In fact the beginning of a new "classic" growth drinking California sap.[27]

44 "Carpenter Toole," photograph of Maryon E. Toole, date unknown

45 JACOB KORSEN BUNGALOW COURT (project),
Los Angeles, 1921–22. Presentation drawing

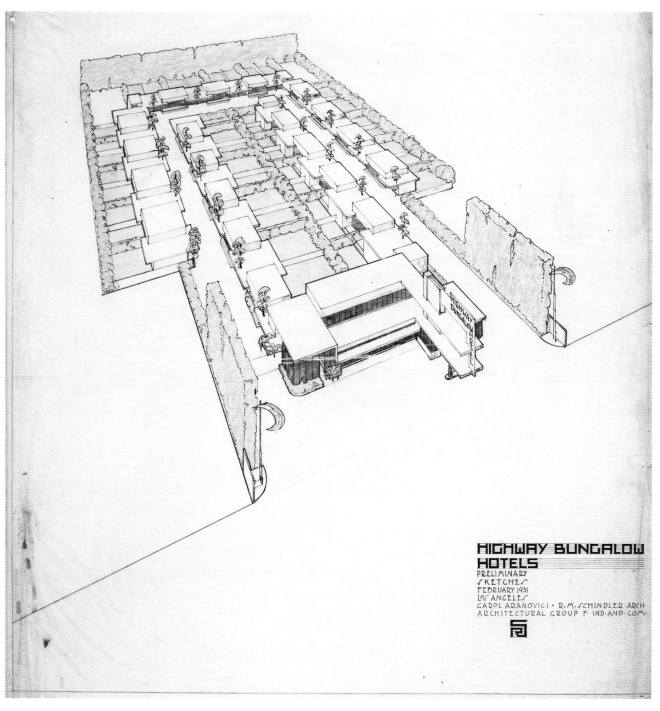

HIGHWAY BUNGALOW
HOTELS
PRELIMINARY
SKETCHES
FEBRUARY 1931
LOS ANGELES
CAROL ARANOVICI · R·M·SCHINDLER·ARCH
ARCHITECTURAL GROUP F· IND·AND·COM·

46 HIGHWAY BUNGALOW HOTELS
(project with AGIC/Carol Aronovici),
location unknown, 1931. Presentation drawing

Notes

1 R. M. Schindler to Arthur Drexler, Curator of Architecture at The Museum of Modern Art, 15 April 1952, Rudolph M. Schindler Collection, Architecture and Design Collection, University Art Museum, University of California, Santa Barbara (hereafter "RMS at ADC/UCSB").

2 Charles Moore, "Schindler: Vulnerable and Powerful," *Progressive Architecture* 54, no. 1 (January 1973): 132, 136.

3 *Ibid.*, 136.

4 *Ibid.*

5 Unpublished document, "Talk on Architecture by Michael Schindler for Creative Class," 4 June 1938, RMS at ADC/UCSB.

6 Schindler's sole European building was the Clubhouse for Actors, built in Vienna in 1912 while he worked as a draftsman for the firm Mayr and Mayer. David Gebhard, *Schindler* (1971; reprint, San Francisco: William Stout, 1997), 12.

7 "The house to be built in one of the vast plains of the West, has to reach the scale of the landscape that means to be either very high or very broad. For this reason the house will be a low stretched mass of adobe walls, with a rather severe expression for the outside." Schindler to Dr. P. T. [*sic*] Martin, 14 December 1915, RMS at ADC/UCSB.

8 *Ibid.*, 3.

9 *Ibid.*, 2.

10 Lionel March, "Log House, *Urhutte* and Temple," in March and Judith Sheine, eds., *R. M. Schindler: Composition and Construction* (London: Academy Editions, 1993), 103.

11 March, 108.

12 *See* Lionel March's thorough history of this house in "Residential Masterpieces: R. M. Schindler," *GA Houses* 56 (April 1998): 32-53, for more information.

13 Schindler to Neutra, October 1921, in Esther McCoy, *Vienna to Los Angeles: Two Journeys* (Santa Monica: Arts + Architecture Press, 1979), 137.

14 From a 1922 description of the house, Kings Road House project files, RMS at ADC/UCSB.

15 Schindler to McCoy, n.d., RMS at ADC/UCSB.

16 I am indebted to architect Thomas Stahl, who translated the mostly German correspondence between Schindler and the Von Koerbers. Letters from 4 and 23 September 1931 suggest Schindler's role in site selection. RMS at ADC/UCSB.

17 Schindler to Mrs. E. M. Von Koerber Boettlicher [*sic*], 4 September 1931, RMS at ADC/UCSB. A specialist in Asian languages, Hans Von Koerber had a dual appointment in the Department of Oriental Studies at the University of Southern California, and as an Associate Curator of Oriental Art at the Los Angeles County Museum of History, Science and Art; the Von Koerbers had an extensive personal collection of Asian art.

18 E. M. Von Koerber-Boetticher to Schindler, 23 September 1931, RMS at ADC/UCSB.

213

19 From Schindler's own architectural summary of the house, RMS at ADC/UCSB.

20 Elizabeth Mock to Schindler, 16 May 1941, RMS at ADC/UCSB.

21 Mock to Schindler, 22 May 1941, RMS at ADC/UCSB.

22 Kenneth Frampton, *Modern Architecture: A Critical History*, 3rd. ed. (London: Thames and Hudson, 1992), 225.

23 Colin St. John Wilson, *The Other Tradition of Modern Architecture: The Uncompleted Project* (London: Academy Editions, 1995), 102-109.

24 *Ibid.*, 109.

25 *Ibid.*, 103.

26 From Schindler's own architectural summary of the house, Box 24/Architectural Writing/Article/Research Material/"House with Sloping Walls ....," Esther McCoy Papers, Archives of American Art, Smithsonian Institution, Washington, D.C.

27 Schindler to Esther McCoy, 4-5, 18 February 1952, Box 26/Architects Files/Correspondence with McCoy/R. M. Schindler, Esther McCoy Papers, Archives of American Art, Smithsonian Institution, Washington, D.C.

47, 48 TRAILER PROJECT (for George S. Gordon Sturdy Built Trailer Company), prototype, 1942. Photographs by Julius Shulman

CHARLES H. WOLFE RESIDENCE, Avalon,
Catalina Island, California, 1928–31

CHECKLIST OF THE EXHIBITION

Note: The Architecture and Design Collection at the University Art Museum, University of California, Santa Barbara, has been abbreviated to "ADC at UCSB."

CREMATORIUM AND CHAPEL FOR
A CITY OF FIVE MILLION (project),
Vienna, 1912-13
Photograph
8 x 10 inches reproduced
ADC at UCSB, CP.1967.100.75.d.2

CREMATORIUM AND CHAPEL FOR
A CITY OF FIVE MILLION (project),
Vienna, 1912-13
Photograph
8 x 10 inches reproduced
ADC at UCSB, CP.1967.100.75.d.3

HOTEL RONG (project),
Vienna, 1912
Photograph
10 x 8 inches reproduced
ADC at UCSB, CP.1967.100.176.d.1

HUNTING LODGE (project),
location unknown, 1912
Photograph
10 x 8 inches reproduced
ADC at UCSB, CP.1967.100.431.d.1

NEIGHBORHOOD CENTER (project),
Chicago, 1914
Pencil, ink, gouache, and watercolor on paper
24 ½ x 14 ½ in.
ADC at UCSB, 1967.100.293.d.3

SUMMER RESIDENCE (project),
Vienna, 1914
Pencil, ink, and gouache on paper
9 x 12 ½ in.
ADC at UCSB, 1967.100.431.d.1

DRAWING OF ADOBE BUILDING,
Taos, New Mexico, 1915
Pencil on paper
14 x 7 ⅝ in.
ADC at UCSB, 1999.57

DRAWING OF ADOBE BUILDING,
Taos, New Mexico, 1915
Pencil on paper
9 ⅞ x 13 ½ in.
ADC at UCSB, 1999.58

R. M. SCHINDLER FOR
OTTENHEIMER, STERN, AND REICHERT
HOTEL (project), Chicago, 1915
Pencil, ink, and gouache on paper on board
19 ½ x 10 ½ in.
ADC at UCSB, 1967.100.506.d.1

PHOTOGRAPH OF ADOBE BUILDING,
Taos, New Mexico, 1915
Photograph by R. M. Schindler
8 x 10 in.
ADC at UCSB, 1967.100.614.1(B)9.p.49

PHOTOGRAPH OF GOVERNOR'S PALACE,
Santa Fe, New Mexico, 1915
Photograph by R. M. Schindler
8 x 10 in.
ADC at UCSB, 1967.100.614.1(B)8.p.5

THOMAS PAUL MARTIN RESIDENCE
(project), Taos, New Mexico, 1915
Pencil, ink, gouache, and gold on paper
15 x 13 in.
ADC at UCSB, 1967.100.265.d.1

THOMAS PAUL MARTIN RESIDENCE
(project), Taos, New Mexico, 1915
Pencil, ink, gouache, and gold on paper
15 x 13 in.
ADC at UCSB, 1967.100.265.d.2

THOMAS PAUL MARTIN RESIDENCE
(project), Taos, New Mexico, 1915
Pencil, ink, gouache, and gold on paper
28 ¾ x 15 ¾ in.
ADC at UCSB, 1967.100.265.d.4

UNIDENTIFIED BAR (project),
Chicago, c. 1915
Pencil and gouache on paper on board
18 ½ x 11 in.
ADC at UCSB, 1967.100.498.d.1

R. M. SCHINDLER FOR
OTTENHEIMER, STERN, AND REICHERT
BUENA SHORE CLUB,
Chicago, 1916–18
Colored ink on paper
15 x 11 in.
ADC at UCSB, 1967.100.48.d.5

R. M. SCHINDLER FOR
OTTENHEIMER, STERN, AND REICHERT
BUENA SHORE CLUB,
Chicago, 1916–18
Pencil, ink, watercolor, and
paint on board
13 ¼ x 10 in.
ADC at UCSB, 1967.100.48.d.11

R. M. SCHINDLER FOR
OTTENHEIMER, STERN, AND REICHERT
BUENA SHORE CLUB,
Chicago, 1916–18
Photograph by R. M. Schindler
10 x 8 in.
ADC at UCSB, 1967.100.48.p.1

R. M. SCHINDLER FOR
OTTENHEIMER, STERN, AND REICHERT
BUENA SHORE CLUB,
Chicago, 1916–18
Photograph by R. M. Schindler
10 x 8 in.
ADC at UCSB, 1967.100.48.p.4

LOG HOUSE (project),
location unknown, 1916–18
Ink and watercolor on linen
12 x 19 in.
ADC at UCSB, 1967.100.246.d.1

LOG HOUSE (project),
location unknown, 1916–18
Ink and watercolor on linen
12 x 19 in.
ADC at UCSB, 1967.100.246.d.5

LOG HOUSE (project),
location unknown, 1916–18
Ink and watercolor on linen
12 x 19 in.
ADC at UCSB, 1967.100.246.d.6

LOG HOUSE (project),
location unknown, 1916–18
Scale model
5¾ x 17½ x 10 in.
Collection of Judith Sheine, Los Angeles

UNIDENTIFIED RESIDENCE (project),
Oak Park, Illinois, c. 1917
Pencil on paper
8½ x 12 in.
ADC at UCSB, 1967.100.511.d.2

UNIDENTIFIED RESIDENCE (project),
Oak Park, Illinois, c. 1917
Pencil on paper
7½ x 14 in.
ADC at UCSB, 1967.100.511.d.3

R. M. SCHINDLER FOR
FRANK LLOYD WRIGHT
MONOLITH HOME (project),
location unknown, 1919
Pencil and ink on paper
12¾ x 12½ in.
ADC at UCSB, 1967.100.285.d.1

R. M. SCHINDLER FOR
FRANK LLOYD WRIGHT
MONOLITH HOME (project),
location unknown, 1919
Pencil and colored pencil on paper
11 x 9½ in.
ADC at UCSB, 1967.100.285.d.4

R. M. SCHINDLER FOR
FRANK LLOYD WRIGHT
J. P. SHAMPAY RESIDENCE
(project), Chicago, 1919
Pencil and colored pencil on paper
25 x 14 in.
ADC at UCSB, 1967.100.396.d.1

R. M. SCHINDLER FOR
FRANK LLOYD WRIGHT
J. P. SHAMPAY RESIDENCE
(project), Chicago, 1919
Pencil and ink on paper
22 x 16¾ in.
ADC at UCSB, 1967.100.396.d.3

R. M. SCHINDLER FOR
FRANK LLOYD WRIGHT
DIRECTOR'S RESIDENCE,
OLIVE HILL, FOR ALINE BARNSDALL,
Los Angeles, 1920
Pencil on paper
16½ x 11½ in.
ADC at UCSB, 1967.100.17.d.1

FREE PUBLIC LIBRARY,
BERGEN BRANCH COMPETITION
(project), Jersey City, New Jersey, 1920
Ink on paper
19 x 15 in.
ADC at UCSB, 1967.100.127.d.1

FREE PUBLIC LIBRARY,
BERGEN BRANCH COMPETITION
(project), Jersey City, New Jersey, 1920
Ink on paper
19 x 15 in.
ADC at UCSB, 1967.100.127.d.2

KINGS ROAD HOUSE,
West Hollywood, California, 1921–22
Pencil and crayon on paper
19½ x 34 in.
ADC at UCSB, 1967.100.213.d.2

KINGS ROAD HOUSE,
West Hollywood, California, 1921–22
Pencil on paper
18 x 19½ in.
ADC at UCSB, 1967.100.213.d.3

KINGS ROAD HOUSE,
West Hollywood, California, 1921–22
Pencil and colored pencil on paper
19½ x 28¼ in.
ADC at UCSB, 1967.100.213.d.15

KINGS ROAD HOUSE,
West Hollywood, California, 1921–22
Pencil, ink, and watercolor on vellum
26 x 10½ in.
ADC at UCSB, 1967.100.213.d.17

KINGS ROAD HOUSE,
West Hollywood, California, 1921–22
Photograph by Ernest M. Pratt
and Viroque Baker
10 x 8 in.
ADC at UCSB, 1967.100.213.p.5

KINGS ROAD HOUSE,
West Hollywood, California, 1921–22
Photograph
8 x 10 in.
ADC at UCSB, 1967.100.213.p.14

KINGS ROAD HOUSE,
West Hollywood, California, 1921–22
Photograph
8 x 10 in.
ADC at UCSB, 1967.100.213.p.16

KINGS ROAD HOUSE,
West Hollywood, California, 1921–22
Photograph of R. M. Schindler, and
Richard and Dione Neutra, c. 1925
8 x 10 in.
Collection of the Friends of the Schindler House

KINGS ROAD HOUSE,
West Hollywood, California, 1921–22
Photograph by Grant Mudford
32 x 40 x 4 in.
Courtesy of Grant Mudford

KINGS ROAD HOUSE,
West Hollywood, California, 1921–22
Photograph by Grant Mudford
16 x 20 in.
Courtesy of Grant Mudford

KINGS ROAD HOUSE,
West Hollywood, California, 1921–22
Photograph by Grant Mudford
16 x 20 in.
Courtesy of Grant Mudford

KINGS ROAD HOUSE,
West Hollywood, California, 1921–22
Photograph by Julius Shulman
8 x 10 in.
Courtesy of Julius Shulman

KINGS ROAD HOUSE BOX CHAIR,
West Hollywood, California, 1921–22
Redwood and canvas
24 x 26 ½ x 28 in.
Collection of the Friends of the Schindler House

KINGS ROAD HOUSE,
West Hollywood, California, 1921–22
Scale model
12 x 32 x 24 in.
Collection of the Friends of the Schindler House

PHILIP LOVELL BEACH HOUSE,
Newport Beach, California, 1922–26
Pencil and ink on vellum
21 x 30 ½ in.
ADC at UCSB, 1967.100.249.d.2

PHILIP LOVELL BEACH HOUSE,
Newport Beach, California, 1922–26
Pencil and ink on vellum
21 x 30 in.
ADC at UCSB, 1967.100.249.d.21

PHILIP LOVELL BEACH HOUSE,
Newport Beach, California, 1922–26
Pencil on paper
7 ½ x 23 ½ in.
ADC at UCSB, 1967.100.239.d.26

PHILIP LOVELL BEACH HOUSE,
Newport Beach, California, 1922–26
Photograph
10 x 8 in.
ADC at UCSB, 1967.100.249.p.2

PHILIP LOVELL BEACH HOUSE,
Newport Beach, California, 1922–26
Photograph
8 x 10 in.
ADC at UCSB, 1967.100.249.p.4

PHILIP LOVELL BEACH HOUSE,
Newport Beach, California, 1922–26
Photograph by R. M. Schindler
8 x 10 in.
ADC at UCSB, 1967.100.249.p.10

PHILIP LOVELL BEACH HOUSE
END TABLE/STOOL,
Newport Beach, California, 1922–26
Plywood, built in 1996
16 x 17 x 15 in.
Courtesy Modernica, Los Angeles

PHILIP LOVELL BEACH HOUSE
LOUNGE CHAIR,
Newport Beach, California, 1922–26
Plywood and upholstery, built in 1996
24 ⅛ x 32 x 32 in.
Courtesy Modernica, Los Angeles

PHILIP LOVELL BEACH HOUSE
STANDING LAMP,
Newport Beach, California, 1922–26
Plywood and glass
57 ¾ x 12 x 4 in.
Collection of Dr. Bobby Lovell

CHARLES P. LOWES RESIDENCE,
Los Angeles, 1923
Pencil on paper
21 x 13½ in.
ADC at UCSB, 1967.100.253.d.7

CHARLES P. LOWES RESIDENCE,
Los Angeles, 1923
Ink and pencil on linen
28 x 34 ½ in.
ADC at UCSB, 1967.100.253.d.11

CHARLES P. LOWES RESIDENCE,
Los Angeles, 1923
Photograph by Viroque Baker
8 x 10 in.
ADC at UCSB, 1967.100.253.p.1

CHARLES P. LOWES RESIDENCE,
Los Angeles, 1923
Photograph
8 x 10 in.
ADC at UCSB, 1967.100.253.p.4

CHARLES P. LOWES RESIDENCE,
Los Angeles, 1923
Photograph by Marvin Rand
8 x 10 in.
Courtesy Marvin Rand

PUEBLO RIBERA COURTS FOR
W. LLEWELLYN LLOYD,
La Jolla, California, 1923–25
Ink and colored pencil on paper
18 ½ x 12 in.
ADC at UCSB, 1967.100.340.d.3

PUEBLO RIBERA COURTS FOR
W. LLEWELLYN LLOYD,
La Jolla, California, 1923–25
Pencil and ink on linen
24 x 27 in.
ADC at UCSB, 1967.100.340.d.4

PUEBLO RIBERA COURTS FOR
W. LLEWELLYN LLOYD,
La Jolla, California, 1923–25
Pencil and ink on paper on linen
20½ x 33½ in.
ADC at UCSB, 1967.100.340.d.5

PUEBLO RIBERA COURTS FOR
W. LLEWELLYN LLOYD,
La Jolla, California, 1923–25
Photograph by R. M. Schindler
10 x 8 in.
ADC at UCSB, 1967.100.340.p.5

PUEBLO RIBERA COURTS FOR
W. LLEWELLYN LLOYD,
La Jolla, California, 1923–25
Photograph by David Gebhard
10 x 8 in.
ADC at UCSB, 1967.100.340.p.23

PUEBLO RIBERA COURTS FOR
W. LLEWELLYN LLOYD,
La Jolla, California, 1923–25
Photograph by R. M. Schindler
8 x 10 in.
ADC at UCSB

PUEBLO RIBERA COURTS FOR
W. LLEWELLYN LLOYD,
La Jolla, California, 1923–25
Photograph by Marvin Rand
10 x 8 in.
Courtesy of Marvin Rand

PUEBLO RIBERA COURTS FOR
W. LLEWELLYN LLOYD,
La Jolla, California, 1923–25
Scale model, built in 2000
57 ½ x 44 x 48 ¼ in.
The Museum of Contemporary Art,
Los Angeles

GOULD & BANDINI
WORKMEN'S COLONY (project),
Los Angeles, 1924
Ink and colored pencil on vellum
17 x 7 in.
ADC at UCSB, 1967.100.146.d.2

HARRIMAN'S COLONY (project),
San Gabriel, California, 1924–25
Pencil, ink, and colored pencil on vellum
20 x 36 ½ in.
ADC at UCSB, 1967.100.156.d.9

JOHN COOPER PACKARD RESIDENCE,
South Pasadena, California, 1924
Pencil and ink on paper
21 x 31 in.
ADC at UCSB, 1967.100.316.d.4

JOHN COOPER PACKARD RESIDENCE,
South Pasadena, California, 1924
Ink and pencil on paper on linen
20 ½ x 40 in.
ADC at UCSB, 1967.100.316.d.5

JOHN COOPER PACKARD RESIDENCE,
South Pasadena, California, 1924
Ink on paper
29 x 40 ¼ in.
ADC at UCSB, 1967.100.316.d.6

JOHN COOPER PACKARD RESIDENCE,
South Pasadena, California, 1924
Photograph by Viroque Baker
10 x 8 in.
ADC at UCSB, 1967.100.316.p.9

JOHN COOPER PACKARD RESIDENCE,
South Pasadena, California, 1924
Photograph by Viroque Baker
10 x 8 in.
ADC at UCSB, 1967.100.316.p.13

JOHN COOPER PACKARD RESIDENCE,
South Pasadena, California, 1924
Scale model, built in 1999
20 ⅛ x 38 ¾ x 20 in.
The Museum of Contemporary Art,
Los Angeles

JAMES EADS HOW RESIDENCE,
Los Angeles, 1925–26
Pencil and ink on paper on linen
62 ¼ x 20 ½ in.
ADC at UCSB, 1967.100.177.d.1

JAMES EADS HOW RESIDENCE,
Los Angeles, 1925–26
Pencil and ink on paper on linen
62 ½ x 20 ½ in.
ADC at UCSB, 1967.100.177.d.2

JAMES EADS HOW RESIDENCE,
Los Angeles, 1925–26
Pencil on paper
15 x 18 in.
ADC at UCSB, 1967.100.177.d.18

JAMES EADS HOW RESIDENCE,
Los Angeles, 1925–26
Photograph by Viroque Baker
8 x 10 in.
ADC at UCSB, 1967.100.177.p.3

JAMES EADS HOW RESIDENCE,
Los Angeles, 1925–26
Photograph by Viroque Baker
10 x 8 in.
ADC at UCSB, 1967.100.177.p.4

JAMES EADS HOW RESIDENCE,
Los Angeles, 1925–26
Photograph by Grant Mudford
16 x 20 in.
Courtesy of Grant Mudford

JAMES EADS HOW RESIDENCE,
Los Angeles, 1925–26
Photograph by Grant Mudford
24 x 30 x 4 in.
Courtesy of Grant Mudford

JAMES EADS HOW RESIDENCE,
Los Angeles, 1925–26
Scale model, built in 1999
41 x 30 x 35 in.
The Museum of Contemporary Art,
Los Angeles

R. M. SCHINDLER AND RICHARD NEUTRA
LEAGUE OF NATIONS BUILDING (project),
Geneva, Switzerland, 1926
Pencil on tracing paper
8 x 18 ¾ in.
University of California Los Angeles Library,
Special Collections Department

R. M. SCHINDLER AND RICHARD NEUTRA
LEAGUE OF NATIONS BUILDING (project),
Geneva, Switzerland, 1926
Pencil on tracing paper
21 x 30 ¼ in.
University of California Los Angeles Library,
Special Collections Department

R. M. SCHINDLER AND RICHARD NEUTRA
LEAGUE OF NATIONS BUILDING (project),
Geneva, Switzerland, 1926
Pencil on tracing paper
8 x 16 ½ in.
University of California Los Angeles Library,
Special Collections Department

R. M. SCHINDLER AND RICHARD NEUTRA
LEAGUE OF NATIONS BUILDING (project),
Geneva, Switzerland, 1926
Pencil on tracing paper
4 ½ x 10 ½ in.
University of California Los Angeles Library,
Special Collections Department

219 R. M. SCHINDLER AND RICHARD NEUTRA
LEAGUE OF NATIONS BUILDING (project),
Geneva, Switzerland, 1926
Pencil and ink on paper
35½ x 45½ in.
University of California Los Angeles Library,
Special Collections Department

R. M. SCHINDLER AND RICHARD NEUTRA
LEAGUE OF NATIONS BUILDING (project),
Geneva, Switzerland, 1926
Limewood, cardboard, and plastic scale model,
built in 1994
19½ x 48¼ x 43½ in.
Collection of Architektur Zentrum, Vienna

R. M. SCHINDLER WITH AGIC
LEAH-RUTH GARMENT SHOP,
Long Beach, California, 1926
Pencil on paper
15 x 12 in.
ADC at UCSB, 1967.100.229.d.1

R. M. SCHINDLER WITH AGIC
LEAH-RUTH GARMENT SHOP,
Long Beach, California, 1926
Photograph
10 x 8 in.
ADC at UCSB, 1967.100.229.p.1

ALINE BARNSDALL
TRANSLUCENT HOUSE (project),
Palos Verdes, California, 1927–28
Pencil, watercolor, and colored pencil on
blueline print
17 x 28 in.
ADC at UCSB, 1967.100.25.d.23

ALINE BARNSDALL
TRANSLUCENT HOUSE (project),
Palos Verdes, California, 1927–28
Pencil, ink, watercolor, crayon, and
colored pencil on board
26 x 31½ in.
ADC at UCSB, 1967.100.25.d.28

R. M. SCHINDLER WITH AGIC
HENRY BRAXTON AND VIOLA
BROTHERS SHORE RESIDENCE
(project), Venice, California, 1928
Pencil, watercolor, and paint on linen
25 x 29 in.
ADC at UCSB, 1967.100.40.d.12

R. M. SCHINDLER WITH AGIC
HENRY BRAXTON AND VIOLA
BROTHERS SHORE RESIDENCE
(project), Venice, California, 1928
Ink and pencil on linen
30 x 18 in.
ADC at UCSB, 1967.100.40.d.13

HENRY BRAXTON GALLERY,
Los Angeles, 1928–29
Ink on linen
11 x 28 in.
ADC at UCSB, 1967.100.39.d.2

HENRY BRAXTON GALLERY,
Los Angeles, 1928–29
Photograph
10 x 8 in.
ADC at UCSB, 1967.100.39.p.2

HENRY BRAXTON GALLERY,
Los Angeles, 1928–29
Photograph by Viroque Baker
10 x 8 in.
ADC at UCSB, 1967.100.39.p.4

CHARLES H. WOLFE RESIDENCE,
Avalon, Catalina Island, California,
1928–31
Ink on linen
39 x 26 in.
ADC at UCSB, 1967.100.477.d.1

CHARLES H. WOLFE RESIDENCE,
Avalon, Catalina Island, California,
1928–31
Pencil and ink on paper
20½ x 30 in.
ADC at UCSB, 1967.100.477.d.14

CHARLES H. WOLFE RESIDENCE,
Avalon, Catalina Island, California,
1928–31
Pencil, ink, colored pencil, and
watercolor on paper
32½ x 18 in.
ADC at UCSB, 1967.100.477.d.24

CHARLES H. WOLFE RESIDENCE,
Avalon, Catalina Island, California,
1928–31
Photograph
10 x 8 in.
ADC at UCSB, 1967.100.477.p.4

CHARLES H. WOLFE RESIDENCE,
Avalon, Catalina Island, California,
1928–31
Photograph
8 x 10 in.
ADC at UCSB, 1967.100.477.p.13

CHARLES H. WOLFE RESIDENCE
STANDING LAMP,
Avalon, Catalina Island, California,
1928–31
Redwood and glass, reproduced in 1990
48 x 25½ x 16 in.
Collection of Robert Nicolais

CHARLES H. WOLFE RESIDENCE,
Avalon, Catalina Island, California,
1928–31
Plywood model by R. M. Schindler
36 x 24 x 24 in.
Collection of Friends of the Schindler House

R. M. SCHINDLER WITH AGIC
LAVANA STUDIO BUILDING (project),
Beverly Hills, California, 1929–30
Pencil, ink, colored pencil, and
watercolor on vellum
13 x 11 in.
ADC at UCSB, 1967.100.228.d.1

PARK MODERNE MODEL CABINS FOR
WILLIAM LINGENBRINK,
Calabasas, California, 1929–38
Pencil, colored pencil, and ink on paper
19¼ x 17 in.
ADC at UCSB, 1967.100.323.d.1

PARK MODERNE MODEL CABINS FOR
WILLIAM LINGENBRINK,
Calabasas, California, 1929–38
Pencil on paper
21 x 18 ½ in.
ADC at UCSB, 1967.100.323.d.4

PARK MODERNE MODEL CABINS FOR
WILLIAM LINGENBRINK,
Calabasas, California, 1929–38
Photograph
8 x 10 in.
ADC at UCSB, 1967.100.323.p.1

PARK MODERNE MODEL CABINS FOR
WILLIAM LINGENBRINK,
Calabasas, California, 1929–38
Promotional brochure
10 x 8 in.
ADC at UCSB, Project Files,
Park Moderne Model Cabins

R. M. SCHINDLER WITH
AGIC/CAROL ARONOVICI
HIGHWAY BUNGALOW HOTELS (project),
location unknown, 1931
Pencil, ink, lead white, and colored pencil on
linen
33 ½ x 30 in.
ADC at UCSB, 1967.100.165.d.1

HANS N. VON KOERBER RESIDENCE,
Torrance, California, 1931–32
Ink on paper
30 ¼ x 21 in.
ADC at UCSB, 1967.100.457.d.2

HANS N. VON KOERBER RESIDENCE,
Torrance, California, 1931–32
Ink on paper
21 x 31 in.
ADC at UCSB, 1967.100.457.d.3

HANS N. VON KOERBER RESIDENCE,
Torrance, California, 1931–32
Photograph
8 x 10 in.
ADC at UCSB, 1967.100.374.p.12

HANS N. VON KOERBER RESIDENCE,
Torrance, California, 1931–32
Photograph
8 x 10 in.
ADC at UCSB, 1967.100.457.p.14

HANS N. VON KOERBER RESIDENCE,
Torrance, California, 1931–32
Photograph by Marvin Rand
10 x 8 in.
Courtesy of Marvin Rand

SARDI'S RESTAURANT REMODELING
FOR A. EDDIE BRANDSTATTER,
Los Angeles, 1932–34
Pencil, ink, colored pencil, and
watercolor on linen
37 ½ x 21 in.
ADC at UCSB, 1967.100.374.d.1

SARDI'S RESTAURANT REMODELING
FOR A. EDDIE BRANDSTATTER,
Los Angeles, 1932–34
Photograph
8 x 10 in.
ADC at UCSB, 1967.100.374.p.2

SARDI'S RESTAURANT REMODELING
FOR A. EDDIE BRANDSTATTER,
Los Angeles, 1932–34
Photograph by Mott Studios
8 x 10 in.
ADC at UCSB, 1967.100.374.p.9

SARDI'S RESTAURANT REMODELING
FOR A. EDDIE BRANDSTATTER CHAIR,
Los Angeles, 1932–34
Anodized aluminum, rubber, and upholstery
34 ½ x 24 ½ x 24 ½ in.
Collection of Michael and Gabrielle Boyd

LINDY'S RESTAURANT,
Los Angeles, 1932–34
Ink on paper
11 ½ x 33 ½ in.
ADC at UCSB, 1967.100.240.d.12

LINDY'S RESTAURANT,
Los Angeles, 1932–34
Photograph
8 x 10 in.
ADC at UCSB, 1967.100.240.p.1

STANDARD OIL COMPANY
SERVICE STATION (project),
location unknown, 1932
Pencil and colored pencil on paper
20 x 28 ¼ in.
ADC at UCSB, 1967.100.421.d.1

UNION OIL COMPANY SERVICE STATION
(project), location unknown, 1932–34
Pencil, colored pencil, and silver-toned tempera
on paper
19 x 30 in.
ADC at UCSB, 1967.100.450.d.7

WILLIAM E. OLIVER RESIDENCE,
Los Angeles, 1933–34
Pencil, ink, colored pencil, and
gouache on linen
21 ½ x 25 ½ in.
ADC at UCSB, 1967.100.304.d.2

WILLIAM E. OLIVER RESIDENCE,
Los Angeles, 1933–34
Photograph
10 x 8 in.
ADC at UCSB, 1967.100.304.p.6

WILLIAM E. OLIVER RESIDENCE,
Los Angeles, 1933–34
Photograph by Axel F. Fog
8 x 10 in.
ADC at UCSB, 1967.100.304.p.10

WILLIAM E. OLIVER RESIDENCE,
Los Angeles, 1933–34
Photograph
8 x 10 in.
ADC at UCSB, 1967.100.304.p.18

WILLIAM E. OLIVER RESIDENCE,
Los Angeles, 1933–34
Scale model
14 x 25 ⅜ x 33 in.
Architektur Museum,
Technische Universität, Munich

221 SCHINDLER SHELTERS (project),
Los Angeles, 1933–39
Ink on paper
21 x 23 ½ in.
ADC at UCSB, 1967.100.384.d.6

SCHINDLER SHELTERS (project),
Los Angeles, 1933–39
Blueline print
16 ½ x 33 in.
ADC at UCSB, 1967.100.384.d.9

A. GISELA BENNATI CABIN,
Lake Arrowhead, California,
1934–37
Pencil on vellum
18 ½ x 22 in.
ADC at UCSB, 1967.100.26.d.1

A. GISELA BENNATI CABIN,
Lake Arrowhead, California,
1934–37
Ink, pencil, and crayon on paper
21 x 23 ½ in.
ADC at UCSB, 1967.100.26.d.2

A. GISELA BENNATI CABIN,
Lake Arrowhead, California,
1934–37
Pencil on paper
14 ½ x 21 in.
ADC at UCSB, 1967.100.26.d.14

A. GISELA BENNATI CABIN,
Lake Arrowhead, California,
1934–37
Photograph by W. P. Woodcock
10 x 8 in.
ADC at UCSB, 1967.100.26.p.1

A. GISELA BENNATI CABIN,
Lake Arrowhead, California,
1934–37
Photograph by W. P. Woodcock
8 x 10 in.
ADC at UCSB, 1967.100.26.p.4

JOHN J. BUCK RESIDENCE,
Los Angeles, 1934
Pencil on paper
21 ½ x 29 ½ in.
ADC at UCSB, 1967.100.47.d.12

JOHN J. BUCK RESIDENCE,
Los Angeles, 1934
Ink on paper
19 x 17 in.
ADC at UCSB, 1967.100.47.d.19

JOHN J. BUCK RESIDENCE,
Los Angeles, 1934
Photograph by Grant Mudford
16 x 20 in.
Courtesy of Grant Mudford

JOHN J. BUCK RESIDENCE,
Los Angeles, 1934
Photograph by Julius Shulman
8 x 10 in.
Courtesy of Julius Shulman

ELIZABETH VAN PATTEN RESIDENCE,
Los Angeles, 1934–36
Pencil on paper
21 x 31 in.
ADC at UCSB, 1967.100.454.d.16

ELIZABETH VAN PATTEN RESIDENCE,
Los Angeles, 1934–36
Ink on paper
14 x 25 ½ in.
ADC at UCSB, 1967.100.454.d.18

ELIZABETH VAN PATTEN RESIDENCE,
Los Angeles, 1934–36
Photograph by W. P. Woodcock
8 x 10 in.
ADC at UCSB, 1967.100.454.p.12

ELIZABETH VAN PATTEN RESIDENCE,
Los Angeles, 1934–36
Photograph by Julius Shulman
8 x 10 in.
Courtesy of Julius Shulman

ELIZABETH VAN PATTEN RESIDENCE,
Los Angeles, 1934–36
Photograph by Julius Shulman
10 x 8 in.
Courtesy of Julius Shulman

ELIZABETH VAN PATTEN RESIDENCE
DINING CHAIR, Los Angeles, 1934–36
Wood, metal, and carpeting, restored 1996
34 x 24 ½ x 24 ½ in.
ADC at UCSB, Gift of John E. Beach Estate

ELIZABETH VAN PATTEN RESIDENCE
UNIT CHAIR, Los Angeles, 1934–36
Wood, metal, and upholstery
28 x 36 x 33 ½ in.
ADC at UCSB

JOHN DEKEYSER DOUBLE RESIDENCE,
Los Angeles, 1935
Pencil on paper
21 x 24 ½ in.
ADC at UCSB, 1967.100.80.d.1

JOHN DEKEYSER DOUBLE RESIDENCE,
Los Angeles, 1935
Ink on paper
15 ¼ x 21 in.
ADC at UCSB, 1967.100.80.d.13

JOHN DEKEYSER DOUBLE RESIDENCE,
Los Angeles, 1935
Photograph by Grant Mudford
20 x 16 in.
Courtesy of Grant Mudford

JOHN DEKEYSER DOUBLE RESIDENCE,
Los Angeles, 1935
Photograph by Grant Mudford
30 x 24 x 4 in.
Courtesy of Grant Mudford

PANEL-POST METHOD (project),
1935–42
Ink on paper
34 ¼ x 20 ¾ in.
ADC at UCSB, 1967.100.319.d.2

PANEL-POST METHOD (project),
1935–42
Ink on paper
21 x 31 in.
ADC at UCSB, 1967.100.319.d.3

RALPH G. WALKER RESIDENCE,
Los Angeles, 1935–41
Pencil, ink, and colored crayon
on brownline print
27 ¼ x 17 ¼ in.
ADC at UCSB, 1967.100.459.d.24

RALPH G. WALKER RESIDENCE,
Los Angeles, 1935–41
Photograph by Grant Mudford
30 x 24 x 4 in.
Courtesy of Grant Mudford

RALPH G. WALKER RESIDENCE,
Los Angeles, 1935–41
Photograph by Julius Shulman
8 x 10 in.
Courtesy of Julius Shulman

RALPH G. WALKER RESIDENCE,
Los Angeles, 1935–41
Photograph by Julius Shulman
8 x 10 in.
Courtesy of Julius Shulman

RALPH G. WALKER RESIDENCE,
Los Angeles, 1935–41
Photograph by Julius Shulman
10 x 8 in.
Courtesy of Julius Shulman

GUY C. WILSON RESIDENCE,
Los Angeles, 1935–38
Pencil and gouache on paper
32 ¼ x 24 in.
ADC at UCSB, 1967.100.474.d.1

GUY C. WILSON RESIDENCE,
Los Angeles, 1935–38
Photograph
8 x 10 in.
ADC at UCSB, 1967.100.474.p.7

GUY C. WILSON RESIDENCE,
Los Angeles, 1935–38
Photograph by Grant Mudford
20 x 16 in.
Courtesy of Grant Mudford

GUY C. WILSON RESIDENCE
COFFEE/COCKTAIL TABLE,
Los Angeles, 1935–38
Wood and glass
14 ½ x 38 x 38 in.
Collection of Richard Guy Wilson

GUY C. WILSON RESIDENCE
DINING CHAIR,
Los Angeles, 1935–38
Wood and carpeting
30 x 18 x 21 in.
Collection of Richard Guy Wilson

GUY C. WILSON RESIDENCE,
Los Angeles, 1935–38
Scale model
17 ⅛ x 24 ⅝ x 35 in.
Architektur Museum,
Technische Universität, Munich

WARSHAW RESIDENCE (project),
Los Angeles, 1936–37
Pencil, pastel, and gouache
on paper on board
20 x 30 in.
ADC at UCSB, 1967.100.463.d.1

WARSHAW RESIDENCE (project),
Los Angeles, 1936–37
Pencil on paper
32 x 21 ½ in.
ADC at UCSB, 1967.100.463.d.3

WARSHAW RESIDENCE (project),
Los Angeles, 1936–37
Scale model
16 ⅝ x 22 x 25 ¼ in.
Architektur Museum,
Technische Universität, Munich

A. E. ROSE BEACH COLONY (project),
Santa Monica, California, 1937
Pencil and colored pencils on paper
17 x 32 ½ in.
ADC at UCSB, 1967.100.354.d.1

A. E. ROSE BEACH COLONY (project),
Santa Monica, California, 1937
Pencil on paper
21 x 32 ½ in.
ADC at UCSB, 1967.100.354.d.5

A. E. ROSE BEACH COLONY (project)
PROTOTYPICAL UNIT (built in West
Hollywood), Santa Monica, California, 1937
Photograph by Julius Shulman
8 x 10 in.
Courtesy of Julius Shulman

A. AND LUBY BUBESHKO APARTMENTS,
Los Angeles, 1938–41
Pencil on paper
21 x 35 in.
ADC at UCSB, 1967.100.46.d.1

A. AND LUBY BUBESHKO APARTMENTS,
Los Angeles, 1938–41
Photograph by Julius Shulman
8 x 10 in.
Courtesy of Julius Shulman

A. AND LUBY BUBESHKO APARTMENTS,
Los Angeles, 1938–41
Photograph by Julius Shulman
8 x 10 in.
Courtesy of Julius Shulman

MILDRED SOUTHALL RESIDENCE
AND STUDIO,
Los Angeles, 1938–39
Pencil on blackline print
22 x 17 ¼ in.
ADC at UCSB, 1967.100.416.d.1

MILDRED SOUTHALL RESIDENCE
AND STUDIO,
Los Angeles, 1938–39
Pencil on paper
21 x 32 ⅝ in.
ADC at UCSB, 1967.100.416.d.6

223 MILDRED SOUTHALL RESIDENCE
AND STUDIO,
Los Angeles, 1938–39
Photograph by Maynard Parker
8 x 10 in.
ADC at UCSB, 1967.100.416.p.1

MILDRED SOUTHALL RESIDENCE
AND STUDIO,
Los Angeles, 1938–39
Photograph
10 x 8 in.
ADC at UCSB, 1967.100.416.p.12

JOSÉ RODRIGUEZ RESIDENCE,
Glendale, California, 1940–42
Pencil on paper
17 x 24 ½ in.
ADC at UCSB, 1967.100.353.d.2

JOSÉ RODRIGUEZ RESIDENCE,
Glendale, California, 1940–42
Pencil on paper
21 x 33 in.
ADC at UCSB, 1967.100.353.d.4

JOSÉ RODRIGUEZ RESIDENCE,
Glendale, California, 1940–42
Pencil on paper
21 x 18 ½ in.
ADC at UCSB, 1967.100.353.d.8

JOSÉ RODRIGUEZ RESIDENCE,
Glendale, California, 1940–42
Photograph by Grant Mudford
24 x 30 x 4 in.
Courtesy of Grant Mudford

JOSÉ RODRIGUEZ RESIDENCE,
Glendale, California, 1940–42
Photograph by Marvin Rand
8 x 10 in.
Courtesy of Marvin Rand

TRAILER PROJECT (for George S. Gordon
Sturdy Built Trailer Company), 1942–46
Photograph by Julius Shulman
10 x 8 in.
Courtesy of Julius Shulman

TRAILER PROJECT (for George S. Gordon
Sturdy Built Trailer Company), 1942–46
Photograph by Julius Shulman
8 x 10 in.
Courtesy of Julius Shulman

T. FALK APARTMENTS (project),
Los Angeles, 1943
Pencil on paper
21 x 30 ¾ in.
ADC at UCSB, 1967.100.108.d.2

T. FALK APARTMENTS (project),
Los Angeles, 1943
Ink on paper
21 ⅛ x 26 ¾ in.
ADC at UCSB, 1967.100.108.d.11

T. FALK APARTMENTS (project),
Los Angeles, 1943
Pencil on paper
21 x 26 in.
ADC at UCSB, 1967.100.108.d.12

BETHLEHEM BAPTIST CHURCH,
Los Angeles, 1944–45
Pencil on paper
18 ½ x 29 ½ in.
ADC at UCSB, 1967.100.28.d.7

BETHLEHEM BAPTIST CHURCH,
Los Angeles, 1944–45
Ink on paper
30 ¼ x 21 in.
ADC at UCSB, 1967.100.28.d.23

BETHLEHEM BAPTIST CHURCH,
Los Angeles, 1944–45
Photograph by Julius Shulman
8 x 10 in.
Courtesy of Julius Shulman

BETHLEHEM BAPTIST CHURCH,
Los Angeles, 1944–45
Photograph by Julius Shulman
8 x 10 in.
Courtesy of Julius Shulman

BETHLEHEM BAPTIST CHURCH,
Los Angeles, 1944–45
Scale model
15 x 28 ¾ x 42 ⅝ in.
Architektur Museum,
Technische Universität, Munich

LAURELWOOD APARTMENTS FOR HENRY
G. SCHICK AND MAXIM H. BRADEN,
Studio City, California, 1945–49
Colored pencil on paper
19 x 36 ⅛ in.
ADC at UCSB, 1967.100.226.d.36

LAURELWOOD APARTMENTS FOR HENRY
G. SCHICK AND MAXIM H. BRADEN,
Studio City, California, 1945–49
Photograph by Lotte Nossaman
8 x 10 in.
ADC at UCSB, 1967.100.226.p.1

LAURELWOOD APARTMENTS FOR HENRY
G. SCHICK AND MAXIM H. BRADEN,
Studio City, California, 1945–49
Photograph by Lotte Nossaman
8 x 10 in.
ADC at UCSB, 1967.100.226.p.9

MAURICE KALLIS RESIDENCE
AND STUDIO,
Studio City, California, 1946–48
Pencil on paper
21 x 43 in.
ADC at UCSB, 1967.100.197.d.9

MAURICE KALLIS RESIDENCE
AND STUDIO,
Studio City, California, 1946–48
Photograph by Robert C. Cleveland
8 x 10 in.
ADC at UCSB, 1967.100.197.p.2

MAURICE KALLIS RESIDENCE
AND STUDIO,
Studio City, California, 1946–48
Photograph by Robert C. Cleveland
8 x 10 in.
ADC at UCSB, 1967.100.197.p.3

MAURICE KALLIS RESIDENCE
AND STUDIO,
Studio City, California, 1946–48
Photograph by Robert C. Cleveland
8 x 10 in.
ADC at UCSB, 1967.100.197.p.7

MAURICE KALLIS RESIDENCE
AND STUDIO,
Studio City, California, 1946–48
Scale model, built in 2000
29 ½ x 70 x 26 in.
The Museum of Contemporary Art,
Los Angeles

RICHARD LECHNER RESIDENCE,
Studio City, California, 1946–48
Pencil and ink on vellum
21 x 40 ½ in.
ADC at UCSB, 1967.100.230.d.1

RICHARD LECHNER RESIDENCE,
Studio City, California, 1946–48
Pencil and colored pencil on blackline print
20 ½ x 37 in.
ADC at UCSB, 1967.100.230.d.4

RICHARD LECHNER RESIDENCE,
Studio City, California, 1946–48
Pencil on paper
18 x 23 in.
ADC at UCSB, 1967.100.230.d.13

RICHARD LECHNER RESIDENCE,
Studio City, California, 1946–48
Photograph by Robert A. Lodder
8 x 10 in.
ADC at UCSB, 1967.100.230.p.8

RICHARD LECHNER RESIDENCE,
Studio City, California, 1946–48
Photograph by Robert C. Cleveland
10 x 8 in.
ADC at UCSB, 1967.100.230.p.16

RICHARD LECHNER RESIDENCE
DINING CHAIR,
Studio City, California, 1946–48
Plywood and upholstery
31 x 15 x 23 ¾ in.
ADC at UCSB

MARYON E. TOOLE RESIDENCE,
Palm Springs, California, 1946–48
Ink on vellum
21 x 38 in.
ADC at UCSB, 1967.100.442.d.1

MARYON E. TOOLE RESIDENCE,
Palm Springs, California, 1946–48
Pencil on paper
21 x 39 ½ in.
ADC at UCSB, 1967.100.442.d.6

MARYON E. TOOLE RESIDENCE,
Palm Springs, California, 1946–48
Photograph by Shirley C. Burden
10 x 8 in.
ADC at UCSB, 1967.100.442.p.4

MARYON E. TOOLE RESIDENCE,
Palm Springs, California, 1946–48
Photograph
8 x 10 in.
ADC at UCSB, 1967.100.442.p.6

MARYON E. TOOLE RESIDENCE,
Palm Springs, California, 1946–48
Photograph by Shirley C. Burden
10 x 8 in.
Archives of American Art, Smithsonian
Institution, Washington, D.C.

MARYON E. TOOLE RESIDENCE,
Palm Springs, California, 1946–48
Scale model, built in 2000
21 x 61 ½ x 25 ½ in.
The Museum of Contemporary Art,
Los Angeles

ELLEN JANSON RESIDENCE,
Los Angeles, 1948–49
Pencil on vellum
21 x 31 ½ in.
ADC at UCSB, 1967.100.192.d.2

ELLEN JANSON RESIDENCE,
Los Angeles, 1948–49
Photograph by Lotte Nossaman
10 x 8 in.
ADC at UCSB, 1967.100.192.p.19

ELLEN JANSON RESIDENCE,
Los Angeles, 1948–49
Photograph
8 x 10 in.
ADC at UCSB, 1967.100.192.p.20

ELLEN JANSON RESIDENCE,
Los Angeles, 1948–49
Scale model, built in 1998
48 x 32 x 32 in.
The Museum of Contemporary Art,
Los Angeles

ADOLPH TISCHLER RESIDENCE,
Los Angeles, 1949–50
Ink on linen
40 x 31 in.
ADC at UCSB, 1967.100.440.d.1

ADOLPH TISCHLER RESIDENCE,
Los Angeles, 1949–50
Pencil on paper
21 x 28 ½ in.
ADC at UCSB, 1967.100.440.d.6

ADOLPH TISCHLER RESIDENCE,
Los Angeles, 1949–50
Photograph by Grant Mudford
16 x 20 in.
Courtesy of Grant Mudford

ADOLPH TISCHLER RESIDENCE,
Los Angeles, 1949–50
Photograph by Grant Mudford
16 x 20 in.
Courtesy of Grant Mudford

ADOLPH TISCHLER RESIDENCE,
Los Angeles, 1949–50
Photograph by Grant Mudford
24 x 30 x 4 in.
Courtesy of Grant Mudford

225 ADOLPH TISCHLER RESIDENCE,
Los Angeles, 1949–50
Scale model, built in 2000
26¼ x 17 x 48 in.
The Museum of Contemporary Art,
Los Angeles

MAURICE RIES RESIDENCE,
Los Angeles, 1950–52
Pencil on paper
21 x 22½ in.
ADC at UCSB, 1967.100.349.d.1

MAURICE RIES RESIDENCE,
Los Angeles, 1950–52
Pencil on paper
21 x 21½ in.
ADC at UCSB, 1967.100.349.d.28

MAURICE RIES RESIDENCE,
Los Angeles, 1950–52
Photograph by Lotte Nossaman
10 x 8 in.
ADC at UCSB, 1967.100.349.p.1

MAURICE RIES RESIDENCE,
Los Angeles, 1950–52
Photograph by Lotte Nossaman
8 x 10 in.
ADC at UCSB, 1967.100.349.p.2

MAURICE RIES RESIDENCE,
Los Angeles, 1950–52
Photograph by Lotte Nossaman
8 x 10 in.
ADC at UCSB, 1967.100.349.p.3

SAMUEL SKOLNIK RESIDENCE,
Los Angeles, 1950–52
Pencil on vellum
21 x 40 in.
ADC at UCSB, 1967.100.404.d.13

SAMUEL SKOLNIK RESIDENCE,
Los Angeles, 1950–52
Photograph by Lotte Nossaman
8 x 10 in.
ADC at UCSB, 1967.100.404.p.1

SAMUEL SKOLNIK RESIDENCE,
Los Angeles, 1950–52
Photograph
8 x 10 in.
Archives of American Art, Smithsonian
Institution, Washington, D.C.

SAMUEL SKOLNIK RESIDENCE
DINING CHAIR,
Los Angeles, 1950–52
Plywood and upholstery, reupholstered c. 1990
28 x 16 x 20 in.
ADC at UCSB

BETHLEHEM BAPTIST CHURCH, Los Angeles, 1944–45.
Perspective elevation

BUILDINGS AND PROJECTS

Notes: An asterisk at the end of an entry indicates the existence of a project file. All addresses given reflect the original street and city names of project locations as found in the archives, and therefore may not conform to today's configuration of street and city boundaries.
AGIC stands for Architectural Group for Industry and Commerce.

A

ABERNATHY HOTEL
(project with AGIC)
Los Angeles, 1929*

AESOP'S CHEST AND NOSEGAY
STORE REMODELING
710 South Flower St.,
Los Angeles, 1927–28

MISS F. AIKEN FURNITURE
1600 North Edgemont Ave.,
Los Angeles, c. 1934

ALBERS CHILD'S ROOM (project)
2781 Outpost Dr., Los Angeles, 1942

ALOHA HOTEL (project)
6731 Leland Way, Los Angeles, 1944–46*

AMBASSADOR HOTEL, TYCKO
PHOTOGRAPHIC STUDIO (project)
Los Angeles, 1925

LONNY ANSON HOTEL BUILDING (project)
Los Angeles, 1945

MR. & MRS. JOSEPH L. ARMON
RESIDENCE
470 West Avenue 43, Los Angeles, 1947–50*

ART-MUSIC BUILDING REMODELING
FOR THE LOS ANGELES CO-OPERATIVE
EXCHANGE
233 South Broadway, Los Angeles, 1932*

ARTIST-CONGRESS EXHIBITION ROOM
(project)
Location unknown, 1938

AVON PARK TERRACE APARTMENTS
(project)
Los Angeles, 1945

B

BACHELOR UNIT (project)
5435 Sunset Blvd., Los Angeles, 1949

MRS. M. DAVIS BAKER RESIDENCE
(project)
Los Angeles, 1923

MISS VIROQUE BAKER STUDIO AND
EXTERIOR SIGNAGE
5417 Hollywood Blvd., Los Angeles, 1925

MISS VIROQUE BAKER & ERNEST PRATT
COMMERCIAL BUILDING INTERIOR
(project)
Los Angeles, 1930

TIBOR BALKANY RESIDENCE (project)
3855 Broadlawn Dr., Los Angeles, 1939

MISS ALINE BARNSDALL ACTOR'S
ABODE/RESIDENCE A
(for Frank Lloyd Wright)
Olive Hill, Los Angeles, 1920*

DIRECTOR'S RESIDENCE, OLIVE HILL,
FOR MISS ALINE BARNSDALL
(for Frank Lloyd Wright)
Olive Hill, Los Angeles, 1920*

MISS ALINE BARNSDALL HILL GROVE
PLANTING PLAN
(project for Frank Lloyd Wright)
Olive Hill, Los Angeles, 1920*

MISS ALINE BARNSDALL
OLEANDERS/RESIDENCE B
(for Frank Lloyd Wright)
Olive Hill, Los Angeles, 1920*

MISS ALINE BARNSDALL TERRACE
SHOPS (project for Frank Lloyd Wright)
Olive Hill, Los Angeles, 1920*

MISS ALINE BARNSDALL FOUNTAIN,
WADING POOL, AND PERGOLA
Olive Hill, Los Angeles, 1924–27*

MISS ALINE BARNSDALL FURNITURE AND
FIXTURES, HOLLYHOCK HOUSE
Olive Hill, Los Angeles, 1924–26*

MISS ALINE BARNSDALL
BEDROOM AND BATHROOM REMODEL,
HOLLYHOCK HOUSE
Olive Hill, Los Angeles, 1925*

MISS ALINE BARNSDALL POSTER
EXHIBITION
Olive Hill, Los Angeles, 1927

MISS ALINE BARNSDALL RESIDENCE
A REMODELING
Olive Hill, Los Angeles, 1927

MISS ALINE BARNSDALL
TRANSLUCENT HOUSE (project)
Palos Verdes, California, 1927–28

MISS ALINE BARNSDALL OLEANDERS
RESIDENCE REMODELING
Olive Hill, 1600 North Edgemont Ave.,
Los Angeles, 1928–29*

MR. & MRS. A. GISELA BENNATI CABIN
Lake Arrowhead, California, 1934–37*

GISELA BENNATI SIGNAGE
3281 Oakshire Dr., Los Angeles, n.d.

MRS. BETTY BERKOFF RESIDENCE
(project)
930 North Western Ave.,
Los Angeles, 1936–37*

BETHLEHEM BAPTIST CHURCH
4901 Compton Blvd., Los Angeles, 1944–45*

DR. LEO & ZARA BIGELMAN FURNITURE
11567 Decente Dr., North Hollywood, California,
1944–47*

I. BINDER & H. GROSS APARTMENT
BUILDINGS
103–111 North Soto St., Los Angeles, 1922–23*

MR. & MRS. ALFIO BISSIRI RESIDENCE
(project)
3896 Franklin Ave., Los Angeles, 1939*

R. H. BLAKELEY RESIDENCE (project)
720 Calle De Arboles, Redondo Beach, California,
1952*

LOUIS BLEMBEL RESIDENCE (project)
2103 Sunset Plaza Dr., Los Angeles, 1949–50*

BLOCK APARTMENTS ALTERATION (?)
1724 El Cerrito, Los Angeles, 1943*

ALEXANDER BORISOFF RESIDENCE
(project)
La Presa Dr., Los Angeles, 1947

DR. MAXIM H. BRADEN RESIDENCE
(project)
11837 Laurelwood Dr.,
North Hollywood, California, 1945*

DR. MAXIM H. BRADEN CABIN
REMODELING
8854 Lookout Mountain Ave.,
Los Angeles, 1947–51*

A. EDDIE BRANDSTATTER RESIDENCE
REMODELING (project)
Los Angeles, 1934*

MRS. F. BRAUN APARTMENT BUILDING
REMODELING
6092 Selma Ave., Los Angeles, 1924

HENRY BRAXTON GALLERY
1624 North Vine St., Los Angeles, 1928–29*

MR. HENRY BRAXTON & MRS. VIOLA
BROTHERS SHORE RESIDENCE
(project with AGIC)
5705 Ocean Front Walk,
Venice, California, 1928; 1930*

MR. & MRS. S. BREACHER APARTMENTS
5806 Carlton Way, Los Angeles, 1925*

MR. & MRS. BRIGGS RESIDENCE
(project)
Bay Island, Newport Beach, California, 1926

MR. M. BROWN DUPLEX APARTMENTS
(project)
La Jolla Ave., West Hollywood, California,
1926–27

BROWN MARKET (project)
Los Angeles, 1925

BROWN, SMITH & MOORE STORE FRONT
ALTERATION (project)
Los Angeles, 1932

BRUNDIN RESIDENCE (project)
El Monte, California, 1925

A. & LUBY BUBESHKO APARTMENTS
2036 Griffith Park Blvd., Los Angeles, 1938–41*

MR. & MRS. JOHN J. BUCK RESIDENCE
805 South Genesee St., Los Angeles, 1934

BUENA SHORE CLUB
(for Ottenheimer, Stern, and Reichert)
Chicago, 1916–18*

MR. & MRS. BURKE RESIDENCE
AND APARTMENTS (project)
Balboa, California, 1938

ANNE M. BURRELL APARTMENT
BUILDING (project)
731 North Alexandria, Los Angeles, 1922

ANNE M. BURRELL APARTMENT
BUILDING (project)
1818–1820 Whitley St., Los Angeles, 1922–23

ANNE M. BURRELL DUPLEX (project?)
North New Hampshire Ave., Los Angeles, 1923

DR. WILLIAM BYERS RESIDENCE
(project)
15041 Sherman Way, Van Nuys, California, 1941*

C

CAFE MONTMARTRE RESTAURANT
REMODELING (project)
Los Angeles, 1931

MRS. M. S. CAHN FURNITURE
815 Malcolm, Los Angeles, 1934

MALCOMB P. CAMPBELL RESIDENCE
(project)
Los Angeles, 1922

B. CAPLAN, H. YAFFE & S. TUCK
APARTMENT BUILDING REMODELING
2236 West Fifteenth St., Los Angeles, 1922

MR. & MRS. BEN CARRÉ RESIDENCE
(project)
10356 Northvale Rd., Los Angeles, 1941–42*

CELOTEX COMMERCIAL BUILDING
EXTERIOR (project)
Location unknown, c. 1925

CENTRAL ADMINISTRATION BUILDING
(project for Ottenheimer, Stern, and
Reichert)
Chicago, 1916

HENRY BRAXTON GALLERY, Los Angeles, 1928–29

A. GISELA BENNATI CABIN, Lake Arrowhead, California, 1934-37.
Photograph by W. P. Woodcock

BUENA SHORE CLUB (for Ottenheimer, Stern, and Reichert),
Chicago, 1916–18. Photographs by R. M. Schindler

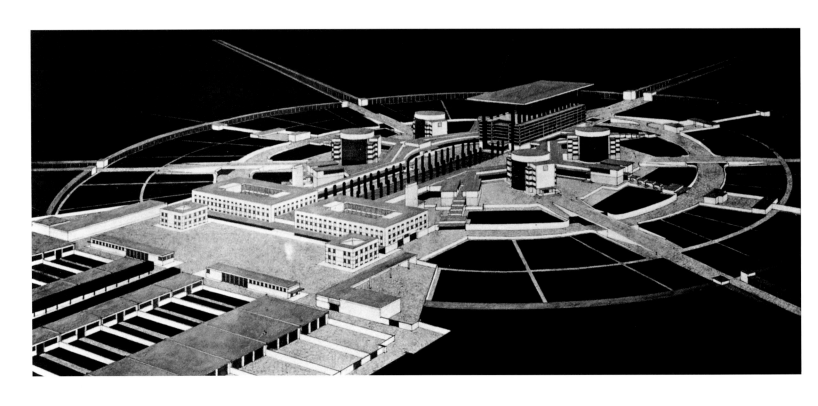

CREMATORIUM AND CHAPEL FOR A CITY OF FIVE MILLION (project),
Vienna, 1912–13. Perspective elevation

RESIDENCE FOR MR & MRS. JOHN DE KEYSER.   R. M. SCHINDLER · ARCHITECT · 1935

JOHN DEKEYSER DOUBLE RESIDENCE, Los Angeles, 1935.
Perspective elevations

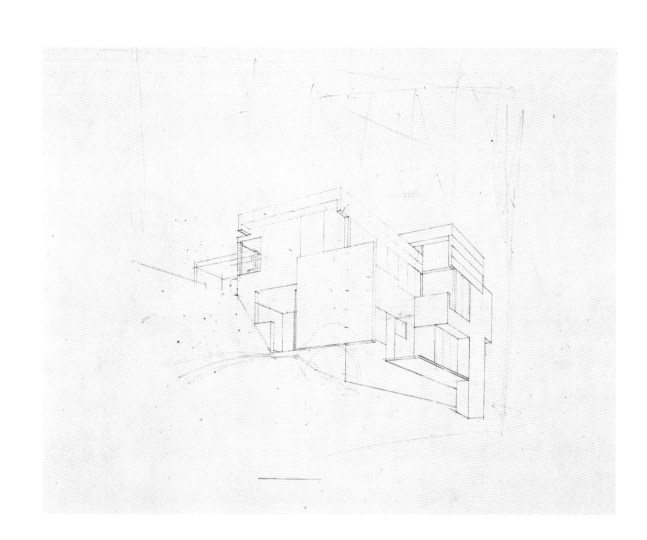

HUNTING LODGE COMPETITION ENTRY (project),
location unknown, 1912. Perspective elevation

JAGDHAUS

R·SCHINDLER·1912

DR. ALFRED GROSS OFFICE REMODELING
Rivkin Medical Building, 12307 Ventura Blvd.,
Studio City, California, 1947*

H

ERNST HAEKEL WORKSHOP
REMODELING (project)
Location unknown, n.d.

HAIN RESIDENCE (project with AGIC)
Los Angeles, 1926

HAIN'S HEALTH FOOD STORE
Third and Hill Streets, Los Angeles, 1926

MR. & MRS. HAINES RESIDENCE
5112 Alishia Dr., Dana Point, California, 1934–35*

MR. & MRS. G. HAMMER RESIDENCE
REMODELING (project)
2253 Kenilworth Ave., Los Angeles, 1943

MR. & MRS. FRANK HANNA RESIDENCE
(project)
Los Angeles, 1938

THOMAS P. HARDY MONOLITH HOMES
(project for Frank Lloyd Wright)
Racine, Wisconsin, 1919

MR. & MRS. JOB HARRIMAN,
HARRIMAN'S COLONY HOUSING
DEVELOPMENT (project)
Langdon Ave. (Longden Dr.), San Gabriel,
California, 1924–25

MR. GEORGE F. & MRS. ROSE L. HARRIS
RESIDENCE
7940 Willow Glen Rd., Los Angeles, 1942–44*

HARTIGAN RESIDENCE (project)
Longview Ave., Los Angeles, 1941

CH. E. HARVEY RESIDENCE REMODELING
2280 Earl St., Los Angeles, 1946

MRS. F. HENDERSON DOUBLE RESIDENCE,
commissioned by O. S. Floren
Los Angeles, 1922

HENNESSY BROTHERS APARTMENT
BUILDING (project with AGIC)
Mariposa St., Los Angeles, c. 1926

HENRY'S RESTAURANT REMODELING
(project)
6321 Hollywood Blvd., Los Angeles, c. 1932

PHIL HERATY RESIDENCE (project)
Los Angeles, 1935

G. HERBOLD RESIDENCE REMODELING
(project)
6406 Varene Ave., Los Angeles, n.d.

MONTI HICKS RETAIL COMMERCIAL
BUILDING (project)
Los Angeles, 1931

HIGHWAY BUNGALOW HOTELS
(project with AGIC/Carol Aronovici)
Location unknown, 1931*

HILAIRE HILER RESIDENCE AND STUDIO
1215 North Alta Loma Dr., Los Angeles, 1941–42*

WILLIAM HILLER STUDIO (project)
Los Angeles, 1931

WILLIAM HILLER PLAYROOM (project)
1134 Serra, North Hollywood, California, c. 1941

MR. & MRS. G. H. HODEL FURNITURE
1800 Huntington Dr.,
San Marino, California, 1940

HOLLYWOOD CARPENTER SHOP
"TRADE HUB" BUILDING (project)
Los Angeles, 1932*

HOLLYWOOD PUBLIC LIBRARY ART ROOM
REMODELING (project)
Los Angeles, 1923

HOLLYWOOD RIVIERA BUILDING
ASSOCIATION APARTMENT BUILDING
(project)
Los Angeles, 1931

HOLLYWOOD WOMEN'S CLUB
REMODELING (project)
7078 Hollywood Blvd.,
Los Angeles, 1944*

HOMER EMUNIM TEMPLE AND SCHOOL
(project for Ottenheimer, Stern, and
Reichert)
Chicago, 1915–16

LESTER HORTON DANCE STUDIO
REMODELING (project)
7566 Melrose Ave., Los Angeles, 1947*

HORTON & CONVERSE DRUG STORE
(project)
Los Angeles, 1932

HOTEL (project for Ottenheimer,
Stern, and Reichert)
Chicago, 1915

HOTEL ELSINORE (project with
A. R. Brandner)
Lake Elsinore, California, 1925–27*

HOTEL RONG (project)
Vienna, 1912

MR. & MRS. JAMES EADS HOW
RESIDENCE AND FURNITURE
2422 Silver Ridge Ave., Los Angeles,
1925–26*

FRANCES MCLALLEN HOWATT
RESIDENCE (project)
Temple Hills Dr., Laguna Beach, California, 1946*

KARL & DORIS HOWENSTEIN
RESIDENCE REMODELING
2083 Hanscom Dr., South Pasadena, California,
1942–46*

HUB OFFICE BUILDING, A. E. ENGLAND
(project?)
Hollywood Blvd., Los Angeles, 1939–40*

HUDSON MARKET (project)
Los Angeles, 1937

JAMES EADS HOW RESIDENCE, Los Angeles, 1925–26.
Photograph by Viroque Baker

MAURICE KALLIS RESIDENCE AND STUDIO, Studio City, California, 1946–48.
View of façade from terrace. Photograph by Robert C. Cleveland

MR. HUMPHREY RESIDENCE (project)
Los Angeles, 1952

MRS. B. HUNTER RESIDENCE (project)
Location unknown, c. 1934

HUNTING LODGE COMPETITION ENTRY
(project)
Location unknown, 1912

HURLEY FURNITURE
Location unknown, n.d.

HUTSEN RESIDENCE (project)
Location unknown, c. 1927

H. HYMAN REMODELING
253 South Palm Dr., Los Angeles, 1944–45*

I

BEATA INAYA FURNITURE
Los Angeles, c. 1946

BEATA INAYA RESIDENCE (project)
Sierra Mar Dr., Los Angeles, 1946*

BEATA INAYA APARTMENT BUILDING
REMODELING (project)
1932–1938 Cheremoya St., Los Angeles, 1948*

BEATA INAYA DUPLEX REMODELING
(project)
1760 Cerrito Place, Los Angeles, 1949

BEATA INAYA RESIDENCE (project)
1462–1468 Altridge Dr.,
Beverly Hills, California, 1950*

INDEPENDENT GERMAN-AMERICAN
WOMAN'S CLUB PLAYBILL
Deutsches Theater, Chicago, 1916*

MICHIO ITO STUDIO FURNITURE
5653½ Hollywood Blvd., Los Angeles, 1930*

JAMES B. IRVING TEMPORARY
RESIDENCE (project for
Frank Lloyd Wright)
Wilmette, Illinois, 1920

J

MR. & MRS. WILLIAM JACOBS
RESIDENCE (project)
Stradella Rd., Los Angeles, 1936*

ELLEN JANSON RESIDENCE
8704 Skyline Dr., Los Angeles, 1948–49*

JARDIN APARTMENTS, EIGHT-STORY
CLASS "A" APARTMENTS (project with
J. H. Miller and AGIC)
Van Ness and Harold Way, Los Angeles, 1927

MISS JEFFRIES RESIDENCE (project)
Los Angeles, 1951*

L. C. JOHNSON DESERT CABIN COLONY
(project)
Location unknown, 1937*

K

GUS KAHN RESIDENCE REMODELING
(project)
917 Benedict Canyon Dr.,
Beverly Hills, California, 1937*

MANYA KAHN RESIDENCE (project)
First St. and Harper Ave, Los Angeles, 1936*

MANYA KAHN RESIDENCE REMODELING
(project)
Lake Elsinore, California, 1946*

MR. & MRS. MAURICE KALLIS
RESIDENCE AND STUDIO
3580 Multiview Dr., Los Angeles, 1946–48;
additions 1948–51*

MR. KARZ APARTMENT BUILDING
(project)
533 North Cummings, Los Angeles, 1941

DR. & MRS. ALEXANDER KAUN
BEACH HOUSE
125 Western Dr., Richmond, California, 1934–35*

DR. & MRS. ALEXANDER KAUN
RESIDENCE REMODELING
1431 Le Roy Ave., Berkeley, California, 1940

KAYNAR MANUFACTURING COMPANY
FACTORY REMODELING
813 East Seventeenth St., Los Angeles, 1950*

ELSIE KELLIS RESIDENCE REMODELING
1212 Green Acre, Los Angeles, 1943–44*

J. KENT RESIDENCE REMODELING
1821 Edgecliff Dr., Los Angeles, 1945*

W. E. KENT RESIDENCE (project)
4939 (4947) Malta St., Los Angeles, 1922*

EUGENE L. KERMIN RESIDENCE (project)
McConnell Dr., Los Angeles, 1946–47*

HENRY KERMIN MEDICAL BUILDING
REMODELING (project)
9215 Venice Blvd., Los Angeles, 1946

HENRY KERMIN RESIDENCE (project)
Glenroy Ave., Los Angeles, 1946

KERR RUG COMPANY RECEPTION ROOM
(project)
Los Angeles, c. 1935

MR. KESSLER COMMERCIAL BUILDING
(project)
512 South Victory Blvd.,
Burbank, California, 1945*

MR. KESSLER APARTMENT BUILDING
(project)
Los Angeles, 1946

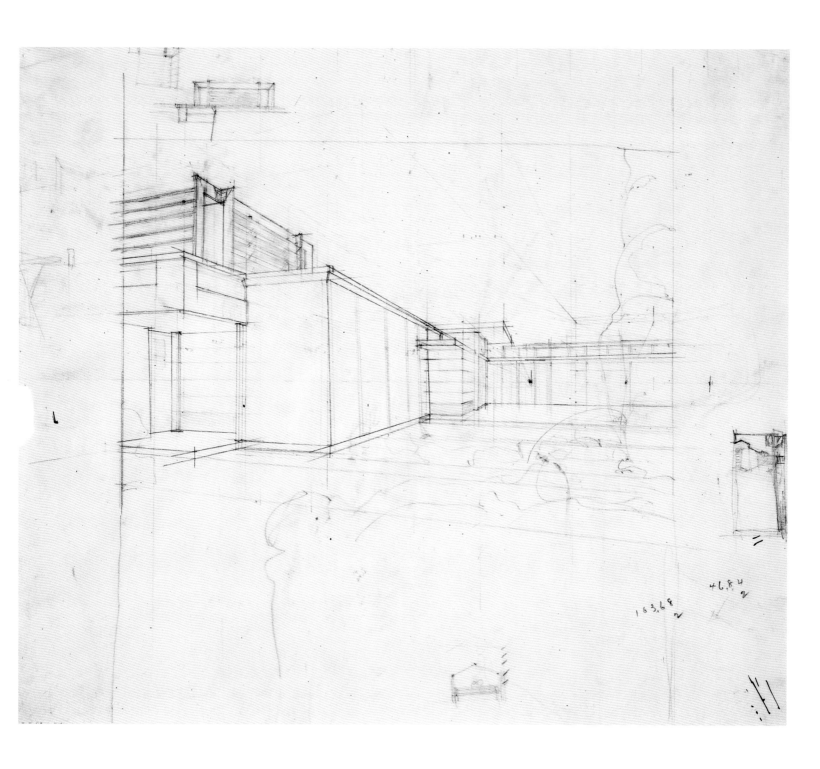

KINGS ROAD HOUSE, West Hollywood, California, 1921–22.
View of entrance with sleeping "basket"

KINGS ROAD HOUSE, West Hollywood, California, 1921–22.
Perspective elevation

LEAH–RUTH GARMENT SHOP (with AGIC), Long Beach, California, 1926

RICHARD LECHNER RESIDENCE, Studio City, California, 1946–48.
Perspective elevation

RICHARD LECHNER RESIDENCE, Studio City, California, 1946–48.
Sketch of fireplace

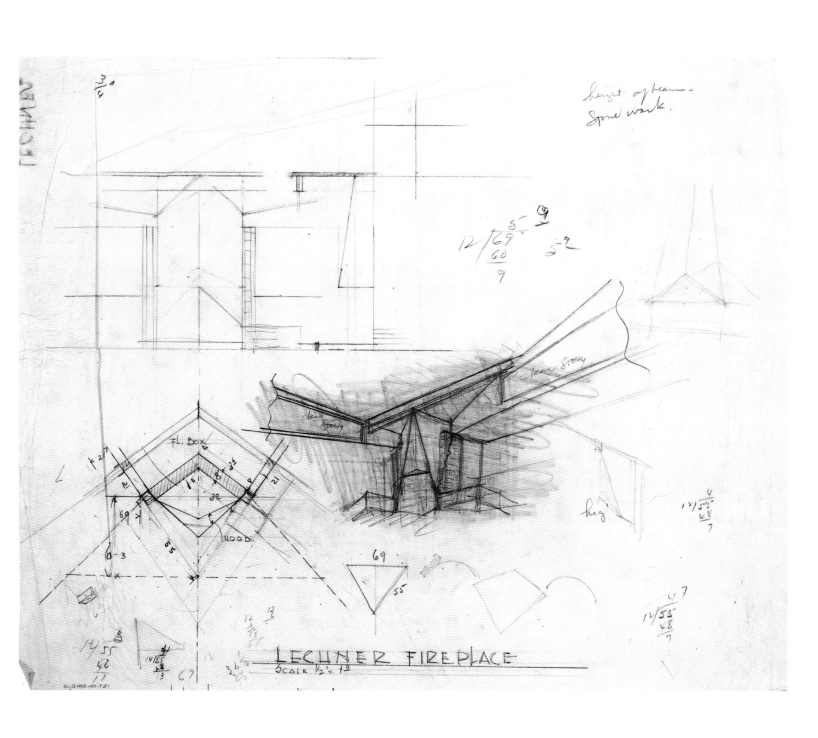

LECHNER FIREPLACE
SCALE ½" = 1°

height of beam—
Stone work.

clear story

FL. BOX

WOOD

high

RICHARD LECHNER RESIDENCE, Studio City, California, 1946–48.
Photograph by Robert C. Cleveland

· FRONT FOR A STEAK HOUSE ·   · R.M. SCHINDLER ARCHITECT ·

LINDY'S RESTAURANT, Los Angeles, 1932–34.
Photograph by W. P. Woodcock

LINDY'S RESTAURANT, Los Angeles, 1932–34

DR. HARRY B. FRIEDGOOD & ROBERT SLOAN MEDICAL BUILDING (project?)
119 North San Vicente Blvd., Beverly Hills, California, 1945; 1950*

FRANK MELINE COMPANY PLAYMART/PHOTOPLAY OFFICE SKYSCRAPER (project)
Los Angeles, 1922

MELROSE PUBLIC PARK LAYOUT (project)
Melrose Park, Illinois, 1917

MEMORIAL COMMUNITY CENTER (project for Frank Lloyd Wright)
Wenatchee, Washington, 1919

LEAH MIDDLETON STORE INTERIOR (project)
Long Beach, California, 1926

ALICE MILLARD RESIDENCE (for Frank Lloyd Wright)
Pasadena, California, 1923

MRS. F. MILLER RESIDENCE FOR MRS. RUTH SHEP (project)
Los Angeles, 1935–36

J. H. MILLER APARTMENT BUILDING (project with AGIC)
Shenandoah Dr., Los Angeles, 1927

J. H. MILLER FIVE-STORY CLASS "B" APARTMENT BUILDING (project with AGIC)
1807 Wilton Pl., Los Angeles, 1927

J. H. MILLER FOUR-STORY CLASS "C" APARTMENT BUILDING (project with AGIC)
Marathon St. and Manhattan Pl., Los Angeles, 1927 [constructed by Neutra as Jardinette Apartments]

SAMUEL MILLER VETERAN'S APARTMENTS (project)
Tulare, California, 1946*

PORT L. MIX BUNGALOW (project)
3804 South Grand Ave., Los Angeles, 1922

MODEL HOUSE (project)
Los Angeles, 1936*

MODERN SCHOOL LIBRARY BUILDING (project)
Los Angeles, 1921

MODERN SHOP (project)
12338 Ventura Blvd., North Hollywood, California, 1946–47*

MONOLITH HOME/WORKER'S HOUSING (project for Frank Lloyd Wright)
Location unknown, 1919*

NATHAN MOORE RESIDENCE REMODELING (for Frank Lloyd Wright)
Oak Park, Illinois, 1923

MR. S. & MRS. ROSE MOREHEAD RESIDENCE (project)
1340 Marianna Rd., Pasadena, California, 1949–50*

MORGAN-PHOTOGRAPHIC SHOP (project)
6305 Sunset Blvd., Los Angeles, 1938*

JESSICA MORGENTHAU STUDIO (project)
Palm Springs, California, 1926

MR. & MRS. KEN O. MUMFORD RESIDENCE (project)
Location unknown, 1936

ALFRED T. MURRAY RESIDENCE (project)
Location unknown, c. 1940

MRS. BARBARA MYERS RESIDENCE REMODELING
2038 Oakstone Way, Los Angeles, 1949–50*

HENRY I. & BARBARA MYERS RESIDENCE REMODELING AND FURNITURE
1286 Sunset Plaza Dr., Los Angeles, 1942–43*

J. NAPOLITANO OLIVE OIL MILL (project with AGIC)
676 Clover St., Los Angeles, 1927

NEIGHBORHOOD CENTER CIVIC COMPLEX COMPETITION FOR THE CITY CLUB OF CHICAGO (project)
Chicago, 1914

MRS. NERENBAUM SERVICE STATION (project)
Los Angeles, 1934

JAMES E. NEVILLE STORE AND HOTEL (project)
6501 Sunset Blvd., Los Angeles, 1923–24*

J. J. NEWBERRY STORE FRONT (project with Herman Sachs)
Los Angeles, 1929

DUDLEY NICHOLS RESIDENCE (project)
Location unknown, 1931*

HAZEL NICKERSON RESIDENCE REMODELING
681 South Norton St., Los Angeles, 1944*

NOBBY KNIT STORE FRONT (project)
Los Angeles, c. 1930

NUREMBEGA HEIGHTS HOTEL (project)
Burbank, California, 1924

O

MRS. E. MCGAULEY OAKLAND CULTURAL CENTER/ART GALLERY (project)
Lake Merritt, Oakland, California, 1928

OFFICER'S CLUB FOR MRS. HARRIET CODY (project)
Palm Springs, California, 1942

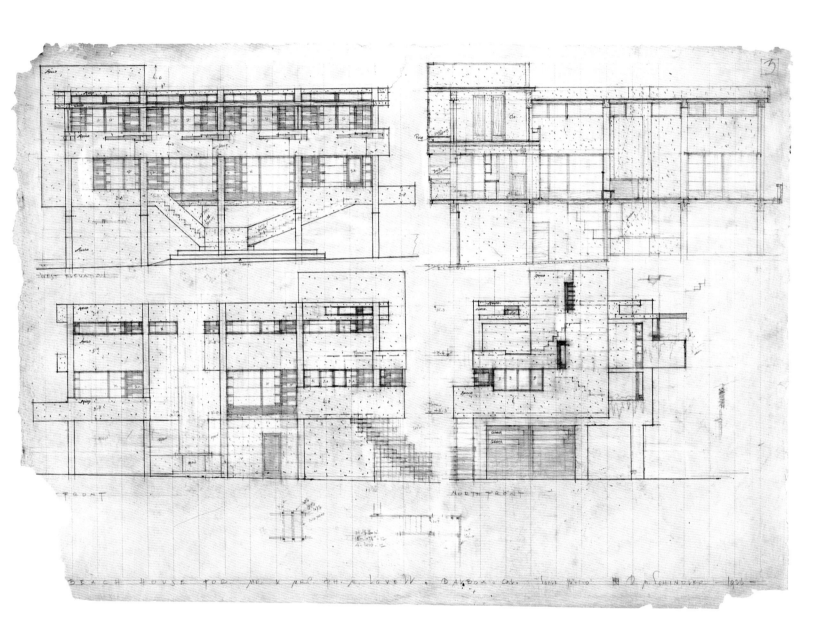

PHILIP LOVELL BEACH HOUSE, Newport Beach, California, 1922–26.
Exterior elevations and section

MR. & MRS. WILLIAM E. OLIVER
RESIDENCE (project)
Crest Trail, Los Angeles, 1931*

MR. & MRS. WILLIAM E. OLIVER
RESIDENCE AND FURNITURE
2236 Micheltorena Ave., Los Angeles, 1933–34*

ONE-ROOM FLAT APARTMENT
(project)
Chicago, 1919

A. OPEGEZ RESIDENCE (project)
5518 Carlton Way, Los Angeles, n.d.

OPERA AND DRAMA GUILD SETS
for "Hotel Imperial," "The Idiot,"
"Monna Vanna," and "Soul of Raphael"
Trinity Auditorium, Los Angeles, 1928–29*

A. G. O'REAR RESIDENCE (project)
Milton Ave., Los Angeles, 1922*

DR. PATRICK S. O'REILLY RESIDENCE
(project)
Glendale, California, 1934

DR. PATRICK S. O'REILLY HOSPITAL
BUILDING (project)
Location unknown, 1935

DR. PATRICK S. O'REILLY MOUNTAIN
CABINS (project)
Wallika Hot Springs, California, 1935*

MRS. O'SULLIVAN & MISS B. KENT
TEAROOM
1765 North Vine St., Los Angeles, 1925–26*

PETER PAUL OTT APARTMENT BUILDING
(project)
153 South Peck Dr., Beverly Hills, California,
1948–49*

MR. & MRS. L. S. OVERPECK RESIDENCE
(project)
Los Angeles, n.d.*

P

MR. & MRS. JOHN COOPER PACKARD
RESIDENCE
East Drive, Pasadena, California, 1924*

PAGE RESIDENCE (project)
Los Angeles, c. 1939

MRS. ANNE L. PAINE DUPLEX,
commissioned by O. S. Floren
1024 Havenhurst Ave., Los Angeles, 1923

K. PALMAN APARTMENT COMPLEX (?)
(project)
5435 Sunset Blvd., Los Angeles, 1949*

PANEL-POST CONSTRUCTION METHOD
(project)
Location unknown, 1935–42

JOSEPH L. FEIL & B. R. PARADISE
PARADISE RESORT/SANITARIUM
(project for Bonwit-Teller?)
Ontario, California, 1929–30*

PARIS-ROME CAFE
(project with Herman Sachs)
Location unknown, 1931

CARLTON PARK RESIDENCE,
commissioned by Dr. Philip Lovell
Fallbrook, California, 1925-26*

PARK MODERNE MODEL CABINS 1 & 3
FOR WILLIAM LINGENBRINK
(first cabin design with AGIC)
Calabasas, California, 1929; 1932; 1938*

EDWARD PAVAROFF RESIDENCE
REMODELING AND FURNITURE
1641 North Crescent Heights Blvd., Los Angeles,
1934–36*

PENNINGTON ESTATE (project)
Pasadena, California, c. 1945

JOHN AND DORIS PENNINGTON
RESIDENCE AND STUDIO REMODELING
Camarillo, California, 1942

JOHN AND DORIS PENNINGTON
FURNITURE
1811 Edgecliff Dr., Los Angeles, 1944

PEOPLE'S BANK (project)
Los Angeles, 1924

M. PERRIERE RESIDENCE (project)
Los Angeles, 1941

PERRY DANCE STUDIO (project)
Los Angeles, c. 1939

MR. PERSTEIN RESIDENCE REMODELING
AND FURNITURE
111 Tamalpais Rd., Berkeley, California, 1933

PHOTOGRAPHS, primarily architecture in
the Chicago area and Schindler projects
1914–26

PHYSICAL EDUCATION CLUB LODGE
(project)
Topanga Ranch, Los Angeles, 1923*

MR. & MRS. A. PLOTKIN RESIDENCE
(project)
Los Angeles, 1924

MR. & MRS. PAUL POPENOE CABIN
Coachella, California, 1922*

MR. & MRS. PAUL POPENOE DESERT
HOTEL (project)
Coachella, California, 1922

POSSON RESIDENCE REMODELING
(project)
Los Angeles, c. 1924

FELIX & GERTRUDE PRESBURGER
RESIDENCE
4255 Agnes St., North Hollywood, California,
1945–47*

WILLIAM E. OLIVER RESIDENCE, Los Angeles, California, 1933–34

JOHN COOPER PACKARD RESIDENCE, South Pasadena, 1924

PUEBLO RIBERA COURTS, FOR W. LLEWELLYN LLOYD, La Jolla, California, 1923–25.
Photograph by R. M. Schindler

MAURICE RIES RESIDENCE, Los Angeles, 1950–52.
Photograph by Lotte Nossaman

THE UNITS

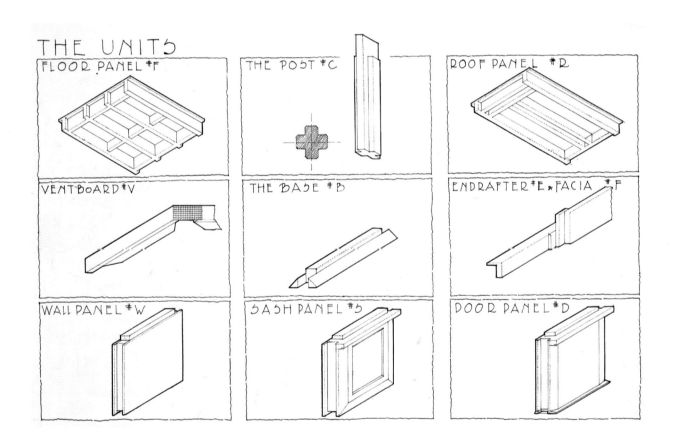

FLOOR PANEL #F

THE POST #C

ROOF PANEL #R

VENTBOARD #V

THE BASE #B

ENDRAFTER #E * FACIA #F

WALL PANEL #W

SASH PANEL #S

DOOR PANEL #D

PANEL-POST METHOD (project), 1935–42

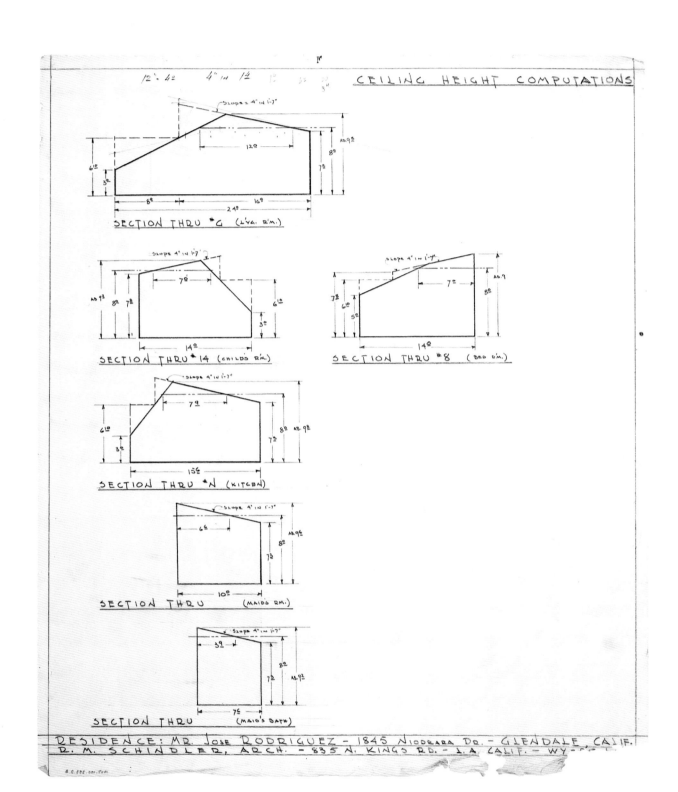

SECTION THRU #G (L'VG. R'M.)

SECTION THRU #14 (CHILD'S R'M.)

SECTION THRU #8 (BED R'M.)

SECTION THRU #N (KITCHEN)

SECTION THRU (MAID'S R'M.)

SECTION THRU (MAID'S BATH)

RESIDENCE: MR. JOSE RODRIGUEZ – 1845 NIOBRARA DR. – GLENDALE, CALIF.
R. M. SCHINDLER, ARCH. – 835 N. KINGS RD. – L.A. CALIF. – WY-

JOSÉ RODRIGUEZ RESIDENCE, Glendale, California, 1940–42.
Ceiling height sections

HERMAN SACHS RESIDENCE (project)
Hacienda Pl., Los Angeles, 1936*

MR. & MRS. SAKS RESIDENCE
REMODELING (project)
14623 Sutton St., Sherman Oaks, California, 1950

DR. SANDERS MEDICAL OFFICE (project)
Location unknown, 1937

J. SANFORD RESIDENCE (project)
Location unknown, n.d.

SARDI'S RESTAURANT NO. I REMODELING
FOR A. EDDIE BRANDSTATTER
6313 Hollywood Blvd., Los Angeles, 1932–34*

SATYR BOOKSHOP SHOW WINDOW
1622 North Vine St., Los Angeles, 1929*

MR. & MRS. ABE M. SAX RESIDENCE AND
FURNITURE (project)
1929 Hollyvista Ave., Los Angeles, 1940*

MRS. MILDRED SAX RESIDENCE (project)
1800 Crescent Heights Blvd., Los Angeles, 1948*

MRS. MILDRED SAX RESTAURANT
(project)
Los Angeles, 1949

BENNO SCHEINER GARDEN
DEVELOPMENT AND RESIDENCE
REMODELING
225 South Maple Dr., Beverly Hills, California,
1944–45*

MR. & MRS. HENRY G. SCHICK
RESIDENCE (project)
11833 Laurelwood Dr.,
North Hollywood, California, 1945*

HENRY SCHICK & ASSOCIATES REST
HOME (project)
12120–12130 Washington Blvd., Los Angeles,
1947–48*

HENRY G. SCHICK RESIDENCE
REMODELING
1932 Cheremoya Ave., Los Angeles, 1948–49*

MR. & MRS. MARK SCHINDLER INTERIOR
REMODELING (project?)
Los Angeles, 1952

SCHINDLER SHELTERS RESIDENCE
PROTOTYPES (project in conjunction with
Panel-Post Construction Method)
Los Angeles, 1933–39*

R. M. SCHINDLER SLAB BLOCK
CONSTRUCTION (project)
Location unknown, 1939

SCHINDLER FRAME WALL
CONSTRUCTION (project)
Location unknown, 1945*

PHILIP J. & PHYLLIS F. SCHLESSINGER
RESIDENCE
1901 Myra Dr., Los Angeles, 1952*

F. SCHMIDT CHICKEN COOP
Evanston, Illinois, 1915

D. SCHNEIDER COMMERCIAL BUILDING
REMODELING
231–235 East Seventh St., Los Angeles,
1945–46*

MR. & MRS. SCHUETTNER RESIDENCE
(project)
Los Tilos St., Los Angeles, 1936*

MR. & MRS. HENRY R. SCHUMACHER
RESIDENCE (project)
Los Angeles, 1953*

CARL SCHURZ, CARL SCHURZ
COOPERATIVE SOCIETY LETTERHEAD
DESIGN
Chicago, 1916

MR. & MRS. M. SEFF REMODELING AND
FURNITURE
605 North Arden Dr., Beverly Hills, California,
1936–37; 1948–49*

SEIBERT CABIN (project with AGIC)
Los Angeles, c. 1926

SAM SELIGSON RESIDENCE
REMODELING
1761 Orange Grove Ave., Los Angeles, 1936*

SEWAGE DISPOSAL PLANT BUILDING
(project)
Los Angeles, 1952

MRS. ROSALUND K. SHAEFER
RESIDENCE REMODELING (project?)
Glencoe Way, Los Angeles, c. 1937

MR. & MRS. J. P. SHAMPAY RESIDENCE
(project for Frank Lloyd Wright)
10401 South Seeley Ave., Chicago, 1919*

ADA MAY SHARPLESS RESIDENCE AND
STUDIO (project)
View Site Terr., Los Angeles, 1938*

MR. & MRS. MILTON SHEP RESIDENCE
AND FURNITURE (project)
1809 Silverwood Terr., Los Angeles, 1934–35*

MRS. RUTH SHEP FURNITURE
Los Angeles, 1932–34*

MRS. RUTH SHEP RESIDENCE (project)
Fanning St., Los Angeles, 1936

MRS. RUTH SHEP RESIDENCE (project)
1809 Silverwood Terr., Los Angeles, 1938

E. H. SHIRLEY HOUSING DEVELOPMENT,
FARM BUILDINGS (project)
Location unknown, 1932*

LUBY SHUTOREV APARTMENT BUILDING
(project)
Griffith Park Blvd., Los Angeles, 1953

MR. & MRS. W. E. SIMS RESIDENCE AND
RANCH BUILDINGS (project)
Ventura, California, 1945

SKETCHES; including nude studies,
travel and landscape drawings
1914–17

SAMUEL SKOLNIK RESIDENCE, Los Angeles, 1950–52.
Photograph by Lotte Nossaman

RESIDENCE:SOUTHALL
R.M.SCHINDLER·ARCHITECT

MILDRED SOUTHALL RESIDENCE AND STUDIO, Los Angeles, 1938–39.
Perspective elevation

MILDRED SOUTHALL RESIDENCE AND STUDIO, Los Angeles, 1938–39.
Photograph by Maynard Parker

SAMUEL & HAIKIN SKOLNIK RESIDENCE
AND FURNITURE
2567 Glendower Ave., Los Angeles, 1950–52*

MR. & MRS. SLEMONS RESIDENCE
(project)
Arcadia, California, 1928

MR. & MRS. PAUL SLOAN RESIDENCE
ALTERATION (project? with AGIC)
8241 De Longpre, Los Angeles, 1930

ROBERT S. SLOAN STUDIO REMODELING
514 North Alta Dr., Beverly Hills, California,
1946–48*

LOU SMITH RESIDENCE (project)
Angelo Dr., Los Angeles, 1947*

SNEGOFF THEATER (project)
Franklin Ave., Los Angeles, 1936

DR. L. E. SNELL HOTEL WIND AND SEA
(project)
La Jolla, California, 1923–24

MR. & MRS. KENNETH SNOKE RESIDENCE
(project)
Hilldale Ave., Los Angeles, c. 1926

MR. & MRS. ALEXANDER SOKOLOW
BEACH COTTAGE (project)
Balboa Island, Newport Beach, California, c. 1932

J. SOLLIN RESIDENCE (Panel-Post
Construction) (project)
Location unknown, 1936

MR. & MRS. ROBERT SONTAG RESIDENCE
(project)
Los Angeles, 1949

DR. MARIE E. SORG RESIDENCE
(with Richard Neutra)
600 South Putney St., San Gabriel, California,
1926–27*

SORRENTO RANCH DEVELOPMENT
APARTMENT BUILDING REMODELING
(project)
San Diego County, California, 1945*

MILDRED SOUTHALL RESIDENCE,
STUDIO, AND FURNITURE
1855 Park Dr., Los Angeles, 1938–39*

MILDRED SOUTHALL SCHOOL OF
TOMORROW AUDITORIUM AND
CLASSROOM BUILDING (project)
Los Angeles, 1944

SPACE DEVELOPMENT RESIDENCE
(project)
Location unknown, c. 1945

RALF M. SPANGLER RESIDENCE (project)
2709 Jalmia Dr., Los Angeles, 1941–46*

SPECULATIVE HOUSING RESIDENCE (with
Edward Lind)
423, 429 and 433 Ellis Ave.,
Inglewood, California, c. 1940

DR. BUELL SPRAGUE MEDICAL BUILDING
REMODELING (project)
6634 Sunset Blvd., Los Angeles, 1936

MR. & MRS. C. E. STALEY RESIDENCE
(project for Frank Lloyd Wright)
Waukegan, Illinois, 1919

STANDARD OIL COMPANY SERVICE
STATION (project)
Location unknown, 1932

LIONEL STANDER DESIGN FOR
APARTMENT (project)
Vine St., Los Angeles, 1935

LIONEL STANDER RESIDENCE
REMODELING
2006 North La Brea Terr., Los Angeles,
1935–36*

MR. & MRS. WILLIAM A. STARKEY
RESIDENCE REMODELING
2330 Merrywood Dr., Los Angeles, 1944–45*

RALPH STEINER RESIDENCE
REMODELING
1264 Hilldale Ave. (8930 Saint Ives Dr.),
Los Angeles, 1946*

JURA STOJANA RESIDENCE GARAGE
ALTERATION
3501 Dahlia St., Los Angeles, 1926; 1931*

JOHN STORER RESIDENCE REMODELING
(project)
8160 Hollywood Blvd., Los Angeles, c. 1925

JANE STORM RESIDENCE (project)
Los Angeles, 1938

JEWEL D. STRADER RESIDENCE (project)
3411 Tareco Dr.,
North Hollywood, California, 1940*

SUMMER RESIDENCE (project)
Vienna, 1914

SUNSET CANYON COUNTRY CLUB
BUILDING (project)
Burbank, California, 1931*

T

HARRY TAYLOR COMMERCIAL BUILDING
REMODELING (Lingenbrink Stores)
12646, 12652, and 12654 Ventura Blvd.,
Studio City, California, 1947–51*

MRS. NETTIE M. TAYLOR RESIDENCE AND
STUDIOS (project)
501 Garfield Ave.,
South Pasadena, California, 1940

MR. EDGAR TEMPLE APARTMENT
BUILDINGS (project)
947 Hyperion St., Los Angeles, 1922

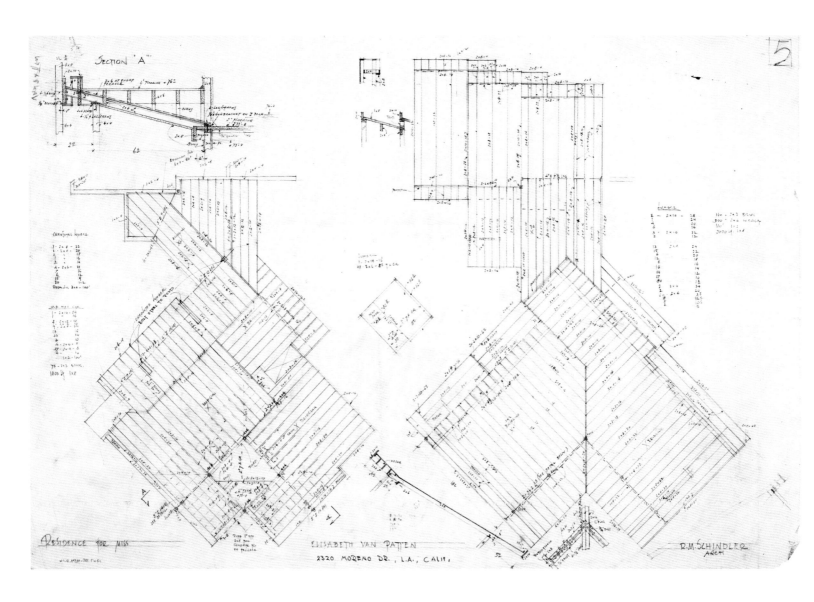

ELIZABETH VAN PATTEN RESIDENCE, Los Angeles, 1934-36.
Framing plans and details

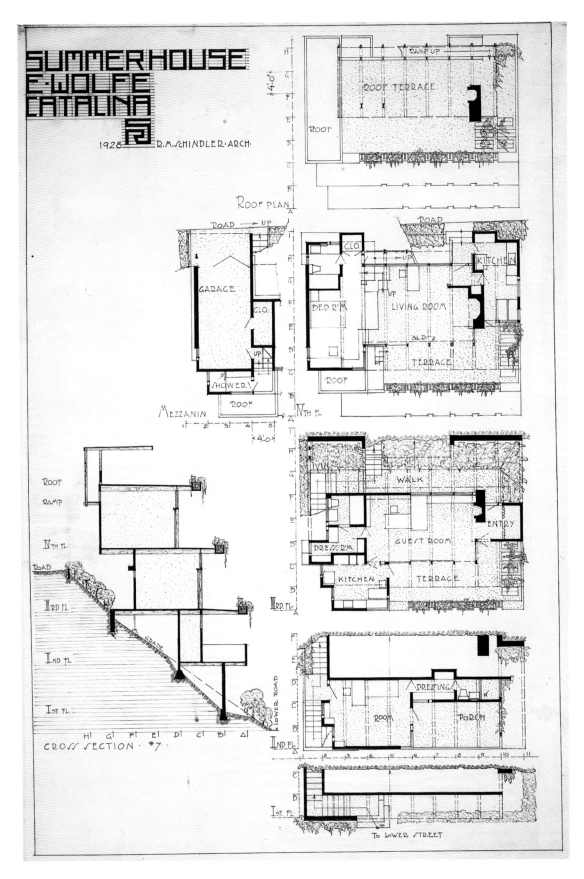

SUMMER HOUSE
E·WOLFE
CATALINA

1928 — R·M·SCHINDLER·ARCH·

ROOF TERRACE

RAMP UP

ROOF

ROOF PLAN

ROAD — UP

GARAGE

CLO.

UP

SHOWER

ROOF

MEZZANIN

CLO.

BED R'M

UP

LIVING ROOM

KITCHEN

ROAD

SL·D·

TERRACE

ROOF

IVTH FL

ROOF RAMP

IVTH FL

ROAD

IIIRD FL

GRADE

IIND FL

IST FL

CROSS SECTION · #7

WALK

DRES·R'M

GUEST ROOM

ENTRY

KITCHEN

TERRACE

IIIRD FL

DRESSING

ROOM

PORCH

IIND FL

IST FL

TO LOWER STREET

LOWER ROAD

CHARLES H. WOLFE RESIDENCE, Avalon, Catalina Island,
California, 1928–31. Plans and section

CHARLES H. WOLFE RESIDENCE, Avalon, Catalina Island,
California, 1928–31

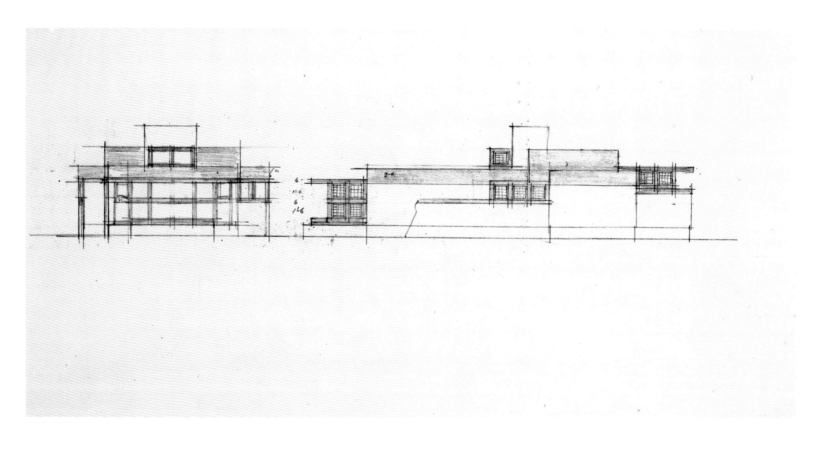

UNIDENTIFIED RESIDENCE (project), Oak Park, Illinois, c. 1917.
Exterior elevations

ANNA [AND OLGA] ZACSEK
BEACH HOUSE
114 Ellen St., Playa Del Rey, California,
1936–38; 1950–51, additions*

ANNA ZACSEK RESIDENCE REMODELING
211 South Muirfield Rd., Playa Del Rey, California,
1950–52*

MRS. T. [OLGA] ZACSEK RESIDENCE
(project with AGIC)
Sayre Lane, Los Angeles, 1927*

I. M. ZAMUDIO RESIDENCE (project)
AND FURNITURE
6113 South Mansfield, Los Angeles, 1941–43

MRS. RESIDENCE ZIEGLER REMODELING
(project)
8307 De Longpre Ave., Los Angeles, 1936

UNIDENTIFIED

UNIDENTIFIED APARTMENT BUILDING
(project)
Los Angeles, 1921

UNIDENTIFIED EIGHT-STORY APARTMENT
BUILDING (project, possibly preliminary
drawings for Jardin Apartments)
Los Angeles, c. 1927

UNIDENTIFIED APARTMENT BUILDING
(project)
127 North Manhattan Ave., Los Angeles, 1952

UNIDENTIFIED APARTMENT BUILDING
(project)
1758–1760 El Cerrito Place, Los Angeles, 1952*

UNIDENTIFIED BAR (project)
Chicago, c. 1915

UNIDENTIFIED EXHIBITION ROOM
(project)
Berkeley, California, c. 1926

UNIDENTIFIED FURNITURE
1919–47

UNIDENTIFIED GARAGE DOOR
MECHANISM
n.d.*

UNIDENTIFIED HOTEL BUILDING
(project, Four-Story Class "C," with AGIC)
Pasadena, California, c. 1927

UNIDENTIFIED HOTEL LOBBY WINDOW
DISPLAY CASE (project)
Chicago, c. 1919

UNIDENTIFIED MARKET INTERIOR
(project)
832 South Broadway, Los Angeles, n.d.

UNIDENTIFIED MEDICAL BUILDING
REMODELING (project)
Location unknown, n.d.

UNIDENTIFIED RESIDENCE (project)
Oak Park, Illinois, c. 1917

UNIDENTIFIED RESIDENCE (project)
Fareholm Dr., Los Angeles, c. 1946

UNIDENTIFIED RESIDENCES (project)
Locations unknown, n.d.

UNIDENTIFIED SASH AND FRAMING
DETAILS (project?)
Locations unknown, 1934–47

UNIDENTIFIED STREET CROSSING
(project)
Location unknown, 1950

UNIDENTIFIED STOREFRONT
(project for Ottenheimer,
Stern & Reichert?)
Van Buren St., Chicago, 1916

UNIDENTIFIED THEATER BUILDING
INTERIOR REMODELING (project)
Location unknown, c. 1930

*The Rudolph M. Schindler Collection in the
Architecture and Design Collection at the University
Art Museum, University of California, Santa
Barbara—which includes his working
drawings, project files, business and personal correspondence, daily planners, client records, and
photographs— is the primary source in
the compilation of this list. Secondary sources frequently consulted include:* The Architectural
Drawings of R. M. Schindler, *edited by David
Gebhard (New York: Garland Publishing, Inc.,
1993);* R. M. Schindler, Architect 1887–1953
*by August Sarnitz (New York: Rizzoli, 1988);
and* Schindler *by David Gebhard (3rd edition,
1997; London: Thames and Hudson, 1971).*

HOTEL (project for Ottenheimer, Stern, and Reichert),
Chicago, 1915. Presentation drawing

SELECTED BIBLIOGRAPHY

"Angles and Rectangles Characterize Plan of Small Studio-Home." *The Architectural Forum* 86 (February 1947): 102.

"The Architecture of R. M. Schindler (1887-1953)." *RIBA Journal* (London) 76, no. 2 (February 1969): 52.

Banham, Reyner. "Rudolf Schindler—A Pioneer Without Tears." *Architectural Design* (London) 37 (December 1967): 578-79.

_____. *The Architecture of the Well-Tempered Environment*, 204-07. Chicago: The University of Chicago Press; and London: The Architectural Press, 1969.

_____. *Los Angeles: The Architecture of Four Ecologies*, 39, 175, 178-89. New York: Harper & Row, 1971.

_____. "The Master Builders: 5. The Gamble House and Schindler House." *The Sunday Times Magazine* (London), 8 August 1971, 26-27.

_____. "Schindler/Chase House, Los Angeles: Rudolph Schindler." In *Age of the Masters: A Personal View of Modern Architecture*, 158-59. 3rd ed., London: Architectural Press, 1975.

"A Beach House for Dr. and Mrs. Alexander Kaun, Richmond, California." *California Arts and Architecture* 51, no. 5 (May 1937): 26.

"A Beach House for Dr. P. Lovell at Newport Beach, California." *Architectural Record* 66, no. 3 (September 1929): 257-61.

Berns, Marla C., ed. *The Furniture of R. M. Schindler*. Santa Barbara, Calif.: University Art Museum, University of California at Santa Barbara, 1997.

Binney, Marcus. "A Viennese in California: Rudolf Schindler at the RIBA." *Country Life* (London) 145 (20 February 1969): 397.

Blauensteiner, Charlotte. "Österreich auf 835 N. King's Road." *Architektur & Bauforum* 29, no. 181 (April 1996): 66-69.

Boeckl, Matthias, ed. "Exhibition Review." *Archis*, no. 4 (April 1995): 10-11.

_____. *Visionäre & Vertriebene: Österreichische Spuren in der modernen amerikanischen Architektur*. Berlin: Ernst & Sohn, 1995.

Brown, T. M. Book review of *Schindler*, by David Gebhard. *Art Bulletin* (London) 55 (June 1973): 309-12; reply by David Gebhard, *Art Bulletin* (London) 56 (March 1974): 150-51.

"A Cabin for Gisela Bennati." *California Arts and Architecture* 61 (February 1944): 21-23.

Cantacuzino, Sherban. "Schindler Shortcomings." Book review of *R. M. Schindler–Architect* by David Gebhard. *The Architectural Review* 143, no. 853 (March 1968): 177.

Chow, Renee Y. "Sharing in a Setting." *Places* 10, no. 4 (Winter 1997): 64-65.

Chusid, Jeffrey M. "The American Discovery of Reinforced Concrete." *Rassegna*, no. 49 (March 1992): 66-73.

Crawford, Margaret. "Forgetting and Remembering Schindler: The Social History of an Architectural Reputation." *2G*, no. 7 (1998): 129-43.

"Design for Sunlight: House for Mr. Henmar Rodakiewicz, Los Angeles." *California Arts and Architecture* 57 (November 1940): 26.

"Dos Casas en Los Angeles, arq. R. M. Schindler." *Nuestra Arquitectura* (December 1938): 440-44.

Filler, Martin. "Schindler's Best." *House Beautiful* 138, no. 1 (May 1996): 48.

Ford, Edward R. "Residential Construction in America: Rudolf Schindler, Walter Gropius, and Marcel Breuer." In *The Details of Modern Architecture*, 289-319. Cambridge, Mass.: The MIT Press, 1990.

Forster, Kurt W. "California Architecture: Now You See It, Now You Don't." *UCLA Architecture Journal* (Los Angeles) (1986): 5-22.

"Four Houses in the Modern Manner." *The Architectural Forum* 61, no. 4 (October 1934): 231-36.

Gebhard, David. *R. M. Schindler–Architect*. Santa Barbara, Calif.: The Art Gallery, University of California, Santa Barbara, 1967.

_____. "Ambiguity in the Work of R. M. Schindler." *Lotus* (Milan), no. 5 (1968): 107-21.

_____. *Schindler*. London: Thames and Hudson; and New York: The Viking Press, 1971.

_____. "R. M. Schindler: Wolfe House, Santa Catalina Island." *Domus* (Milan), no. 689 (December 1987): 56-65, XXII.

Gebhard, David, and Harriette Von Breton. *L. A. in the Thirties: 1931-1941*, 6, 43, 46, 49, 50, 109-16. Layton, Utah: Peregrine Smith, 1975.

Giella, Barbara. "R. M. Schindler's Thirties Style: Its Character (1931-1937) and International Sources (1906-1937)." Ph.D. diss., New York University, 1987.

Giovannini, Joseph. "A Modernist Architect's Home is Restored in Los Angeles." *The New York Times*, 3 December 1987, C-12.

Goldberger, Paul. "A House of the Future, Now Part of Our Past." *The New York Times*, 13 December 1987, 48-52.

Graf, Otto Antonia. *Die vergessene Wagnerschule, Schriften des Museums des 20. Jahrhunderts*, 25-27, 34. Vienna: Verlag Jugend und Volk, 1969.

Hertzberger, Herman. "Dedicato a Schindler: Some notes on two works by Schindler." *Domus* (Milan), no. 454 (September 1967): [2]-7.

Hilberseimer, Ludwig. *Internationale neue Baukunst*, 9, 55. Stuttgart: Verlag J. Hoffmann, 1928.

_____. *Contemporary Architecture: Its Roots and Trends*, 169. Chicago: Paul Theobald & Co., 1964.

Hilberseimer, Ludwig, and Julius Vischer. *Beton als Gestalter*, 78. Stuttgart: Julius Hoffmann, 1928.

"Hillside house is a dramatic complex of varied levels and roofs." *The Architectural Forum* 86 (February 1947): 100-01.

Hines, Thomas S. "Conserving the Visible Past: The Schindler House and the Los Angeles Preservation Movement." *L. A. Architect* (Los Angeles) 4, no. 4 (September 1978): n.p.

_____. *Richard Neutra and the Search for Modern Architecture: A Biography and History*. New York and Oxford: Oxford University Press, 1982.

Hitchcock, [Henry-]Russell. "An Eastern Critic Looks at Western Architecture." *California Arts and Architecture* 57 (December 1940): 21-23, 40-41.

Hollein, Hans. "Rudolf M. Schindler: Ein Wiener Architekt in Kalifornien." *Der Aufbau* (Vienna) 16, no. 3 (March 1961): 102-04.

_____. "Rudolf M. Schindler: Ein weiterer Beitrag zur Berichtigung der Architekturgeschichte." *Bau* (Vienna) 21, no. 4 (1966): 67-82.

"House for J. DeKeyser, Hollywood, Calif." *The Architectural Forum* 64, no. 3 (March 1936): 190.

"House for J. J. Buck, Los Angeles, California; R. M. Schindler, Architect." *The Architectural Forum* 65, no. 4 (October 1936): 264-65.

"House for Ralph G. Walker, Los Angeles, Calif." *The Architectural Forum* 69, no. 5 (November 1938): 362-63.

"House for V. McAlmon, Los Angeles, Calif.; R. M. Schindler, Architect." *The Architectural Forum* 66, no. 4 (April 1937): 340-41.

"House for W. E. Oliver, Los Angeles, Calif." *American Architect* 146 (May 1935): 23-26.

"Houses for Outdoor Life. A Vacation Settlement on the Pueblo Ribera, La Jolla, California." *Architectural Record* 68, no. 1 (July 1930): 17-21.

Koenig, Giovanni Klaus. "Dal Danubio blu al viale del Tramonto: Rudolf Michael Schindler e Richard Josef Neutra." *Casabella* (Milan) 34 (November 1970): 29-36; and 35 (January 1971): 36-42.

Kovatsch, Manfred. "Rudolf M. Schindler: Notizen zu acht Bauten." *Bauwelt* (Guetersloh, Germany) 75, no. 39 (19 October 1984): 1685-89.

_____, ed. *R. M. Schindler, Architekt, 1887-1953*. Munich: Museum Villa Stuck, 1985.

Kurrent, Friedrich, ed. *Raummodelle: Wohnhäuser des 20. Jahrhunderts*. Salzburg-Munich: Verlag Anton Pustet, 1995.

Leclerc, David. "Schindler, la maison Wolfe: Les morsures du temps," "Un pionnier sans les larmes," and "À Catalina." *L'architecture d'aujour-d'hui* (Paris), no. 307 (October 1996): 57-71.

Longstreth, Richard. Book review of *R. M. Schindler: Composition and Construction*, edited by Lionel March and Judith Sheine. *Journal of Architectural Education* (May 1996): 264-66.

March, Lionel. "Residential Masterpieces: R. M. Schindler, How House." *GA Houses*, no. 56 (April 1998): 32-53.

March, Lionel, and Judith Sheine, eds. *R. M. Schindler: Composition and Construction*. London: Academy Editions, 1993.

McCoy, Esther. "Schindler, Space Architect." *Direction* 8, no. 1 (Fall 1945): 14-15.

_____. "Four Schindler Houses of the 1920s." *Arts and Architecture* 70, no. 9 (September 1953): 12-14.

_____. "A Work by R. M. Schindler: Visual Expansion of a Small House." *Los Angeles Times Sunday Magazine*, 2 May 1954, 14-15.

_____, ed. "R. M. Schindler." *Arts and Architecture* 71, no. 5 (May 1954): 12-15, 35-36.

_____. "Roots of California Contemporary Architecture." *Arts and Architecture* 73, no. 10 (October 1956): 14-17, 36-39.

_____. "Five California Architects." *Progressive Architecture* 41, no. 7 (July 1960): 129-36.

_____. "R. M. Schindler." In *Five California Architects*, 121-36. New York: Reinhold, 1960.

_____, ed. "Letters of Louis H. Sullivan to R. M. Schindler." *Journal of the Society of Architectural Historians* (Philadelphia) 20, no. 4 (December 1961): 179-84.

_____. "Renewed Interest in Popularity of Schindler's Architecture." *Los Angeles Times*, 22 October 1967, Calendar-46.

_____. "R. M. Schindler." *Lotus* (Milan), no. 5 (1968): 92-105.

_____, ed. "Letters between R. M. Schindler and Richard Neutra, 1914-1924." *Journal of the Society of Architectural Historians* (Philadelphia) 33, no. 3 (October 1974): 219-24.

_____. "Five Houses of R. M. Schindler." *Architecture and Urbanism* (Tokyo) 82, no. 9 (September 1977): 134-35.

_____. "Pauline Schindler, 1893-1977." *Progressive Architecture* 58, no. 9 (September 1977): 28, 33.

_____. *Vienna to Los Angeles: Two Journeys*. Santa Monica, Calif.: Arts + Architecture Press, 1979.

_____. "Schindler: A Personal Reminiscence." *L. A. Architect* (Los Angeles) (November 1987): 5-9.

279 _____. "Second Guessing Schindler." *Progressive Architecture* 70, no. 4 (April 1989): 86-89.

Miralles, Enric. "Schindler-Chase Residence." *Quaderns d'Arquitectura i Urbanisme* 185 (April-June 1990): 4-11.

_____. "'No, I'd Rather Not.' Three Houses by R. M. Schindler." *2G*, no. 7 (1998): 26-28.

Moore, Charles W. "Schindler: Vulnerable and Powerful." *Progressive Architecture* 54, no. 1 (January 1973): 132, 136.

Moore, Charles W., and Gerald Allen. *Dimensions: Space, Shape and Scale in Architecture*, 167-74. New York: Architectural Record Books, 1976.

Moore, Charles W., Peter Becker, and Regula Campbell. *The City Observed: Los Angeles. A Guide to its Architecture and Landscapes*, 128, 136, 157, 233, 256-57, 258-60, 299-301, 359-60. New York: Random House, 1984.

Neutra, Richard J. *Wie Baut Amerika?* Stuttgart: Julius Hoffmann, 1927.

_____. *Amerika: Die Stillbildung des neuen Bauens in den Vereinigten Staaten*, 65, 128-32, 139. Vienna: A. Schroll, 1930.

Noever, Peter, ed. *Rudolf M. Schindler*. Vienna: MAK—Austrian Museum of Applied Arts; and Munich and New York: Prestel, 1995.

Noever, Peter, and William Mohline, eds. *Zugmann: Schindler*. Santa Monica, Calif.: Form Zero Editions, 1996.

Norden, Deborah. Book review of *R. M. Schindler: Composition and Construction*, edited by Lionel March and Judith Sheine. *Sites* (New York), no. 26 (1995): 141-43.

Ohanesian, Paul B. "The Schindler House: 1921 Landmark in Los Angeles." *AIBC Forum* (July 1978): 20-24.

O'Neill, Dan. "Schindler Survey." Book review of *Schindler* by David Gebhard. *The Architectural Review* 152, no. 907 (September 1972): 191.

_____. "The High and Low Art of Rudolph Schindler." *The Architectural Review* 153, no. 914 (April 1973): 242-46.

Park, Jin-Ho. "Schindler, Symmetry and the Free Public Library, 1920." *Arq: Architectural Research Quarterly* (London) 2, no. 2 (Winter 1996): 72-83.

Pastier, John. "Hollywood Classic." *The Architects' Journal* (London) (13 November 1991): 32-39.

Pendexer, Edwin. "America's Own Architecture." *Building Age and National Builder* (New York) 48 (December 1926): 97.

Polyzoides, Stefanos. "Schindler, Lovell, and the Newport Beach House, Los Angeles, 1921-1926." *Oppositions*, no. 18 (Fall 1979): 60-73.

Polyzoides, Stefanos, and Panos Koulermos. "R. M. Schindler—Notes on His Work: Five Houses by R. M. Schindler." *Architecture and Urbanism* (Tokyo) (November 1975): 61-126.

_____. "Response to Esther McCoy's Critical Comments on 'Five Houses of R. M. Schindler.'" *Architecture and Urbanism* (Tokyo) (February 1978): 75-76.

Puga, Anne-Marie. "Schindler, la maison Wolfe: Album photographique." *L'architecture d'aujourd'hui* (Paris), no. 307 (October 1996): 48-56.

"Residence in Los Angeles, California." *Architectural Record* 65, no. 1 (January 1929): 5-9.

"Residence of Mr. and Mrs. W. Oliver, Los Angeles, California." *California Arts and Architecture* 47, no. 1 (January 1935): 8.

"Residences in California; Architect, R. M. Schindler." *Architect and Engineer* 123, no. 3 (December 1935): 16-21, 26-27.

R. M. Schindler, Arquitecto. Madrid: Ministerio de Obras Públicas y Urbanismo, 1984.

"R. M. Schindler Exhibit, Balboa Park, San Diego." *Architect and Engineer* 198, no. 1 (July 1954): 8.

"R. M. Schindler 1887-1953." Issue devoted to Schindler on the occasion of an exhibition at the Stedelijk Museum, Amsterdam, May-June 1969. *Bouwkundig Weekblad* (Amsterdam) 87, no. 8 (29 April 1969).

"RIBA Drawings." *Architectural Design* 42, no. 7 (July 1972): 404.

Rotondi, Michael. "How I Discovered R. M. Schindler." *2G*, no. 7 (1998): 29-31.

Rouillard, Dominique. "Logiques de la pente à Los Angeles: Quelques figures de F. L. Wright et R. M. Schindler." *Cahiers de la recherche architecturale* (Paris), no. 14 (1984): 8-25.

_____. "Schindler: Two Site Systems." In *Building the Slope: Hillside Houses, 1920-1960*, 45-86. Santa Monica, Calif.: Arts + Architecture Press, 1987.

"Rudolf M. Schindler—Ein Wiener Architekt in Kalifornien." *Der Aufbau* 16, no. 3 (March 1961): 102-04.

Sarnitz, August. "Rudolf Michael Schindler—Theory and Design." Master's thesis, Massachusetts Institute of Technology, Cambridge, Mass., 1982.

_____. "Raumarchitektur—Theorie und Praxis eines Prinzips. Über das Entwurfs und Konstruktionsprinzip bei Rudolf M. Schindler." Ph.D. diss., Technische Universität Wien, Vienna, 1983.

_____. "Mythos und Moderne. Rudolf M. Schindler—60 Jahre Strandhaus Lovell." *Bauforum* (Vienna) 18, no. 108 (1985): 19-34.

_____. "Proportion and Beauty—The Lovell Beach House by Rudolph Michael Schindler, Newport Beach, 1922-26." *Journal of the Society of Architectural Historians* (Philadelphia) 45, no. 4 (December 1986): 374-88.

_____. "Rudolf M. Schindler zum 100. Geburtstag." *Bauwelt* (Guetersloh, Germany) 78 (23 October 1987): 1486.

_____. *R. M. Schindler, Architect 1887-1953*. New York: Rizzoli, 1988.

Schindler, Pauline Gibling. "Modern California Architects." *Creative Art* 10, no. 2 (February 1932): 111-15.

_____. "Modern Architecture Acknowledges the Light which Kindled It: Frank Lloyd Wright." *California Arts and Architecture* 47, no. 1 (January 1935): 17.

Schindler, R. M. "Modern Architecture: A Program" (unpublished manuscript). Vienna, 1912.

_____. "Ventilation." *Los Angeles Times Sunday Magazine*, 14 March 1926, 25-26.

_____. "Plumbing and Health." *Los Angeles Times Sunday Magazine*, 21 March 1926, 25-26.

_____. "About Heating." *Los Angeles Times Sunday Magazine*, 4 April 1926, 24-25.

_____. "About Lighting." *Los Angeles Times Sunday Magazine*, 11 April 1926, 30-31.

_____. "About Furniture." *Los Angeles Times Sunday Magazine*, 18 April 1926, 26-27.

_____. "Shelter or Playground." *Los Angeles Times Sunday Magazine*, 2 May 1926, 26-27.

_____. "A Cooperation Dwelling." *T-Square* (Philadelphia) 2, no. 2 (February 1932): 20-21.

_____. "Space Architecture." *Dune Forum* (Oceano, Calif.) (February 1934): 44-46.

_____. "Space Architecture." *California Arts and Architecture* 47, no. 1 (January 1935): 18-19.

_____. "Furniture and the Modern House: A Theory of Interior Design." *Architect and Engineer* 123, no. 3 (December 1935): 22-25; and 124 (March 1936): 24-28.

_____. "A Prefabrication Vocabulary: The Panel-post Construction." *California Arts and Architecture* 60, no. 5 (June 1943): 25-27.

_____. "Reference Frames in Space." *Architect and Engineer* 165, no. 1 (April 1946): 10, 40, 44-45.

_____. "Postwar Automobiles." *Architect and Engineer* 168, no. 2 (February 1947): 12-14.

_____. "The Schindler Frame." *Architectural Record* 101, no. 5 (May 1947): 143-46.

"Schindler-Shelters." *American Architect* 146 (May 1935): 70-72.

Scott, Patrick, and David Dalsass, et al. *Mirrors & Hammers: Eight Germanic Emigres in Los Angeles*. Los Angeles: Los Angeles Educational Partnership, 1988.

Segal, Walter. "The Least Appreciated. Rudolf Schindler: 1887-1953." *The Architects' Journal* (London) 149, no. 8 (19 February 1969): 476-79.

Shand, P. Morton. "A Cantilevered Summer-House." *The Architectural Review* 73, no. 436 (March 1933): 117.

Sheine, Judith. "Schindlerfest: Revising Architectural History." *Architecture and Planning* (1988): 9-11.

_____. "Schindler Reassessed." *Architectural Record* 176, no. 10 (September 1988): 69, 71.

_____. "Residential Masterpieces: R. M. Schindler. Manola Court Apartments." *GA Houses* (Tokyo), no. 53 (June 1997): 32-41.

_____. "R. M. Schindler 1887-1953." *2G*, no. 7 (1998): 4-25.

_____. *R. M. Schindler: Works and Projects*. Barcelona: Editorial Gustavo Gili, 1998.

Sherwood, Roger. "El Pueblo Ribera Court." In *Modern Housing Prototypes*, 31-37. Cambridge, Mass.: Harvard University Press, 1978.

"Sixteen Southern California Architects Exhibit Contemporary Trends in a Group Showing at Scripps College." *Arts and Architecture* 67, no. 4 (April 1950): 22-33.

"Small Desert House." *Arts and Architecture* 68, no. 10 (November 1951): 38.

Small, Kay. "Hollywood Architects in International Contest." *Hollywood Magazine* (Los Angeles) (December 1928): 9.

Smith, Kathryn. "Chicago—Los Angeles: The Concrete Connection." In Marc M. Angelil, ed., *On Architecture, the City, and Technology*, 103-05. Washington, D.C.: Association of Collegiate Schools of Architecture; and Stoneham, Mass.: Butterworth Architecture, 1990.

_____. *The R. M. Schindler House, 1921-22*. West Hollywood, Calif.: Friends of the Schindler House; and Los Angeles: Perpetua Press, 1987.

Steele, James. *How House: R. M. Schindler*. London: Academy Editions, 1996.

Steiner, Dietmar. "Das Bild von Leben ist das Leben." *Die Presse* (Vienna), 21 March 1986, 5.

Stern, Robert A. M. "International Style: Immediate Effects." *Progressive Architecture* 63, no. 2 (February 1982): 106-09.

Storrer, Bradley R. "Schindler—Wright Exchange: The Schindler Licensing Letters." *Journal of the Taliesin Fellows*, no. 9 (Winter 1992-93): 14-19.

Suekane, Shingo. "Spatial Composition of R. Schindler." *Nihon Kenchiku Gakkai keikakukei ronbun hokokushu* (Tokyo), no. 7 (July 1997): 221-27.

281 "A Summer House at Catalina for Mr. and Mrs. E. Wolfe." *California Arts and Architecture* 47, no. 1 (January 1935): 18-19.

"Summer House of C. H. Wolfe, Catalina Island." *The Architectural Record* 70, no. 3 (September 1931): 157-61.

Sundberg, Bo. "Fran Wien till Los Angeles (Rudolf Schindler and Richard Neutra)." *Arkitektur* (Stockholm) 87, no. 8: 60-62.

Sweeney, Robert L. "Interview: Robert Sweeney, Executive Director of the Schindler House." *Sites* (New York), no. 6 (1982): 10-16.

_____. " A Real California Scheme." *GA Houses* (Tokyo), no. 26 (July 1989): 6-28.

Tabor, Philip. "A Man Before His Time." Book review of *R. M. Schindler, Architect 1887-1953* by August Sarnitz. *The Architects' Journal* (London) 190, no. 7 (16 August 1989): 74-75.

Taut, Bruno. *Modern Architecture*, 9, 150-51. London: The Studio, 1929.

_____. *Die neue Baukunst in Europa und Amerika*, 178-79. Stuttgart: Julius Hoffmann, 1929.

Treiber, Daniel. "R. M. Schindler, 1887-1953." *AMC* (Barcelona), no. 54/55 (June/September 1981): 117-30.

Uhl, Ottokar. *Moderne Architektur in Wien von Otto Wagner bis Heute*, 49, 89. Vienna and Munich: Schrollverlag, 1966.

"Unusual Home Is Built of Concrete and Glass." *Popular Mechanics* 47, no. 6 (June 1927): 969.

Visconti, Marco, and Werner Lang. "R. M. Schindler: Kings Road House, West Hollywood, 1921-22." *Domus* (Milan), no. 746 (February 1993): 78-84, XXII.

"Visionäre & Vertriebene." Exhibition review. *Bauwelt* (1995): 562-63.

Walker, Derek, et al. "The Morphology of Los Angeles" and "The Architecture of Los Angeles." *Architectural Design* 51 (August-September 1981): 1-97.

Webb, Michael. "Expulsion into Paradise." *Metropolis* 16, no. 1 (July-August 1996): 72-73, 84-85.

"A Week-end House in California." *The Architects' Journal* (London) 104 (25 July 1946): 65-66.

"White Collar Apartments for a Steep Lakeside Lot." *Interiors* (New York) 103 (January 1944): 41.

Wilson, Richard Guy. "International Style: The MOMA Exhibition." *Progressive Architecture* 63, no. 2 (February 1982): 92-104.

"The Year's Work: R. M. Schindler." *Interiors* (New York) 106, no. 1 (August 1946): 83.

"The Year's Work: R. M. Schindler." *Interiors* (New York) 107, no. 1 (August 1947): 84.

Zevi, Bruno. "R. M. Schindler: Austria e California in una composizione diversa da Richard Neutra." *L'architettura* (Milan) 6 (October 1960): 422-23.

INDEX

This publication accompanies the exhibition
"THE ARCHITECTURE OF R. M. SCHINDLER,"
organized by Elizabeth A. T. Smith and Michael Darling
and presented at The Museum of Contemporary Art, Los Angeles,
25 February—3 June 2001.

"THE ARCHITECTURE OF R. M. SCHINDLER" is made possible
in part by generous support from The Ron Burkle Endowment
for Architecture and Design Programs, Gensler, Cynthia A. Miscikowski
and Douglas Ring, Kelly Lynch and Mitch Glazer, and The Austrian
Cultural Institute.

In-kind support has been provided by Homasote Company.

Exhibition Tour
THE MUSEUM OF CONTEMPORARY ART, LOS ANGELES
25 February–3 June 2001

NATIONAL BUILDING MUSEUM, WASHINGTON, D.C.
29 June–7 October 2001

MAK—AUSTRIAN MUSEUM OF APPLIED ARTS, VIENNA
13 November 2001–10 February 2002

Editor: Stephanie Emerson
Assistant editor: Jane Hyun
Editorial assistant: Elizabeth Hamilton
Designers: Lorraine Wild and Amanda Washburn
Printer: Dr. Cantz'sche Druckerei, Ostfildern, Germany

Copyright © 2001
The Museum of Contemporary Art, Los Angeles
250 South Grand Avenue
Los Angeles, California 90012

*Clothbound edition co-published and distributed by Harry N. Abrams,
Incorporated, New York*

ISBN: 0-8109-4223-2

Printed in Germany

Library of Congress Cataloging-in-Publication Data
Schindler, R. M. (Rudolph M.), 1887-1953.
    The architecture of R. M. Schindler / organized by Elizabeth
A. T. Smith and Michael Darling ; essays by Michael Darling ... [et al.].
    p. cm.
    Exhibition tour, The Museum of Contemporary Art, Los Angeles
25 Feb.–3 June 2001, National Building Museum, Washington, D.C.,
29 June–7 Oct. 2001, MAK, Vienna, 13 Nov. 2001–10 Feb. 2002.
    Includes bibliographical references and index.
    ISBN 0-8109-4223-2
    I.   Schindler, R. M. (Rudolph M.), 1887-1953-Catalogs. 2. Modern
movement (Architecture)-United States-California-Catalogs. 3.
Architecture, Modern-20th century-United States-California-Catalogs. I.
Smith, Elizabeth A. T., 1958- II. Darling, Michael. III. Museum of
Contemporary Art (Los Angeles, Calif.) IV. National Building Museum (U.S.)
V. Österreichisches Museum für Angewandte Kunst. VI. Title.

NA737.S35 A4 2001
720'.92-dc21   00-045595

Photo Credits
Grant Mudford, pp. 2, 30, 40, 53, 58, 62, 78-79, 89-90, 98, 101,
116, 125-26, 132, 134-135, 138, 174, 183 top, 195;
Julius Shulman, pp. 14, 55-56, 63, 70 bottom, 73 bottom, 212-213;
The Frank Lloyd Wright Archives, Scottsdale, Arizona, p. 22;
San Diego Historical Society, San Diego Historical Society Collection,
p. 28 bottom; Courtesy Friends of the Schindler House, gift of
Mrs. Richard Neutra, p. 47; The John Lautner Foundation, p. 82;
Photograph © Tim Street-Porter/Esto. All rights reserved, p. 83 left;
Courtesy Fotoworks—Benny Chan, p. 83 right; Schindler Family
Collection, courtesy Friends of the Schindler House, pp. 93 all,
95 all, 97 all, 102, 111, 113; Archive Werner M. Moser, Eidgenossische
Technische Hochschule Zürich, pp. 94, 96 all; Courtesy of
the Academy of Motion Picture Arts and Sciences, pp. 99 top, 110;
Collection of Robert Sweeney, gift of Dione Neutra, p. 100 all;
Courtesy of Harrison Memorial Library, Carmel, p. 105;
The drawing of Sadakichi Hartmann, from the Sadakichi Hartmann
Collection, is used with the permission of the Special Collections
Library, University of California, Riverside, p. 106; Courtesy Friends
of the Schindler House, gift of Peg Weiss, p. 108; Department of
Special Collections, Charles E. Young Research Library, University
of California, Los Angeles, p. 120 all; Courtesy Pavel Štecha, p. 127;
Jon Miller © Hedrich Blessing, p. 128; Courtesy of Richard Guy Wilson,
pp. 131, 136 all, 139; Stan Reifel, p. 147 top; Courtesy of the
Los Angeles County Museum of Art, p. 147 bottom; Graphische Sammlung
Albertina, Vienna, p. 189; © 2000 Artists Rights Society (ARS),
New York/ADAGP, Paris/FLC, p. 204; and Esther McCoy Papers,
Archives of American Art, Smithsonian Institution, p. 206.

All other photographs appear courtesy of the Architecture
and Design Collection, University Art Museum, University of California,
Santa Barbara.